Skira Architecture Library

Francesco Craca

João Álvaro Rocha

Architectures 1988-2001

Skira

Scientific editor
Francesco Craca

Design
Marcello Francone

Editing
Marina Beretta

Layout
Francesco Craca
Claudio Nasso

Texts of the projects
João Álvaro Rocha

Translations
Fernando Torres (from Portuguese)
Benta Wiley Bombardi (from Italian)
Laura Mulas (from Spanish)

Iconography
João Ventura Lopes
Francesco Craca
Susana Vilela

First published in Italy in 2003 by
Skira Editore S.p.A.
Palazzo Casati Stampa
via Torino 61
20123 Milano
Italy
www.skira.net

Printed and bound in Italy. First edition
ISBN 88-8491-113-3

Distributed in North America and Latin America by Rizzoli International Publications, Inc. through St. Martin's Press, 175 Fifth Avenue, New York, NY 10010.
Distributed elsewhere in the world by Thames and Hudson Ltd., 181a High Holborn, London WC1V 7QX, United Kingdom.

Contents

Antonio Ravalli

In Equilibrium upon Contemporaneity

Confronted with the conditions of contemporary society, architectural thought seems unable to find a correct connection to reality, it lacks the capacity to intervene in determining the manner and the dynamics of development, and is unable to formulate simple responses to the challenges that contemporary society proposes. In this sense signals are plentiful and it's not by chance that architects are often considered throughout the world as carriers of unrealistic requests incomprehensible exactly when they try to confront themes with their particular view point.

The fact that architecture finds a hostile surrounding in contemporary society is not surprising at all. It's enough to think of the prevailing mirage of the virtual compared to the material and the obvious solidity inherent in the act of construction; of the economic and cultural globalization eroding the diversity of local contexts; of the uncertainty of the decision making process. These factors, together with the continuing change in functional needs and tastes, hinder the understanding of permanent spatial assets, thus resulting in absolutely necessary settlements born under the push of high speed transport and media that have threatened the density and cohesion of the existing urban structure. All this means losing the representative function of buildings, now substituted by new and more efficient means of communication.

In such a situation it is difficult to individuate a way to propose oneself in front of reality.

João Álvaro Rocha has decided on a silent position but yet one not at all comfortable; he has decided to follow a path within a specific discipline using the instruments of his profession, convinced that a classical response may still lay strong foundations for the values with which we can live. An underlay that allows us to express our desire to be citizens of an enlarged and complex world.

Such position is one that still believes in the value of words such as *place*, *identity* and *"doing"*, where "doing" reveals the true character of his belief, in the conviction that no research can be developed without a simple but precise adhesion to material culture.

Rocha's architecture is defined by a few phrases: the form seems simple, extremely clear, but any type of representation that demonstrates the finesse and the severity of an object is absolutely unable to transmit the potential of the relations established with its surroundings. A continual connection with material culture of the country in which he was born and works is evident, a search that clearly expresses the evocation of themes both technical and expressive and the capacity to investigate the continuity of the productive processes without necessarily enrolling in the call for contemporary hyper. A reflexive position that in Portugal finds many famous predecessors and that (even if it may seem obvious to collocate Rocha outside the actual debate), demonstrates a profound maturity and intention.

Such position can be clearly located in a process whose points of reference are

Shinkel and Mies, sharing a continual reference to geometric rigour and mathematical strength that constitutes the condition for developing the basis of a project. For Rocha the field of relations between geometric mass and the landscape in which they are located assumes a paradigmatic value, a term that allows to discover, each time, the sense in which to build and organize in a certain time and place.

It is exactly this great concern to circumstances that characterizes the compositions of the Portuguese architect: landscape is the parameter with which his architecture is measured, it moves through built spaces. By taking on the role of protagonist, the project looks in contact with the surroundings.

Rocha's architecture surprisingly reveals the magic of evidence, and lets the viewer learn the basic rules of complexity which manipulate his creativity, transforming it into his professional signature. His work follows this path: the careful dismounting and analysis of complexity to propose it interpreted and rebuilt by way of simple and coherent forms.

In the light of this, it is possible to find the key to the interpretation of the numerous projects illustrated in this book. A cord that ties together his first works – obviously more connected to academia and the period in which they are collocated – to those of complete maturity, arriving at the most recent ones, full of that patient search that has characterized all his work, that we hope may continue to be both long and prolific.

HOUSES

Using our emotions we interpret desires and aspirations; by way of reason we make these aspirations become principles, convinced that the solidity, vitality and strength of a solution are found in the validity of the principle that both inspires and supports it. What may be of interest is that from this never ending dialectic process between sentiment and reason may spring a panorama of significance to the simple existence of things. In a search towards their real essence, at the purest state, allowing the possibility to finalize the disponibility of things, transforming the potential of reality into a tight complex of concreteness and ideals, reason and sentiments. *(F.C.)*

. House in Lugar da Várzea (I)

2. House in Lugar da Várzea (II)

3. House in Lugar da Várzea (III)

Two Houses in Lugar da Várzea (I & II) Vermoim - Maia

Design
João Álvaro Rocha, Architect
1988-90

Construction
1990-93

Collaborators
Maria da Conceição Melo, Architect
Francisco Portugal e Gomes, Architect
Manuel Fernando Santos, Draughtsman

To live in a house, and feel it as yours, is something very special, for it creates intimacy. So is the act of designing it. Building two houses in the same location, and simultaneously, is a great challenge. People may belong to the same family, but are still different. So is the program: the image to be conveyed is that of a whole, but also of individual elements.

In a project, different languages intersect to build one single body.

"The style does not matter. What does matter is the relation between work and life: style is the result of such relationship."[1]

The ground is a narrow and long stretch of land, accessible from two fronts. The allotment foresees the construction of three houses. The project includes only two.

A granite wall is drawn to unite two sides. It's a path, meant to protect from the rain coming from the south, and to safeguard privacy.

The constructions are placed along the wall-path.

The lower house almost occupies all of the ground width. The other, taller, is distributed over three units that mark the path. In the middle lies a space that belongs to both.

The first house is an object of well-defined volume, placed on the land. Inside, the space seems to be only one. The relation with the smaller bodies that complement it generates its exterior space.

In the second house the spatial limits are less precise. The square structure is divided by the granite walls that cross it. Interior and exterior fuse under the roof plane that shelters that part of the land.

Two houses, two images, that complement each other giving form to a whole.

Porto, 1990

[1] Fernando Távora, *Da Organisação do Espaço*.

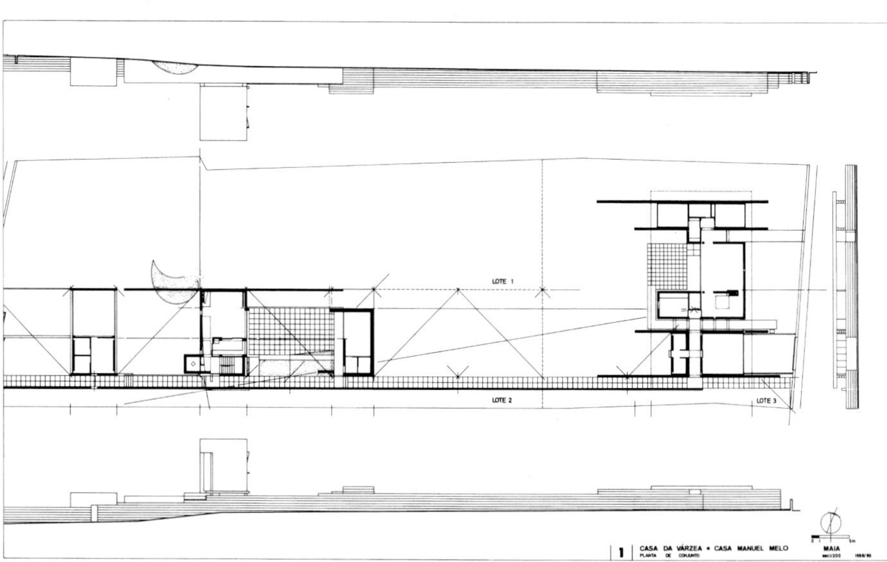

Two houses in Lugar da Várzea (I & II), site plan.

Várzea I house, general view from the street (west).

Várzea II house, general view from the street (west).

1. House in Lugar da Várzea (I)

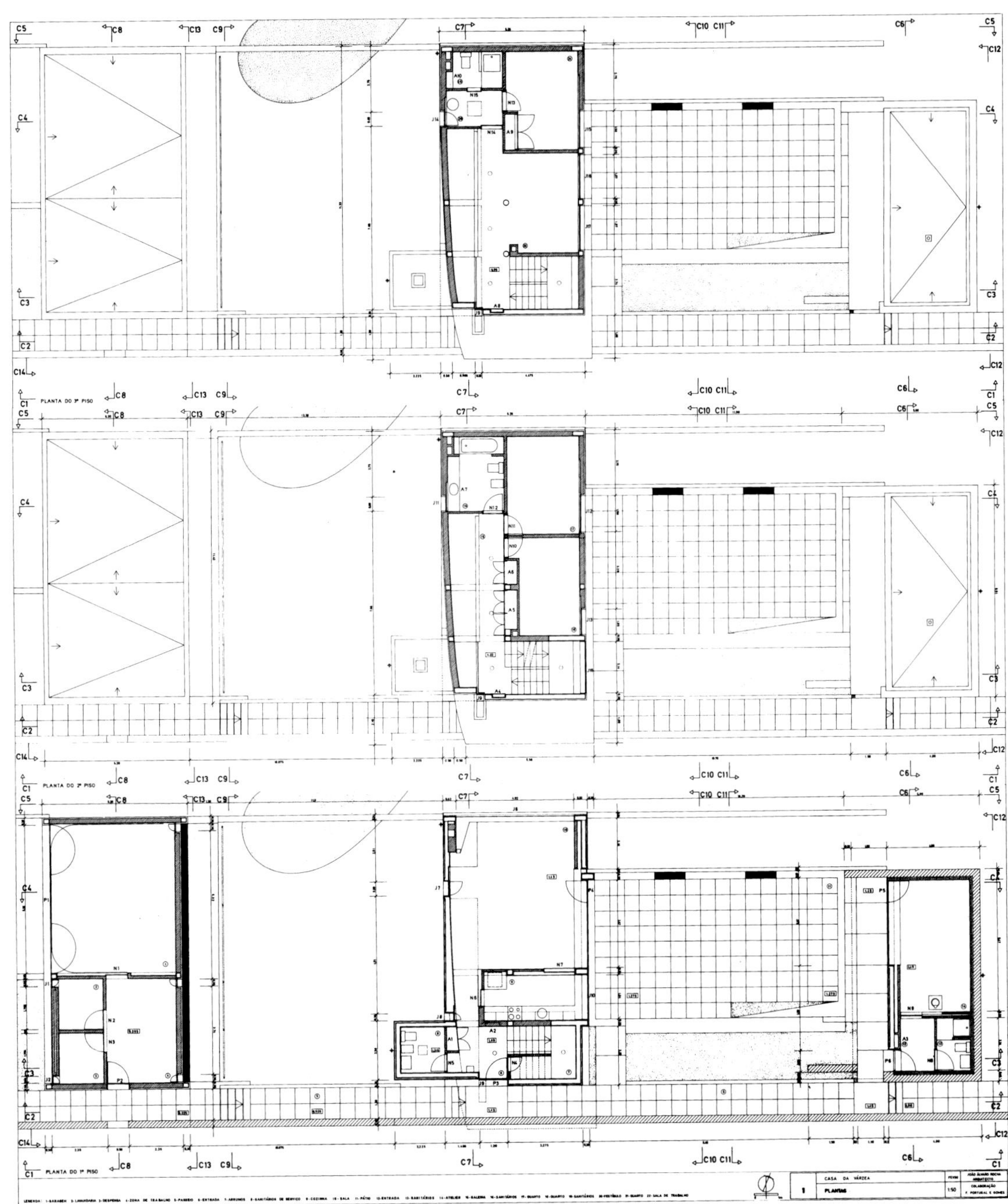

Ground, first and second floor plans.

South façade,
partial view.

East façade, view
from the patio.

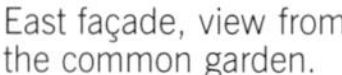

East façade, view from the common garden.

Living room, view towards the fire place and outer patio on the west.

Living room, view from the entry.

Stairs between 1st and 2nd floors.

Library on 2nd floor, view towards the stairs.

Hall of the master bedroom, on 2nd floor.

2. House in Lugar da Várzea (II)

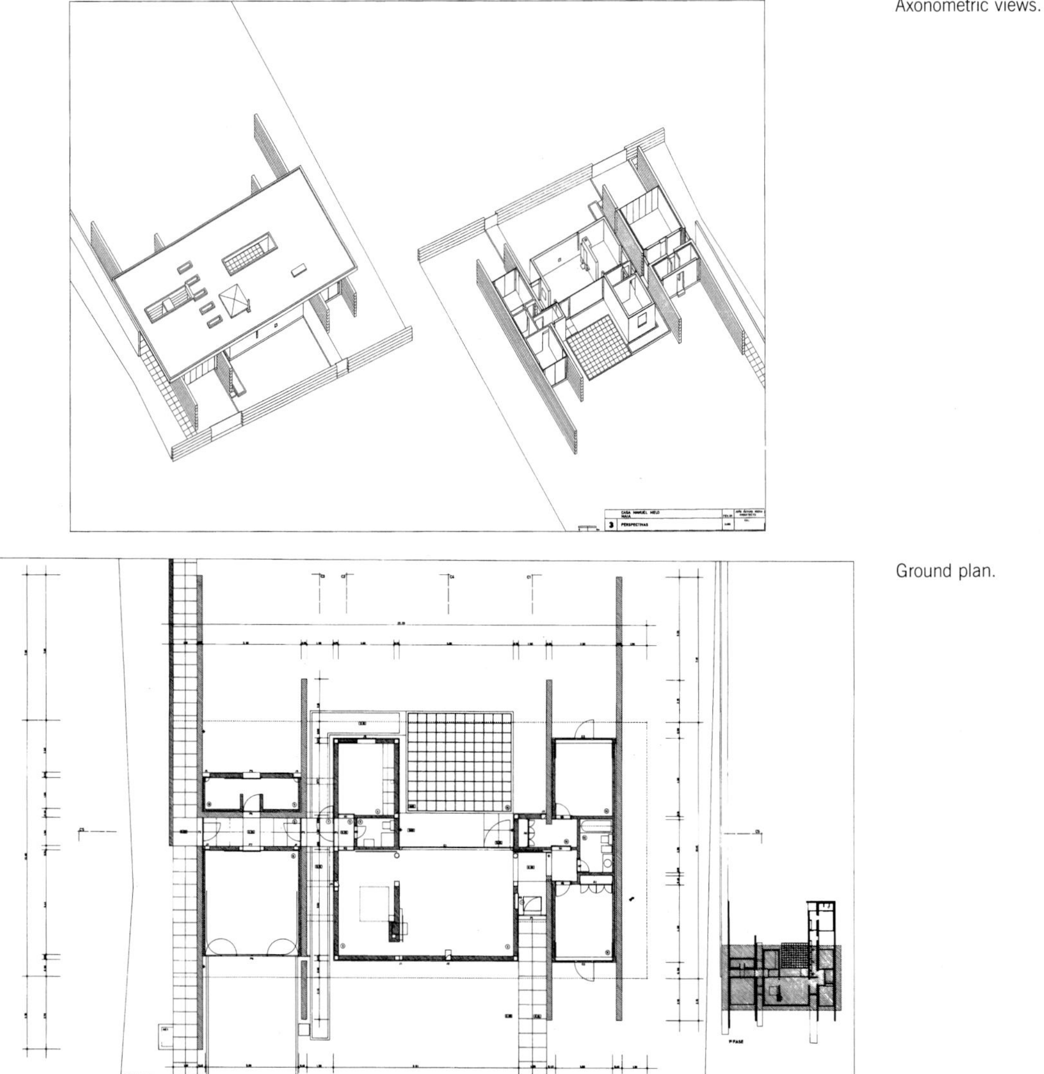

Axonometric views.

Ground plan.

East façade, general view from the street.

West façade, general view from the common garden.

Entry hall, view towards the living room.

Living room.

Living room, view from the outer patio.

Detail of door panel, between the bedroom and inner patio.

3. House in Lugar da Várzea (III) Vermoim - Maia

Design
João Álvaro Rocha, Architect
1996-97

Construction
1999-(underway)

Collaborators
Carla Garrido de Oliveira, Practice Architect

Model
Carla Garrido de Oliveira, Practice Architect

This house completes the layout of an allotment whose arrangement began a few years ago with the construction of two other houses, and thereby fulfills the original project.

The design presented is identical to the one that gave form to the other two existing houses.

The body of the house is organized in a vertical sequence, in two distinct and juxtaposed volumes: the basement, shaped as a podium to assure contact with the ground, contains the garage and service areas; the remaining floors, devoted to domestic spaces, are concentrated in one single volume that stands out as a counterpoint to the slightly sloping land.

The project has given the opportunity to reinterpret the original idea of the complex, and to analyse the interventions and the presumptions on which the architectural conception of the two existing houses was based.

Now as then, the problem has been recognizing the site the house is going to occupy, considering that its "location" depends fundamentally on the interaction that it may establish with the others. The definite expression of that interaction will result almost exclusively from the precision with which the limits that shape it are defined.

The notion of limit proposed here is meant to evaluate the material "presence", while the body of the object answers to the following description:

"It is as if the specificity of the projects were materialized in each of their parts or organizational levels, which no longer need to be subjected to a hierarchy to become meaningful. The part is freed syntactically from the whole, to become a synthesis of it."[1]

The modular character of the project is not aimed at the repetition of any unit; on the contrary, it results from the necessity to establish a rhythm, a cadence that allows the organization of the elements that constitute it.

The unit that is pursued also corresponds to the spatial unity from which the internal organization is drawn.

Porto, November 1997

[1] Alejandro Zaera, "Entre o rosto e a paisagem", in *El croquis*, no. 60.

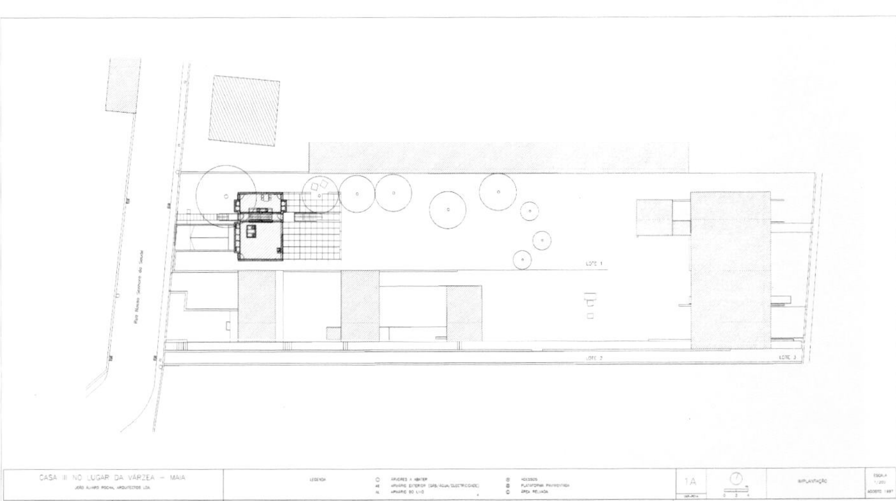

Site plan.

Facing page:
East façade, view from the common garden with Várzea I house to the left.

Ground, first and second floor plans.

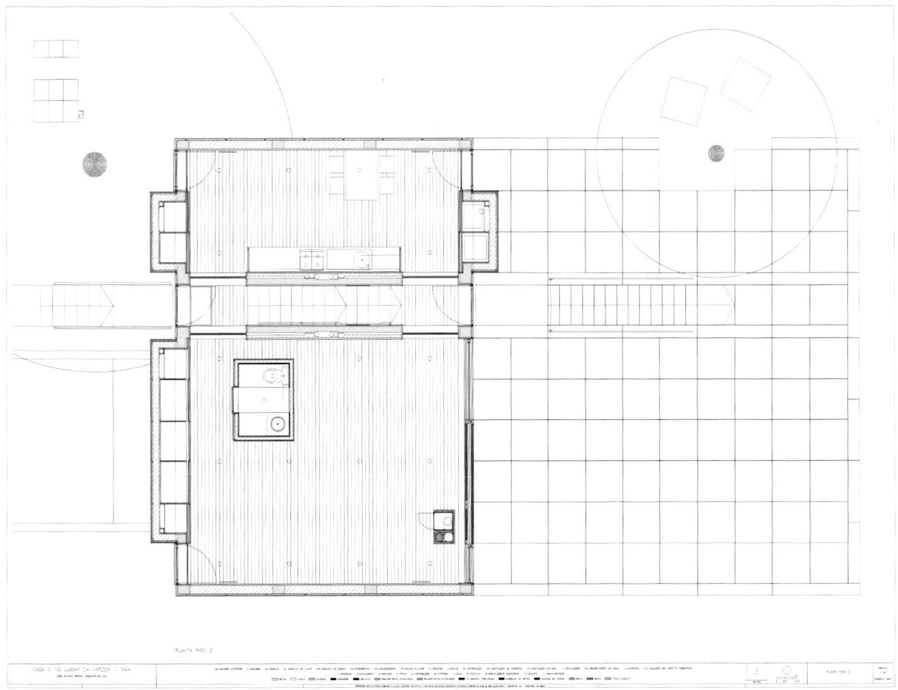

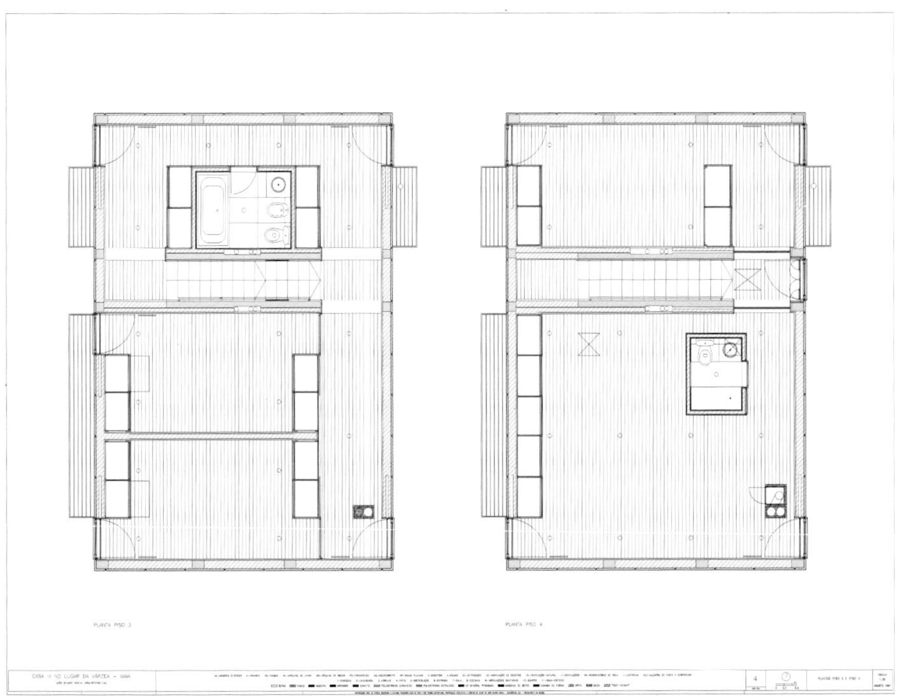

West façade, view
from the street entry.

East façade, view
from the outer patio.

Cross-section through stairs.

Facing page:
West façade, detail.

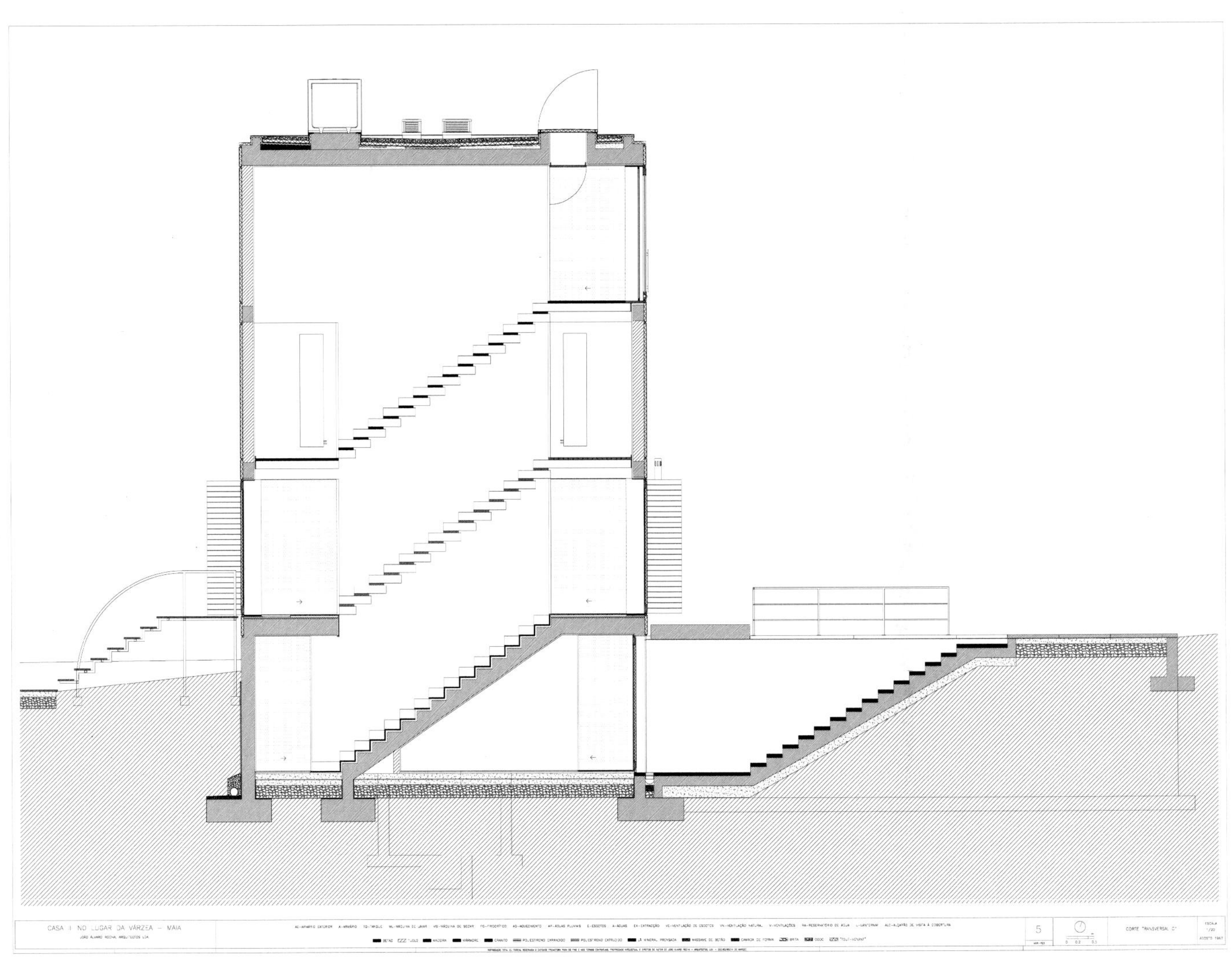

4. House in Lugar do Paçô
Carreço - Viana do Castelo

Design
João Álvaro Rocha, Architect
1994-95

Construction
1995-97

Collaborators
Jorge Pereira Esteves, Architect
Ana Sousa da Costa, Architect

Model
Jorge Pereira Esteves, Architect

This is a house that wants to see the sea...

The construction is located on the highest portion of a hill, where the line that defines its profile is transformed – and merges with the top line of the slope.

It is meant to be expansive and open like the horizon, and soft like the fresh breeze.

It is made of subtle contrasts: the grey of the concrete, the brown of the wood and the earth, the bright green of the grass, the somber green of the trees and the blue of the sky and the sea. And the wind, can it have a colour?

The rest is plain, only the elements necessary to redraw the boundaries of the property and indicate the access – as it has always been there, in Minho.

After all, this is a house that only wants to see the sea.

"[...] We should paint exactly what we have before us.

I say yes. Then a silence:

Besides being necessary to paint the canvas [...]"[1]

Porto, August 1996

[1] Supposed dialogue taken from *The Atelier of Alberto Giacometti* by Jean Genet.

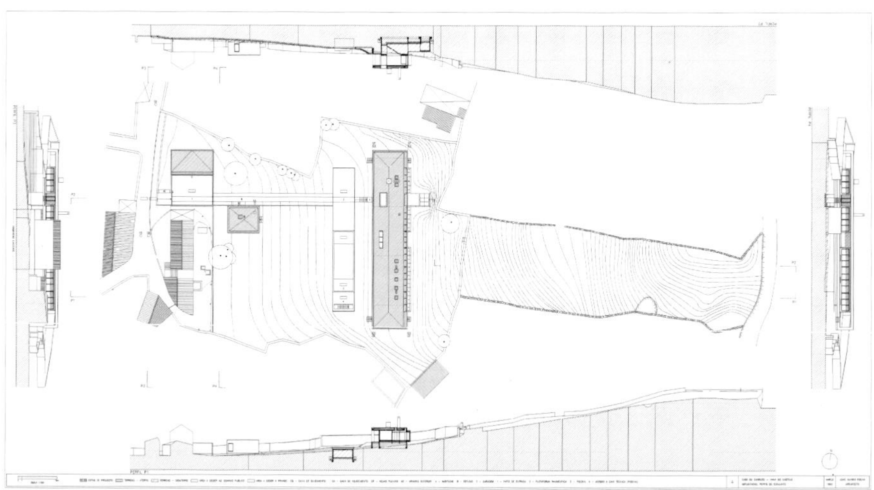

Site plan.

West façade (open) general view from the garden.

West façade (closed) general view from the garden.

Ground floor plan.

Basement plan.

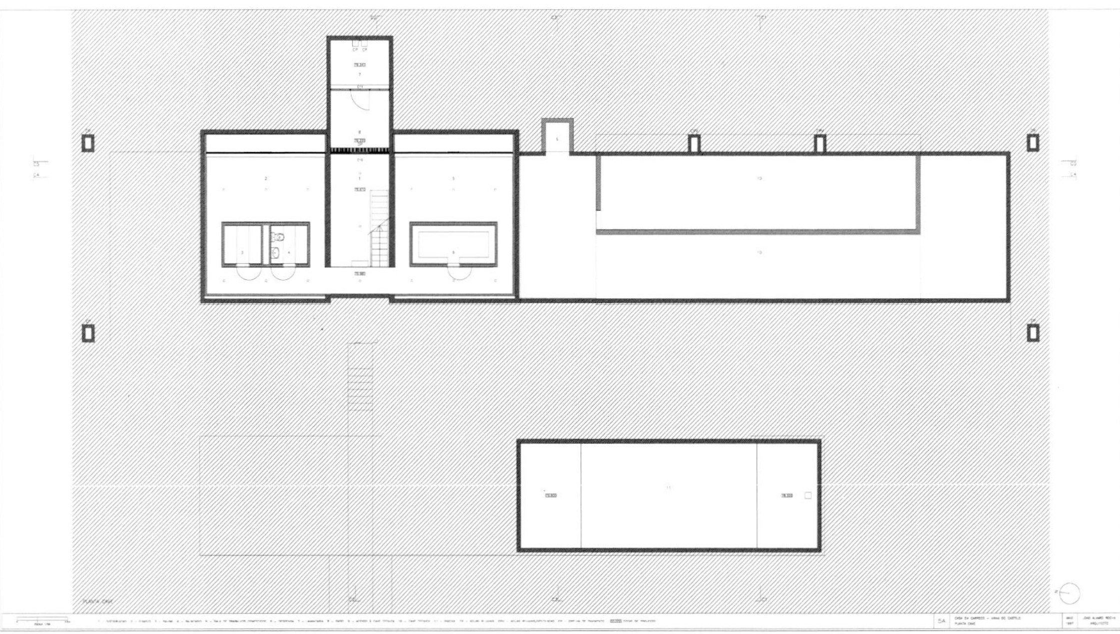

West façade, view from the north side of the garden.

Cross-section through
stairs and service patio.

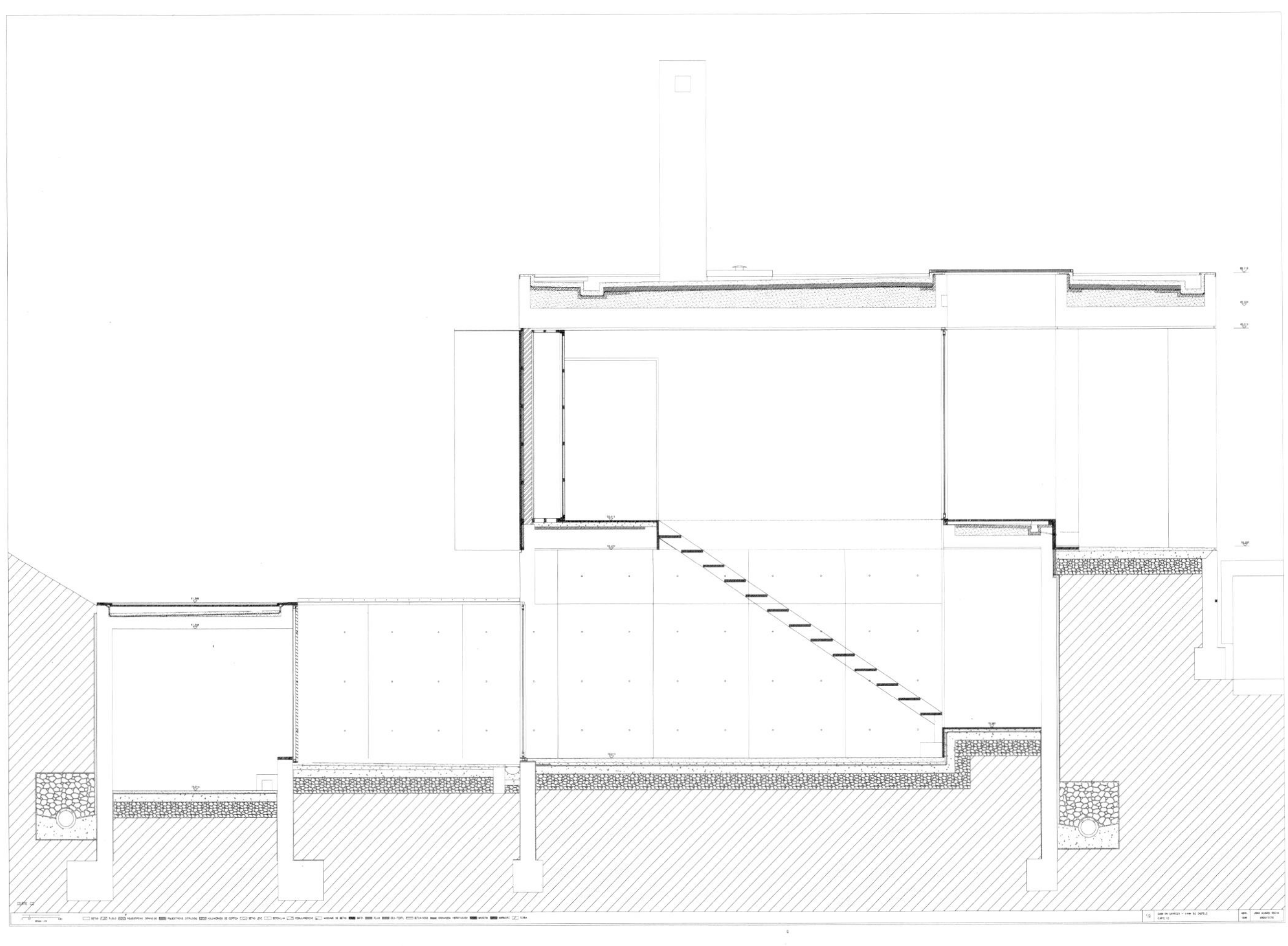

East façade, general view.

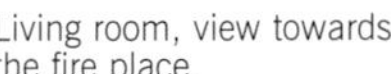

Living room, view towards the fire place.

Living room, general view of the entry hall.

Entry hall.
Corridor.

Hall between corridor and bedroom.
Inner stairs, with service patio behind.

5. House in Santarém

Design
João Álvaro Rocha, Architect
1998-99

Construction
2000-(underway)

Collaborators
António Luís Neves, Architect
Carla Garrido de Oliveira, Architect

Model
Pedro Valentim, Practice Architect

The house is located on the most elevated part of the site, placed on a slope and turned towards the landscape, its front looking onto it.

The viewpoints are reasonably oriented – inside and out, to see everything or just a part of the whole, so that the landscape becomes a painting.

It is organized in three volumes in accordance with the project. On one side, the body of the atelier and the garage; in the centre, a block of bedrooms with higher elevation in order to punctuate the mass; and on the other side, the body of living spaces. In the middle, an unclouding of the parts of the scenery occurs, the separation of elements, but also their connection.

Light unites everything, so that being inside may sometimes give the idea of being outside.

Light is vertical, and strong; it creates harsh contrasts so that differences become identifiable, and colours and textures are enhanced.

Building in the south…

Porto, October 1999

Study sketch, general view from northeast side.

Facing page:
Northeast façade, general view from the surroundings.

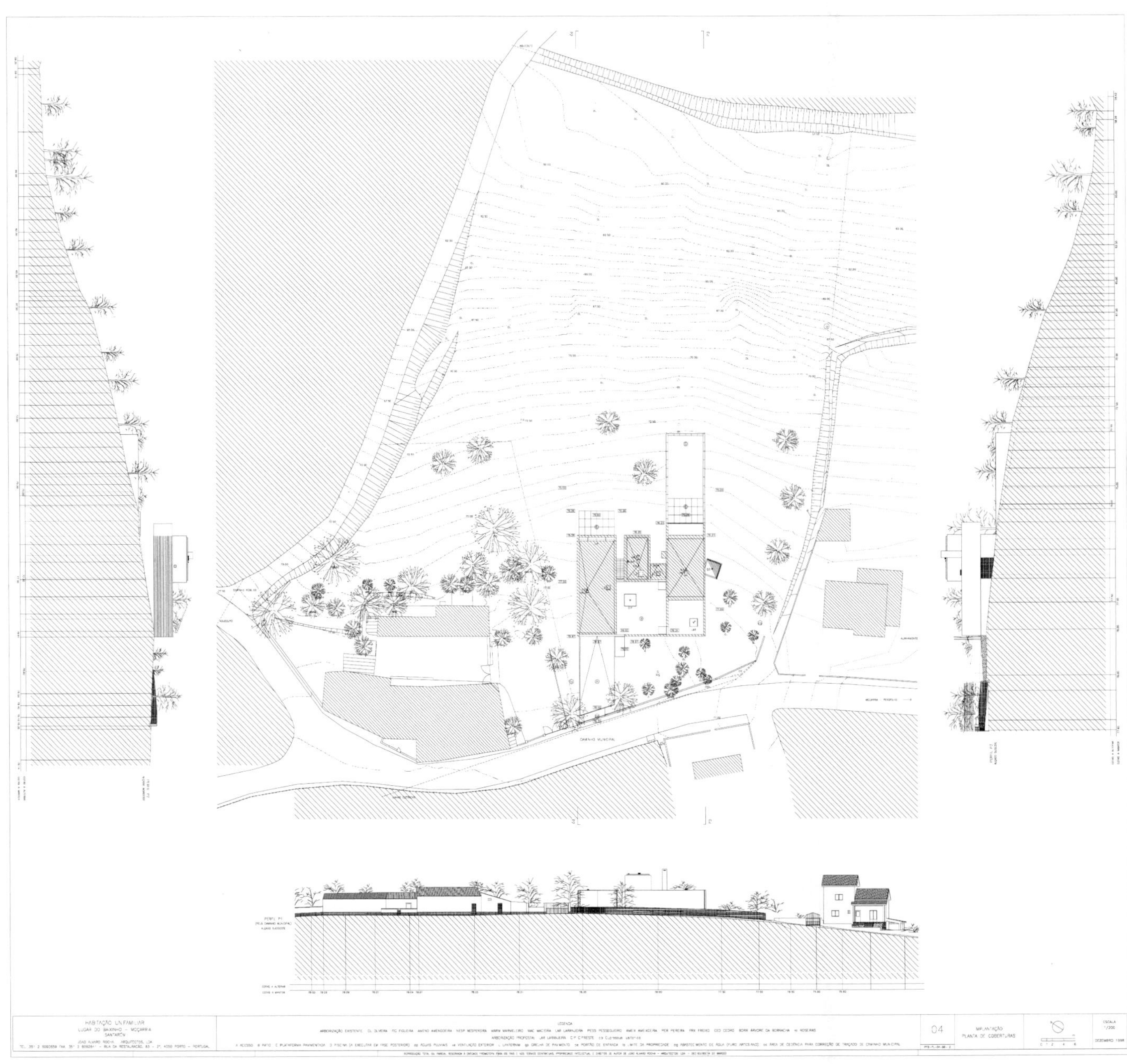

Facing page:
Site plan and general cross-sections.

Model, general view from the south.

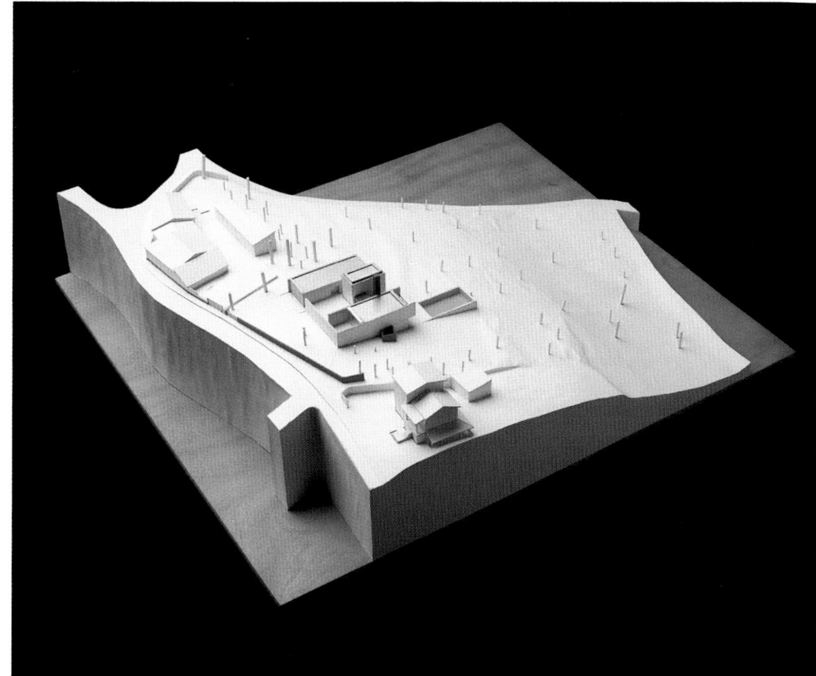

Model, general view from the north.

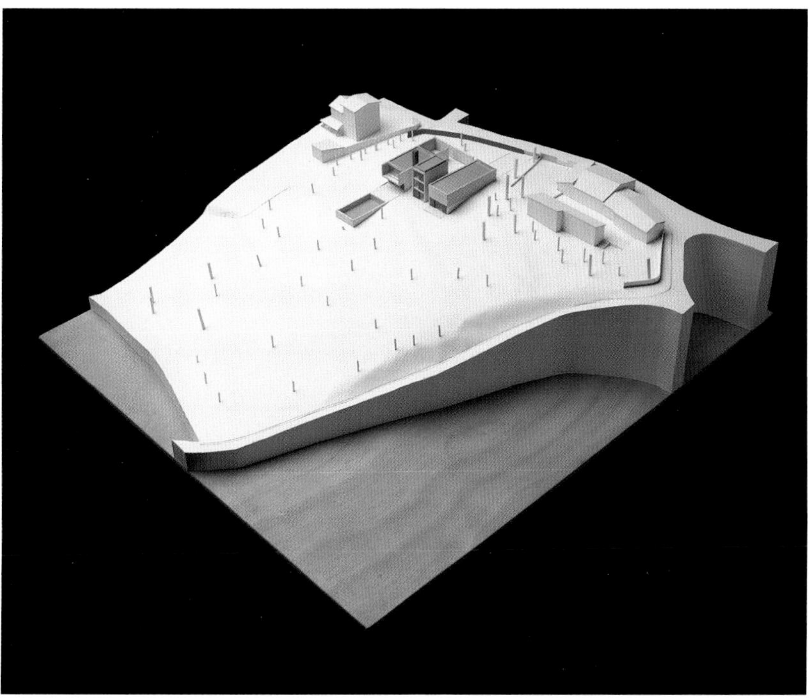

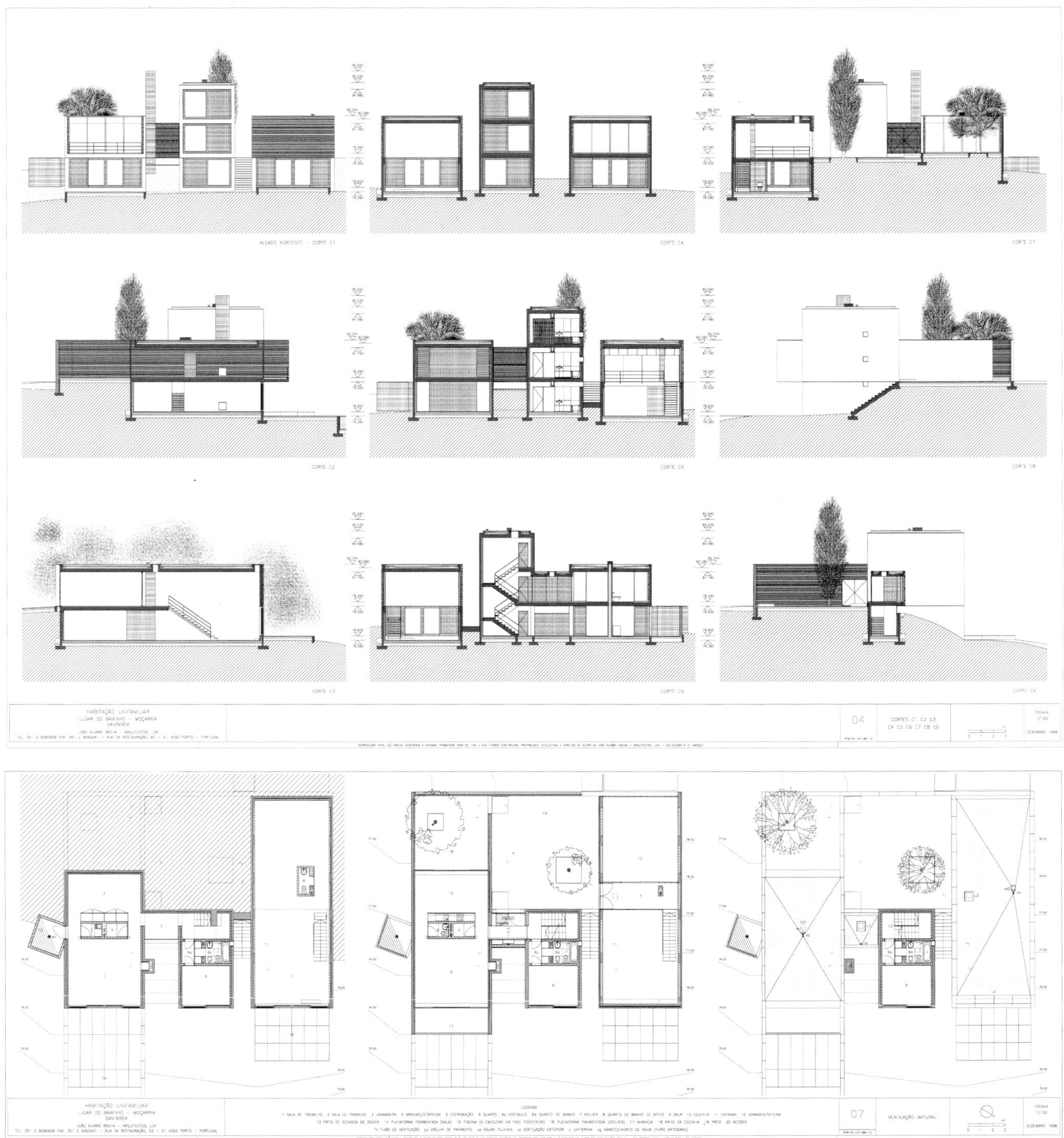

Facing page:
Sections.

Basement, ground and 1st floor plans.

Patio, view from the street entry.

East façade, general view
from the north.

East façade, general view.

6. House in Montenero, Tuscany

Design
João Álvaro Rocha, Architect
2000-02

Collaborators
Francesco Craca, Practice Architect
Stefano Ferracini, Architect

Model
Manuel André Gaspar, Model Maker

The presence of a sublime landscape disquiets me.

I hear the stones that speak to me of a warm, sheltering earth, made of soft tones, as a painting of a great master.

History and Tradition are foretold in this long horizon. There is no need for words. One needs only to look, place hands on the ground and know how to see, *parce qu'il y a des yeux qui ne voient pas*.[1]

A sight wished to be tangible, or a landscape made matter.

The old house, up above, seems distracted from the place on which it stands. Its apparent indifference is also the condition of its honesty and discretion. Maybe, that indifference is what averts it from the landscape, and simultaneously approximates it to the earth.

Maybe, this equilibrium, although precarious, is also part of "the natural order of things".

To find a time in the landscape, and belonging to it, this is the challenge.

A time to "be"; a time that – to avoid the falsity of the picturesque – is to affirm itself as it is today, without any nostalgia.

After all, a painting that cannot be painted because it already exists, with the measure of what is seen and the energy of what isn't visible – somewhere between heaven and earth.

Porto, February 2002

[1] Le Corbusier.

Site view.

Facing page:
Site plan.

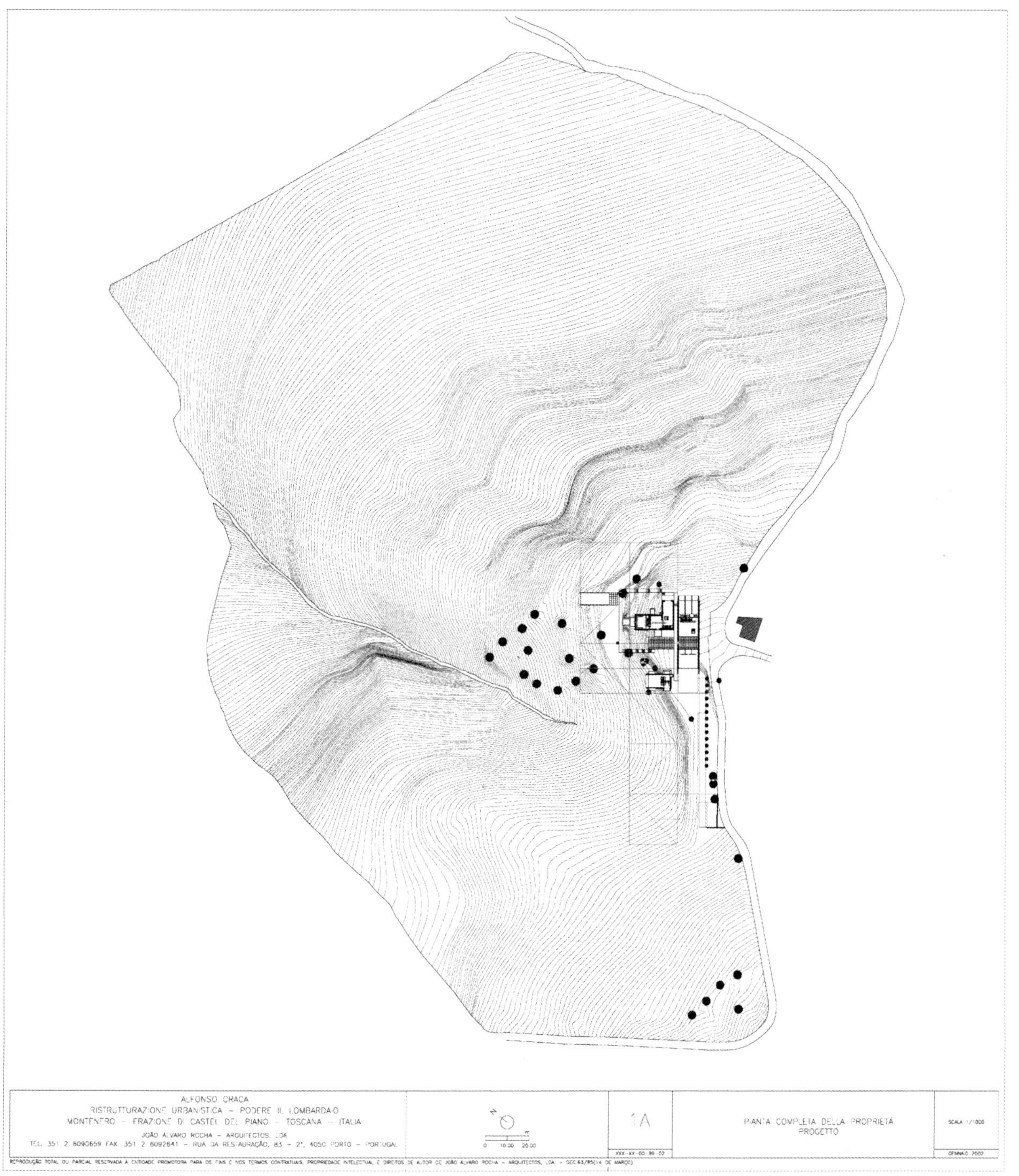
ALFONSO CRACA
RISTRUTTURAZIONE URBANISTICA – PODERE IL LOMBARDAIO
MONTENERO – FRAZIONE DI CASTEL DEL PIANO – TOSCANA – ITALIA
JOÃO ÁLVARO ROCHA – ARQUITECTOS, LDA
TEL. 351 2 6090659 FAX. 351 2 6092641 – RUA DA RESTAURAÇÃO, 83 – 2°, 4050 PORTO – PORTUGAL
N
0 10.00 20.00
m
1A
XXX-XX-00-99-02
PIANTA COMPLETA DELLA PROPRIETÀ
PROGETTO
SCALA 1/1000
GENNAIO 2002
REPRODUÇÃO TOTAL OU PARCIAL RESERVADA À ENTIDADE PROMOTORA PARA OS FINS E NOS TERMOS CONTRATUAIS. PROPRIEDADE INTELECTUAL E DIREITOS DE AUTOR DE JOÃO ÁLVARO ROCHA – ARQUITECTOS, LDA – DEC.63/85(14 DE MARÇO)

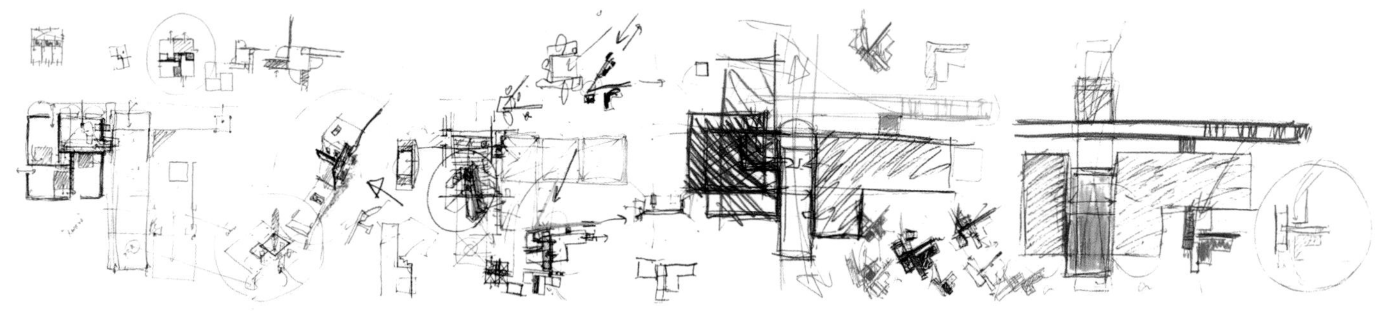

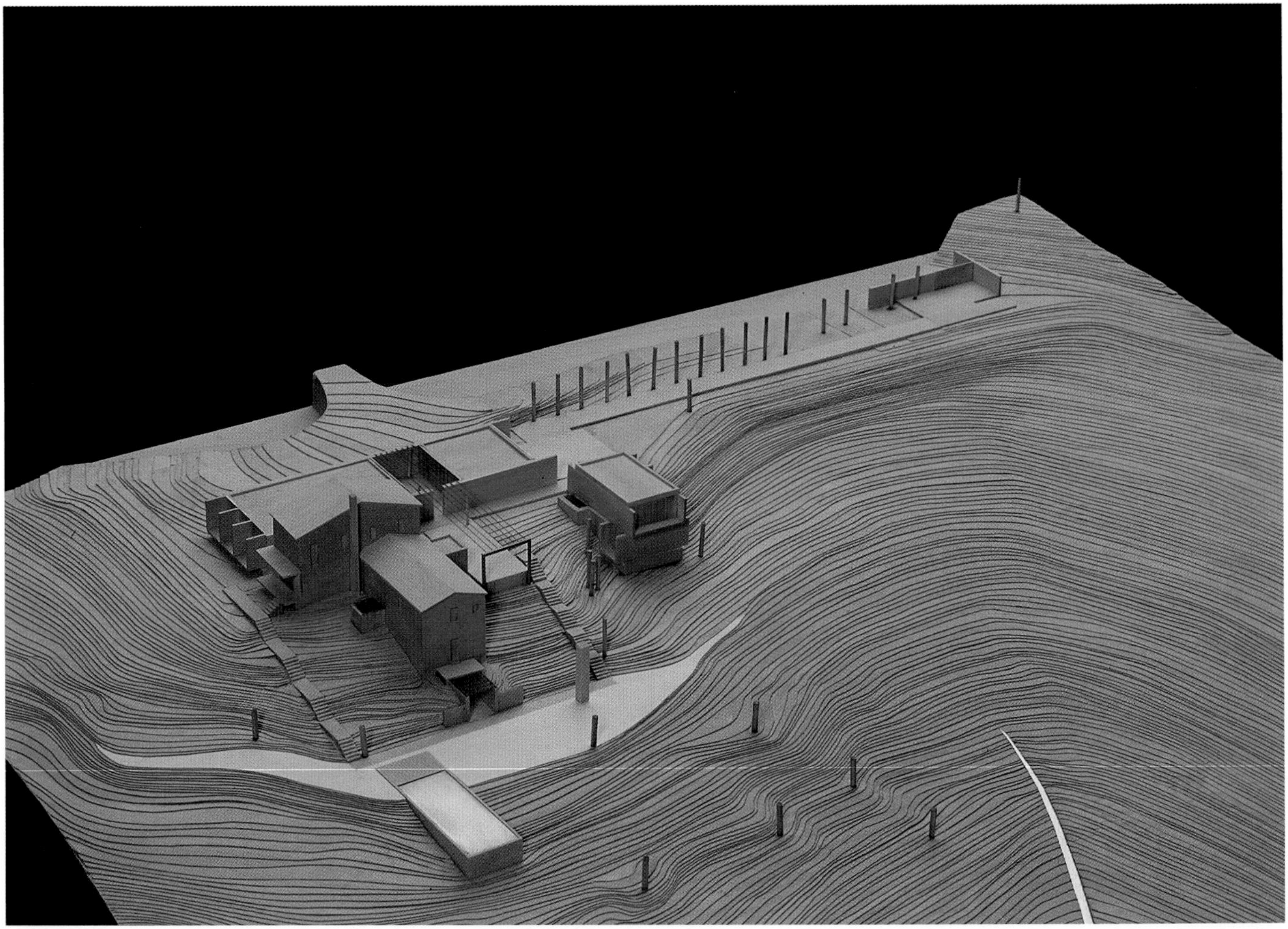

Facing page:
Study sketches and model view from the west.

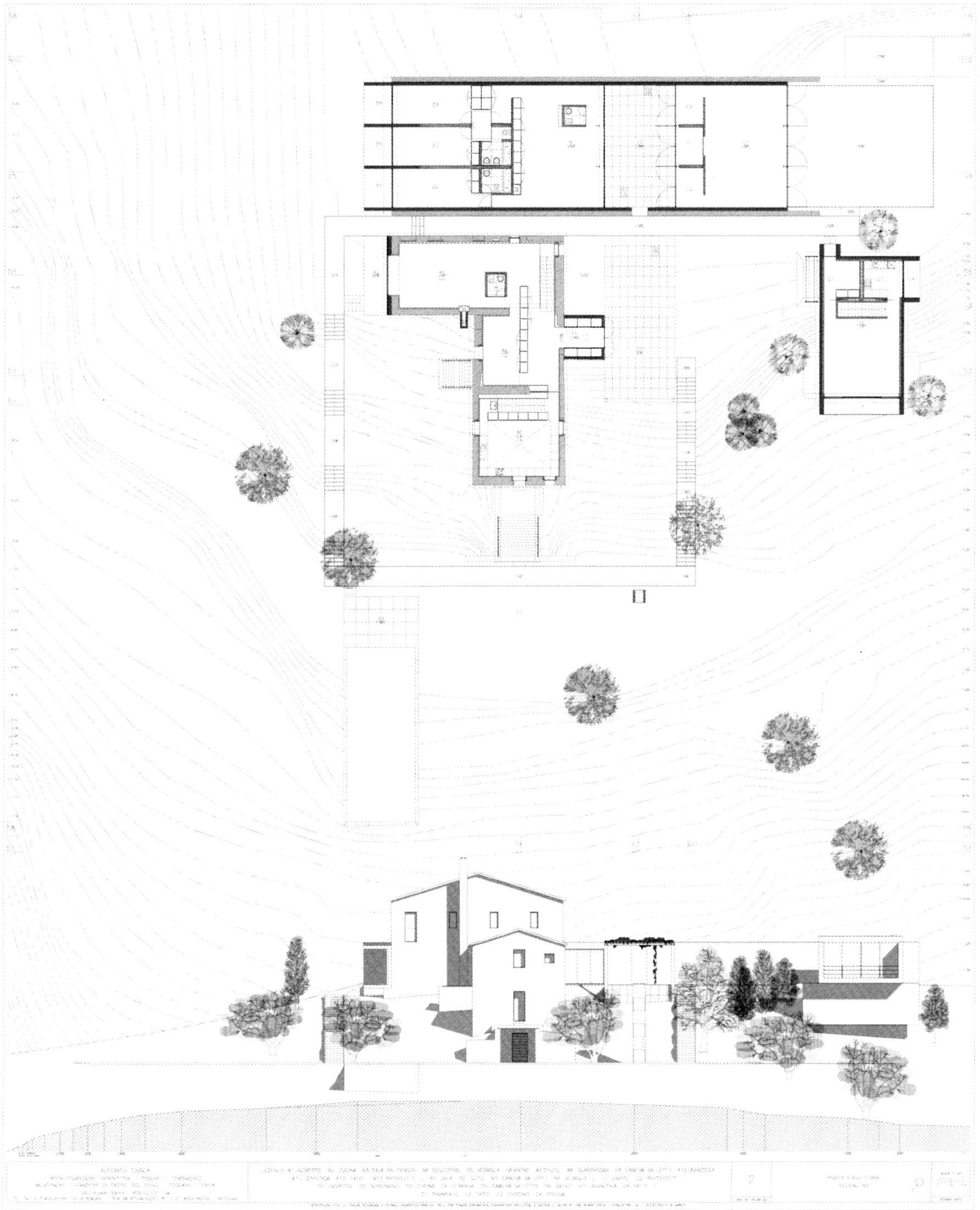

Ground floor plan.

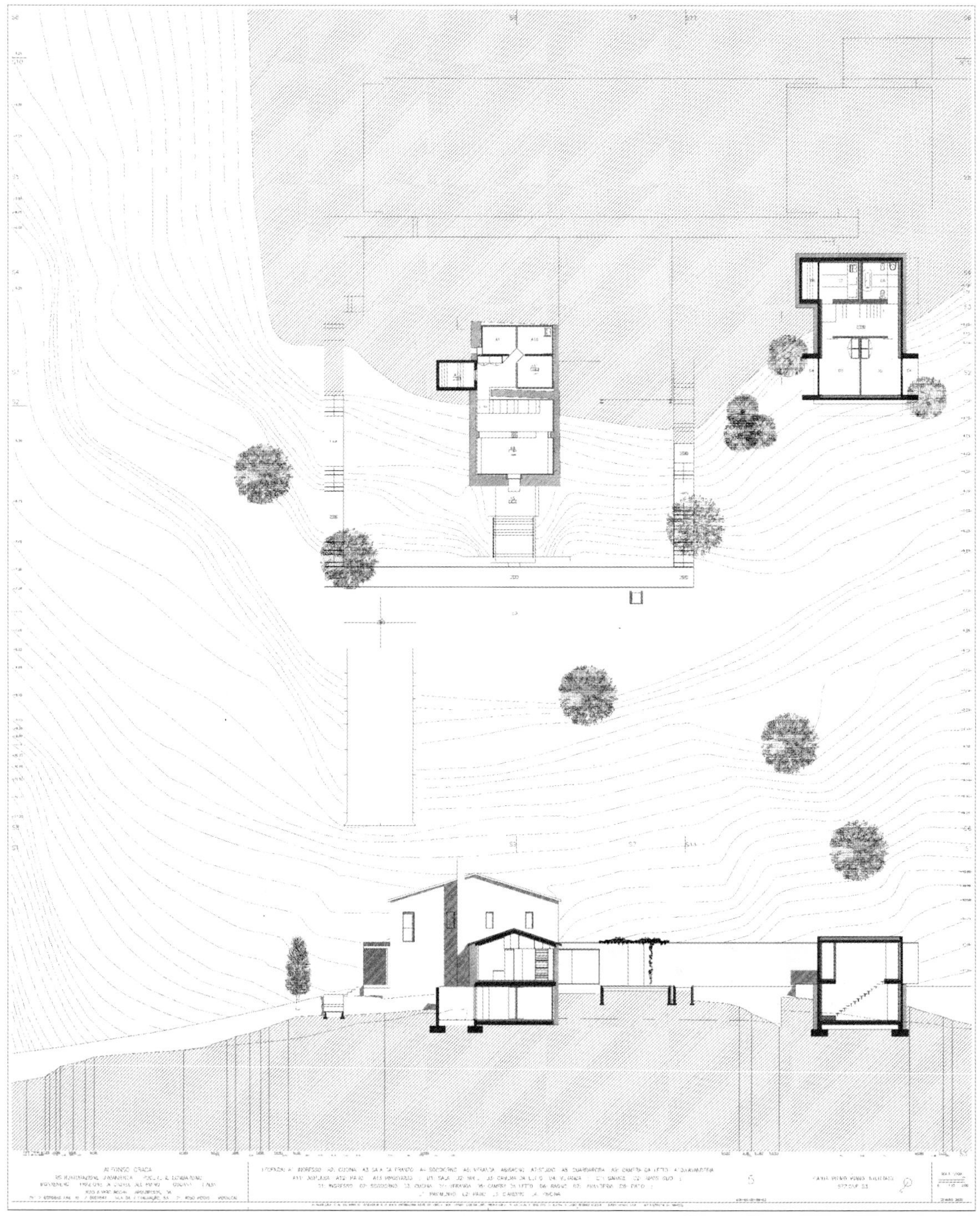

Basement plan.

Sections.

Sections.

Facing page:
Working sketches
and model view from
the south.

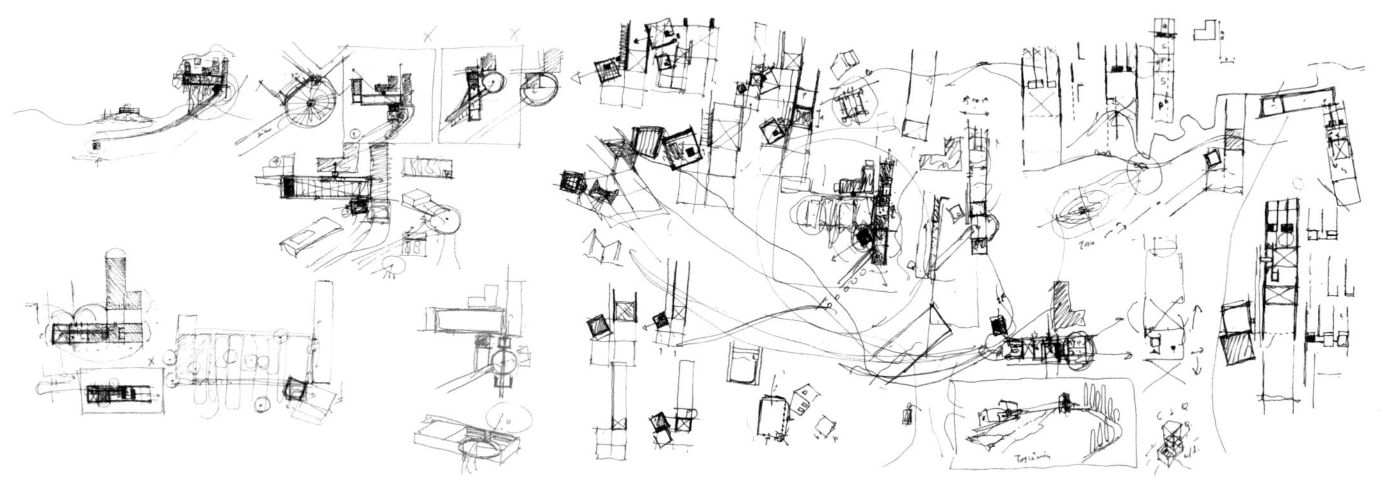

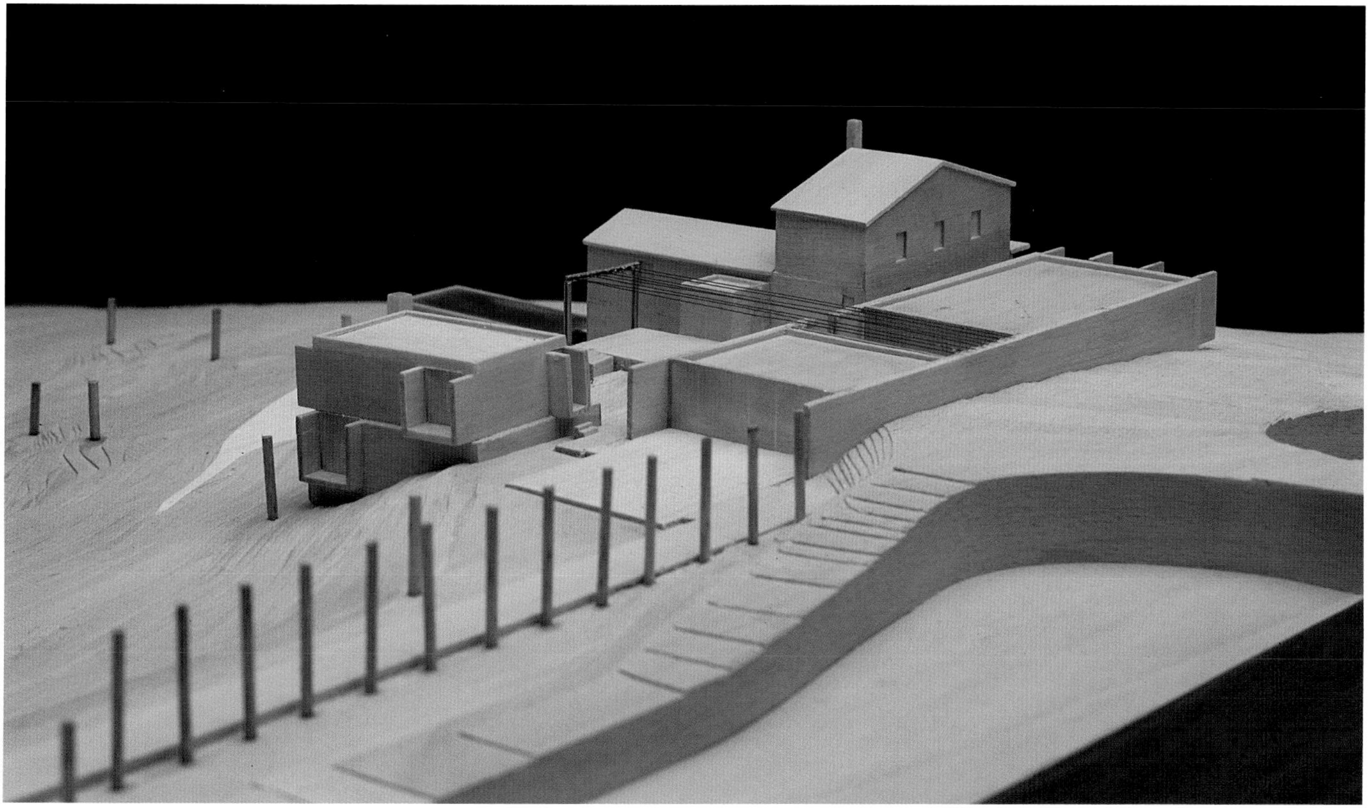

HOUSING

Conscious of the cultural effects of our actions, we represent our time aiming uniquely at solutions to its real necessities, interpreting its aspirations and acting in the knowledge of its limits. Thus, faced with the diversification in the ways of collective living that the contemporary world produces, the design of a habitat is based above all on the capacity to interpret a strategy of transformation of specific contexts by way of a rigorous definition of its elementary structure together with the adoption of an adequate logic in the combination of its parts. A process in which tradition demonstrates to be the most valuable stimulation for renewal. *(F.C.)*

7. Quinta da Barca: Pinhal Houses

8. Quinta da Barca: Marina Houses

9. Social Housing Maia I

10. Social Housing Vila Nova da Telha I

11. Social Housing Gemunde

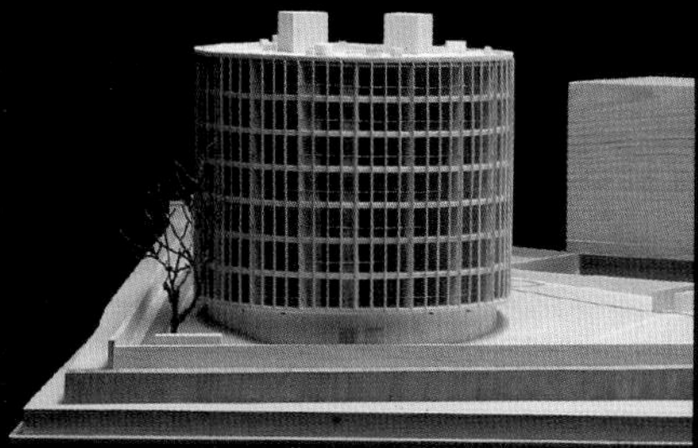

12. Portofino Apartment Building

7. Quinta da Barca: Pinhal Houses Esposende

Design
João Álvaro Rocha, Architect
1995-96

Construction
First phase 1997-2001 / second phase 2000-02

Collaborators
Alberto Barbosa Vieira, Architect
Jorge Pereira Esteves, Architect
José Eurico Salgado dos Santos, Architect

Models
Alberto Barbosa Vieira, Architect
José Eurico Salgado dos Santos, Architect

Almost nothing remains of the original estate: only the boundary walls, part of the garden and the river as a backdrop.

Now the property has been transformed into a housing complex, situated in a charming area of great natural beauty.

By analysing this transformation, the physical space of the estate seems only to make sense as a "precinct" that holds other constructions, and is meant for other uses and other people.

The intervention relating to this project is limited to one portion of the allotment, with no possibility of alterations of the basic elements: the number and dimension of the lots must be integrally respected; the already built roads, and the infrastructures associated to it, must be preserved; and the occupational typology initially foreseen can only be modified circumstantially.

The principles that form the conceptual basis of the project are consequently set starting from this apparently limited scenario.

In this context the idea of a "precinct", both as an affirmation of individuality and of privacy, acquires a meaning to be understood on a double level: the one relating to the precinct meant as a unit and intended to meet living needs; and the one resulting from the repetition of that unit, as a response to the larger precinct that is the estate itself.

This double level can also be seen in the different solutions used for the two floors that constitute the four rows of homes: on the one hand, they guarantee the spatial and functional independence that marks the unit articulation; on the other, they permit the displacement of the different units, allowing a better arrangement of the buildings and the street plan that shape the allotment.

Such arrangement is but a compromise between the basic level of the unit and the more articulated one resulting from its repetition.

The conceptual evolution of the entire complex has been developed from this very compromise, firmly believing that any exception only reveals the elements that compose the unit, making the repetition even more explicit.

The world of forms is very restricted. That is why we repeat them infinitely. What is variable and simultaneously permanent, is the urgency of their combination.

Porto, July 1997

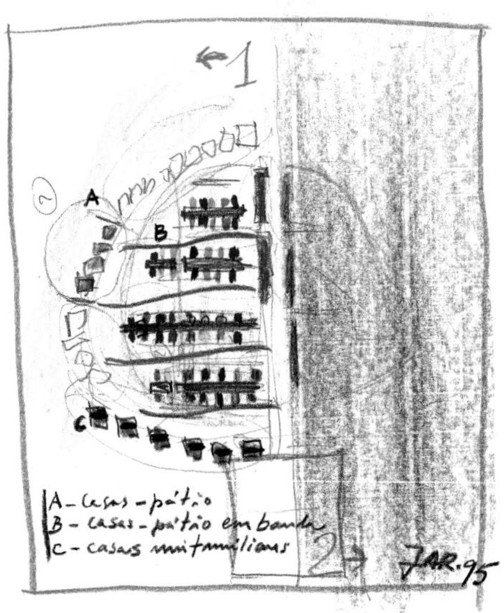

Study sketch,
general settlement.

Site plan.

Ground floor plan.

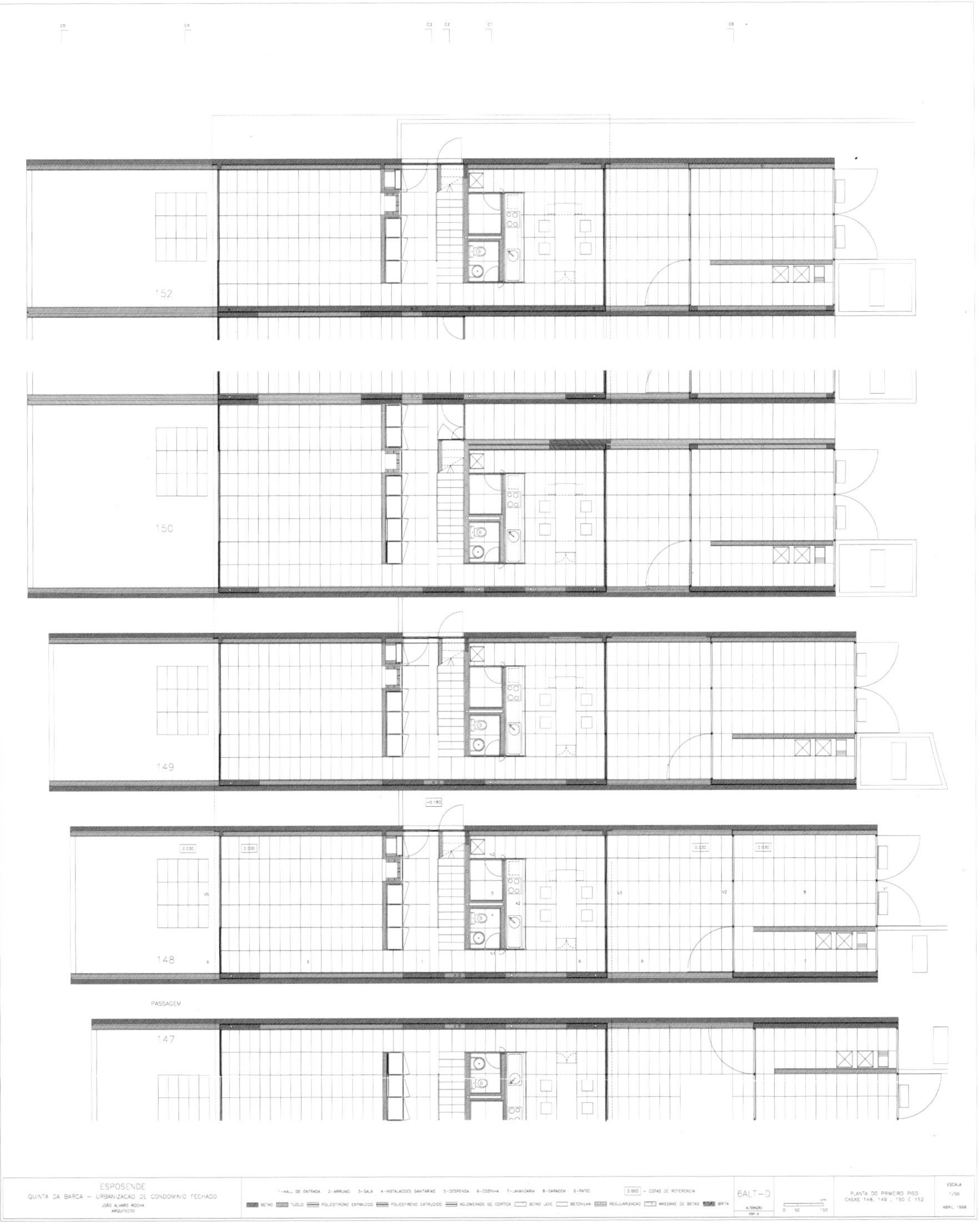

First floor plan.

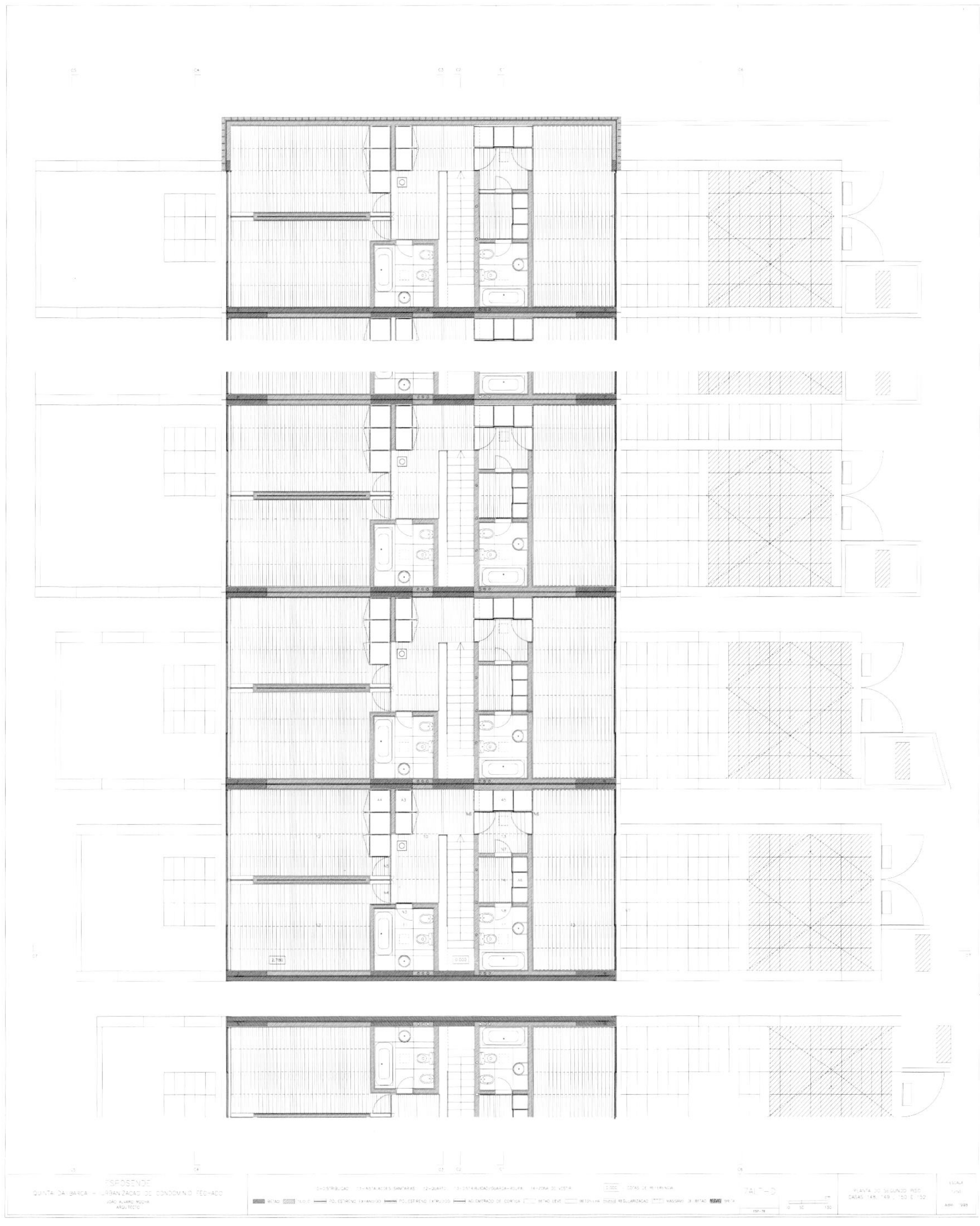

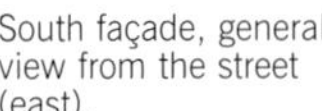

South façade, general view from the street (east).

North façade, general view with garages from the street (east).

South façade, partial view with front patios.

North façade, partial view with garages.

Stairs in entry hall.

Kitchen, general view
towards the living room.

Inner patio between garage and kitchen, general view.

Outer patio, general view from the living room.

Distribution hall in bedroom area.

Distribution hall, detail of the access to bedrooms.

8. Quinta da Barca: Marina Houses Esposende

Design
João Álvaro Rocha Architect
1996-97

Construction
1999-2001

Collaborators
Alberto Barbosa Vieira, Architect
Jorge Pereira Esteves, Architect

Model
Alberto Barbosa Vieira, Architect
Ana Sofia Ribeiro, Practice Architect

This second project of a group of buildings situated in the same housing complex of Quinta da Barca is based essentially on the choice of an occupational pattern different from that of the allotment.

We can therefore affirm that the main objective in redesigning this section of the complex is to physically "erase" the constructions it contains, in order to emphasize the compositional dynamics which gives form to the estate venture.

The choice of materials different to those used in the other buildings adds to this logic of order; at the same time, it tries to emphasize the contact between the actual construction and the ground on which it stands.

The challenge is that of defining a "precinct" suitable on a living scale, and to inscribe it in a territory also defined as a "precinct", which is the estate itself.

The houses are organized on one floor and are linked perpendicularly along the street from which they are accessed. The individual entrances, from that same street, are seen as a way of creating an alternate sequence between the various units forming the two complexes – a rhythm that emphasizes the individuality within each unit.

This compositional strategy results in an inner courtyard onto which the actual entrance to the complex opens. All the compartments are organized sequentially from this courtyard, in a direct spatial relationship with a larger courtyard, situated on the opposite side of the entranceway.

The precinct meant as a living space has two faces: a schist surface on the outside, which reveals the compact nature of the buildings, and their soil engrained character; and a white plaster surface inside, used to create homogeneity and luminosity.

From the outside, the complex appears as a compact, apparently insurmountable bulk, revealing almost nothing of its interior space. From the inside, the inner and outer spaces seems to merge in one single body.

Then there is merely and only the light...

Porto, September 1997

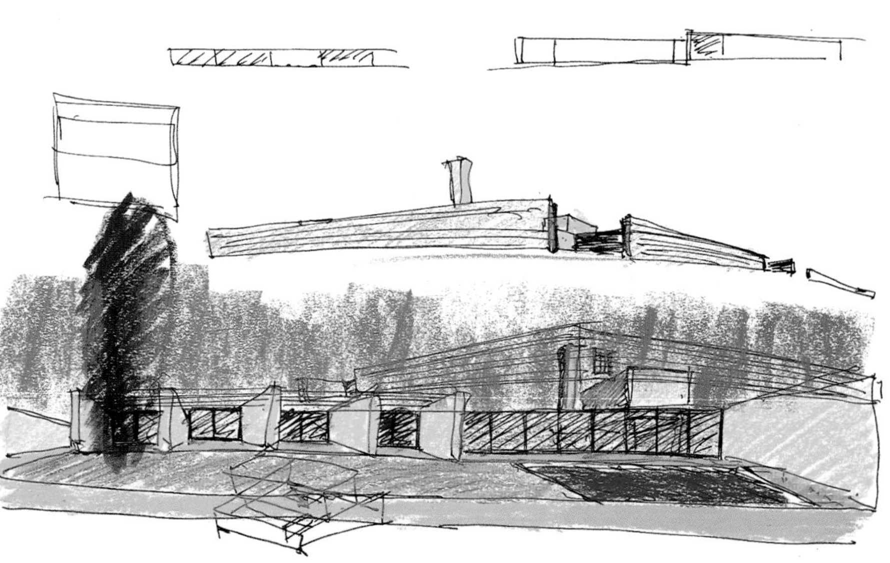

Study sketch, general views.

Site plan

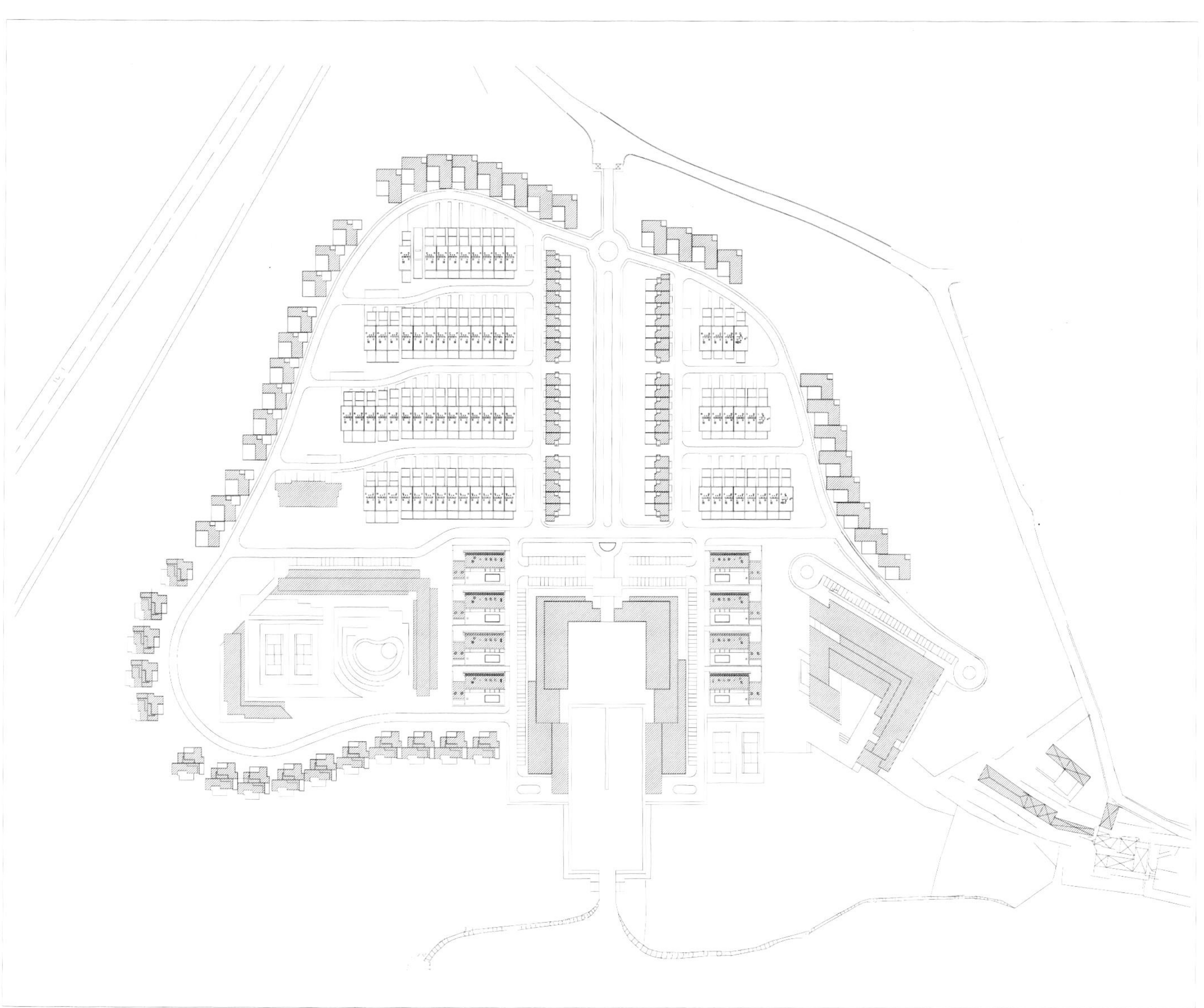

Ground floor plan and general sections of one of the complexes.

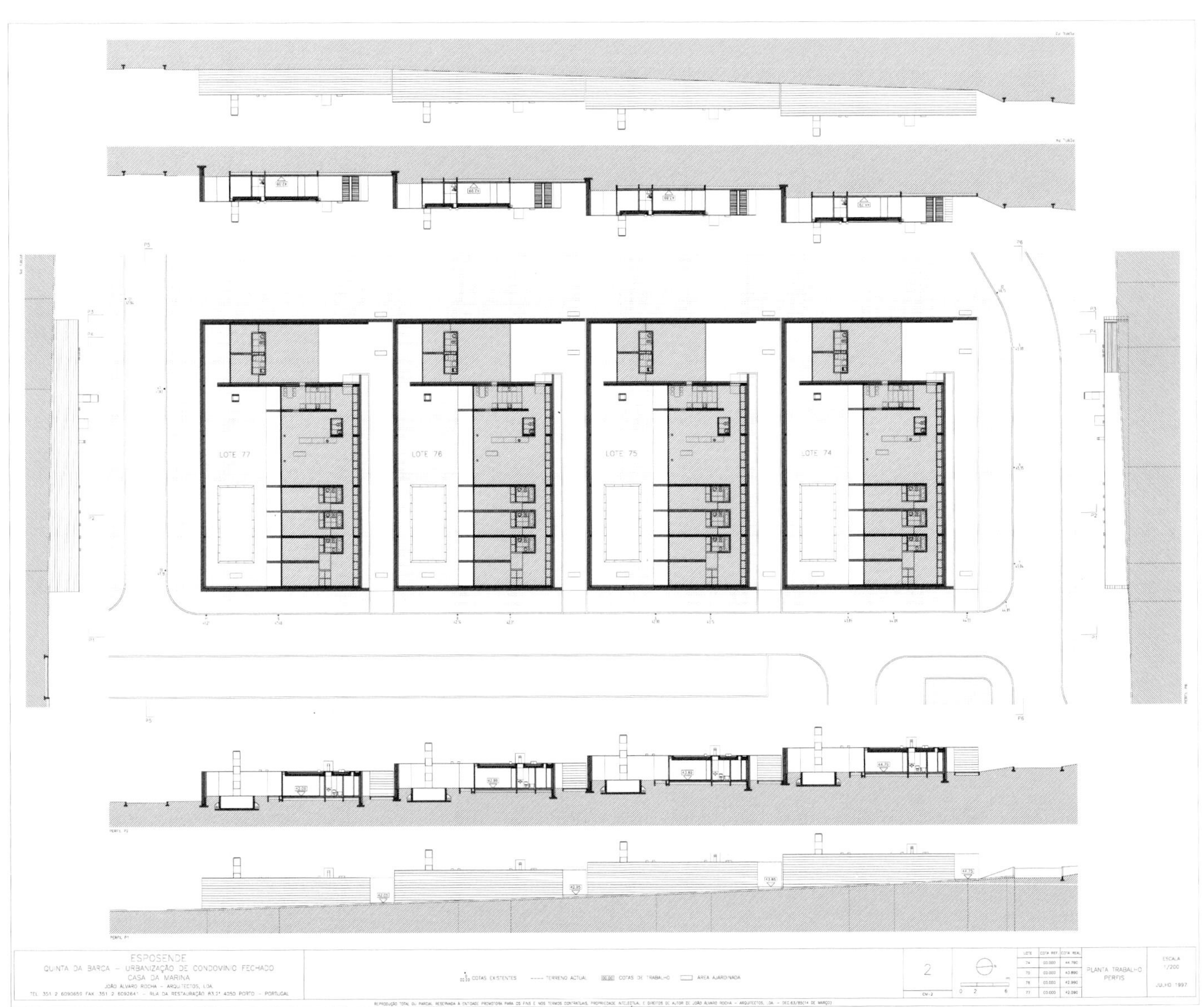

Street façade with the entrance, general view from the east.

Inner patio, general view.

Entry patio, view towards the street.

Entry patio, view from the garage.

Detail of the entry hall.

Corridor, general view of the entry hall.

Kitchen, view towards the exterior (inner patio) with barbecue.

Living room, general view towards the entry hall and the inner patio.

Corridor, general view from the bedroom areas towards the entry hall.

Bedroom, general view
towards the inner patio.

Bedroom, general view
towards the inner patio.

Swimming-pool in
the inner patio.

9. Social Housing Maia I
Special Rehousing Program
Lugar do Outerio - Maia

Design
João Álvaro Rocha, Architect
Francisco Portugal e Gomes, Architect
1996

Construction
1997-99

Collaborators
Ana Sousa da Costa, Architect
Jorge Pereira Esteves, Architect
Pedro Tiago Pimentel, Practice Architect

The land where the housing complex lies is situated inside a low density allotment, in an area close to the centre of the city, a location that confirms the unmistakable dullness of an urban grid lacking any urban design strategy. This is enough to understand the difficulties to be faced in the project.

The choice of the location and the design are the result of an unavoidable compromise between the building scale and the scale characterizing the close surroundings; such compromise should not be detrimental to any spaces of collective use that the project is going to generate.

The complex is placed on the side opposite the entranceway to the allotment, and is directly related to the existing Telephone Exchange building; its location contributes to the "regulation" of the land's inner limits.

The choice to use the same material (brick) of the Telephone Exchange building goes beyond a mere effort of approximation: it is an expression of the will to "regulate", and a way to establish an identity. Such identity is emphasized by the unique and coherent image resulting from the austerity, and the rigour of the complex design.

The conceptual basis of the building is founded on the idea that a portion of urban territory should be internally articulated, capable of generating a collective and balanced occupation of open space, whereby the relation between the parts and this space should provide the necessary hierarchy.

Porto, November 1999

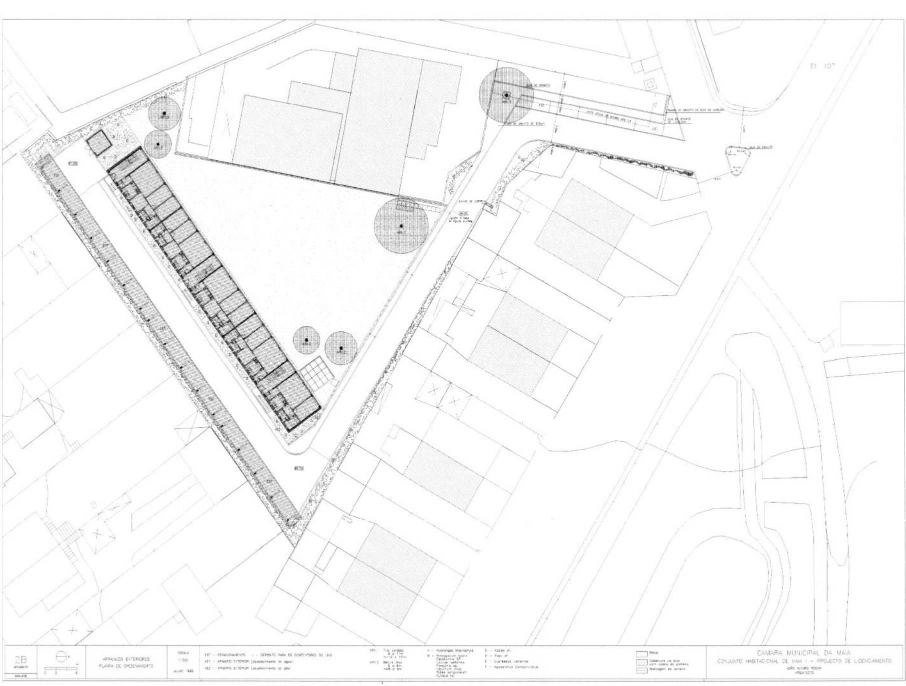

Site plan.

Southwest façade,
general view.

Basement, first, second/third and roof plans.

Facing page:
North east façade, general view from the carport.

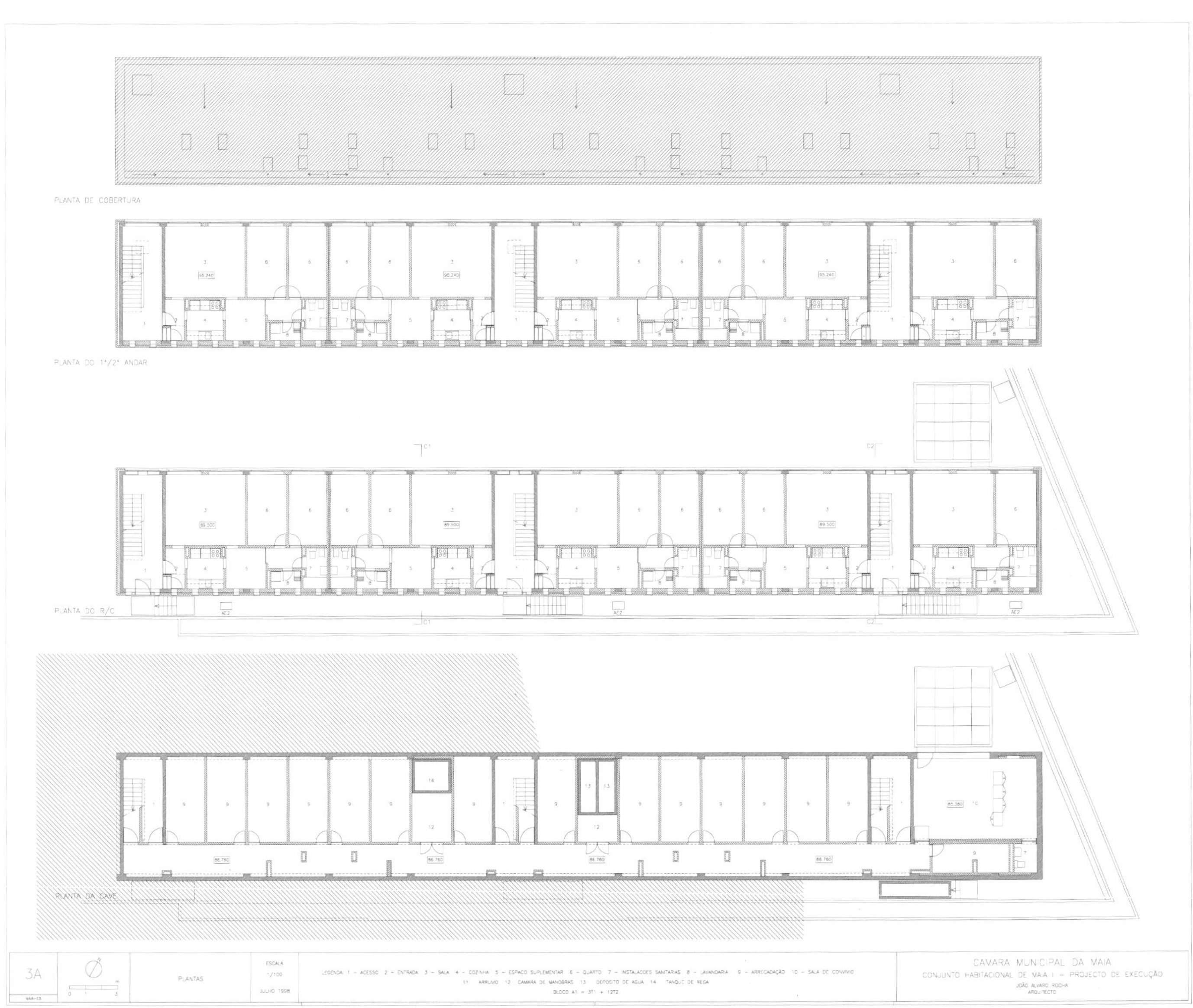

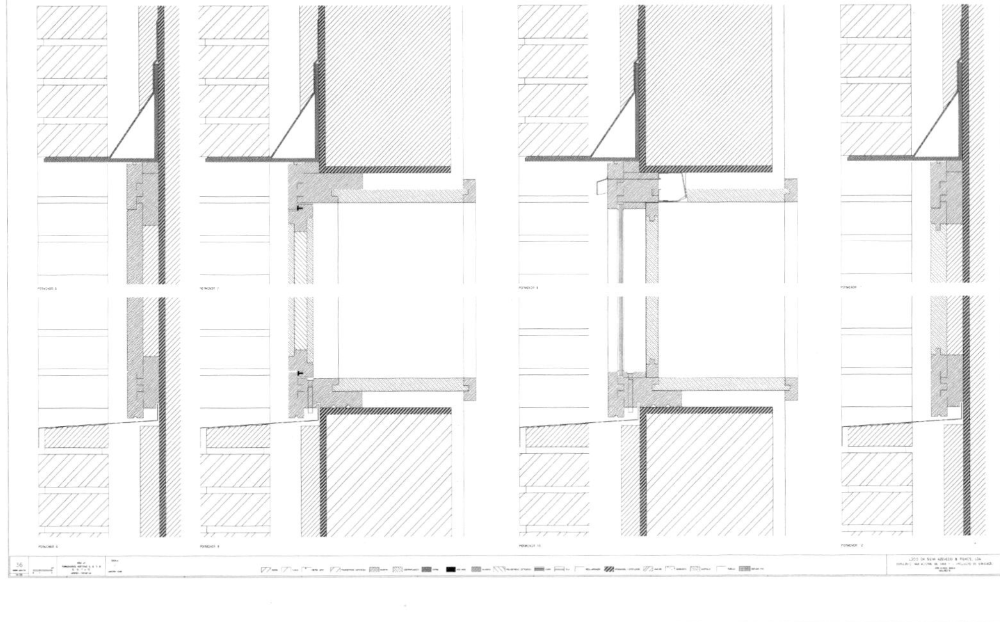

Southwest façade windows, vertical details.

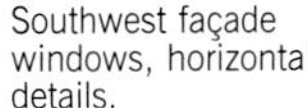

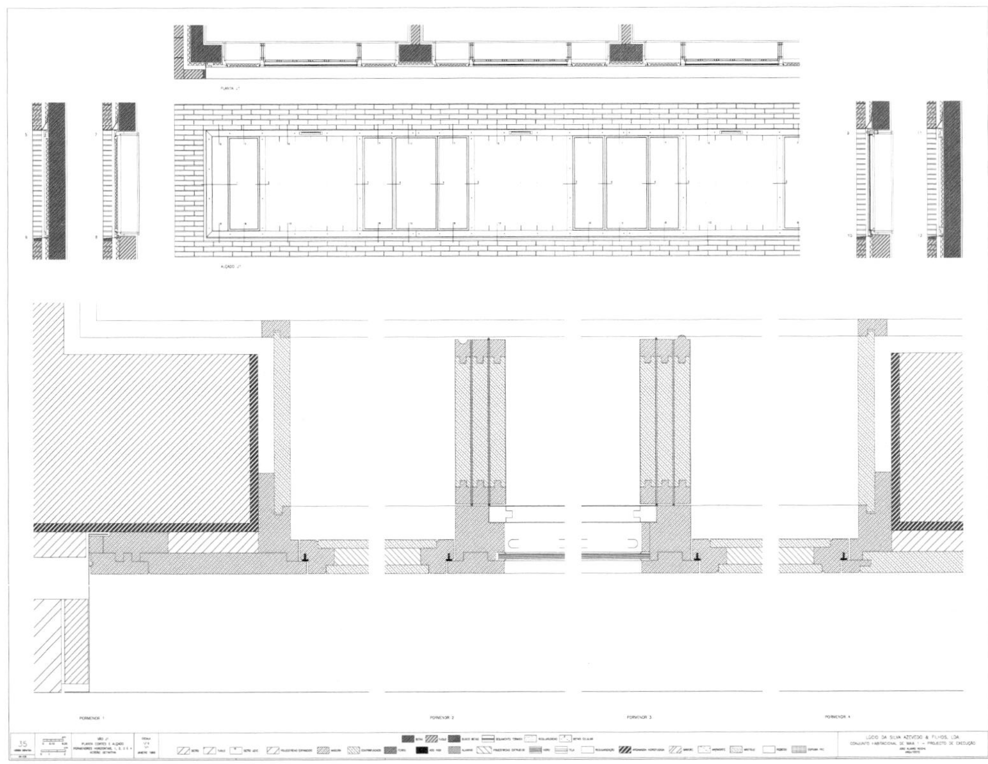

Southwest façade windows, horizontal details.

Southwest façade,
partial view.

Entry hall, general view towards the northeast façade.

Stairs, general view towards the southwest façade.

Dining area, view towards bedroom area.

Southwest façade windows, view from the living room.

10. Social Housing Vila Nova da Telha I
Special Rehousing Program
Vila Nova da Telha - Maia

Design
João Álvaro Rocha, Architect
Francisco Portugal e Gomes, Architect
1996

Construction
1997-2000

Collaborators
Ana Sousa da Costa, Architect
Jorge Pereira Esteves, Architect
Pedro Tiago Pimentel, Practice Architect

The land the housing complex occupies is located in a territory whose morphology results from the unrestrained building of successive lots; the absence of any effort to order and define a hierarchy of the public space is here a tangible reality, which goes beyond any purely speculative process.

The land is bounded by a public street on one side, and the railway on the other, and faces the so-called "civic centre", which should serve as a sort of central point of reference in the area. These physical limits cannot be ignored when defining the project.

Although the living style proposed by the project is different from that which predominantly characterizes this part of the territory (single-family homes), the design aims at overcoming the limits set by the land, as well as contradicting the "centrality" suggested by its location.

The project's approach refuses predominance, and prefers anonymity as opposed to any kind of forefront position.

The regularity with which the buildings are arranged along the public street, and the way they are grouped so as to shape their own exterior space (courtyards), demonstrates an effort to articulate the scale of the complex in relation with its immediate surroundings.

Both compactness and permeability characterize the complex, and reveal a compromise whereby the essential and rigour are the expression of the plainness that is pursued. A plainness which is only apparent, and hides the complexity on which it is constructed, being that the truly simple is obtained through the concentration of that same complexity.

Porto, December 2001

Site plan.

Facing page:
General view from the railroad tracks (west).

Basement and floors plans.

Facing page:
General view from the street.

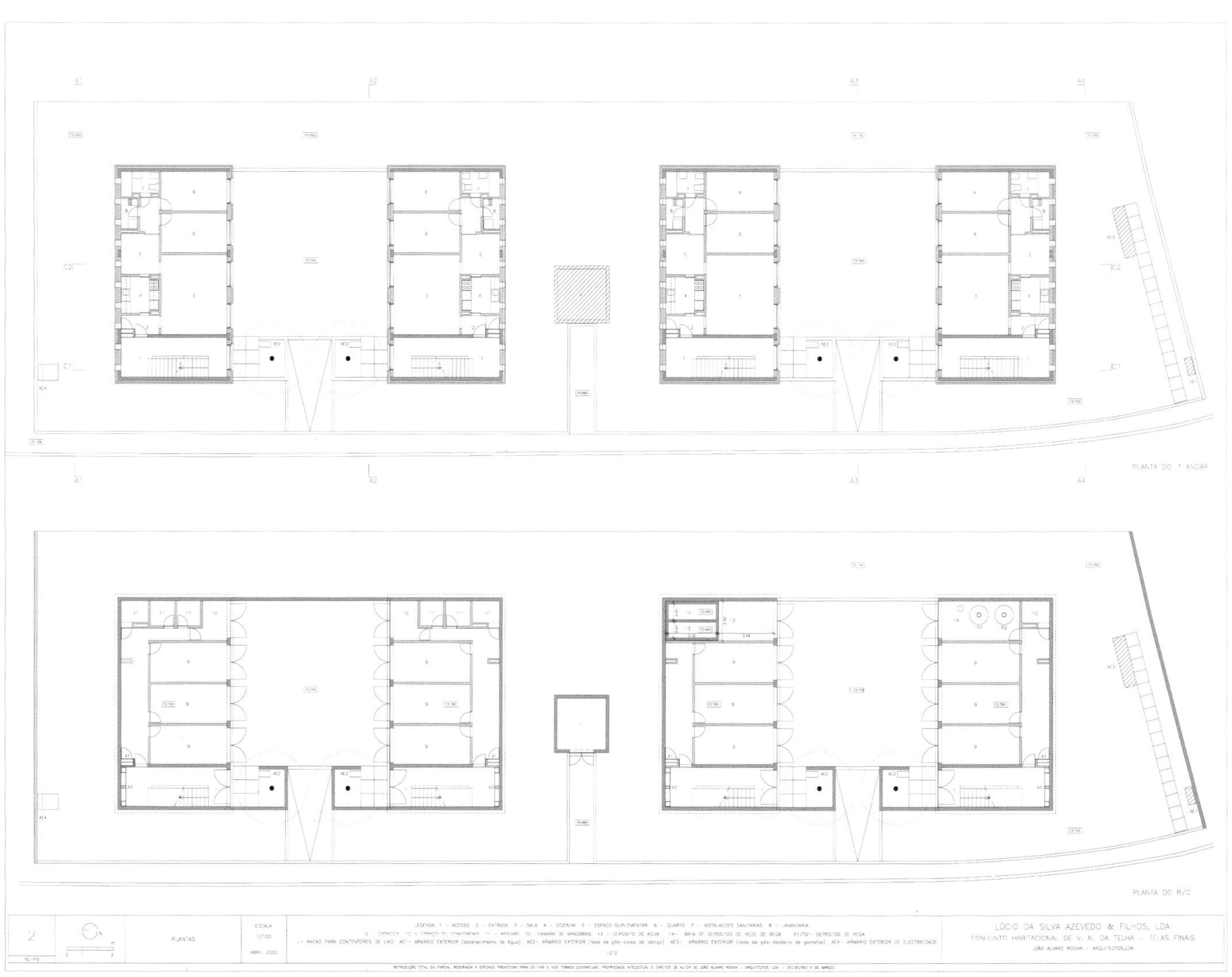

Courtyard façade, partial view.

Courtyard façade, partial view from the outer entry hall.

Entry, general view
towards the outer hall.

Stairs, general view
towards the entry and
the windows of the
courtyard façades.

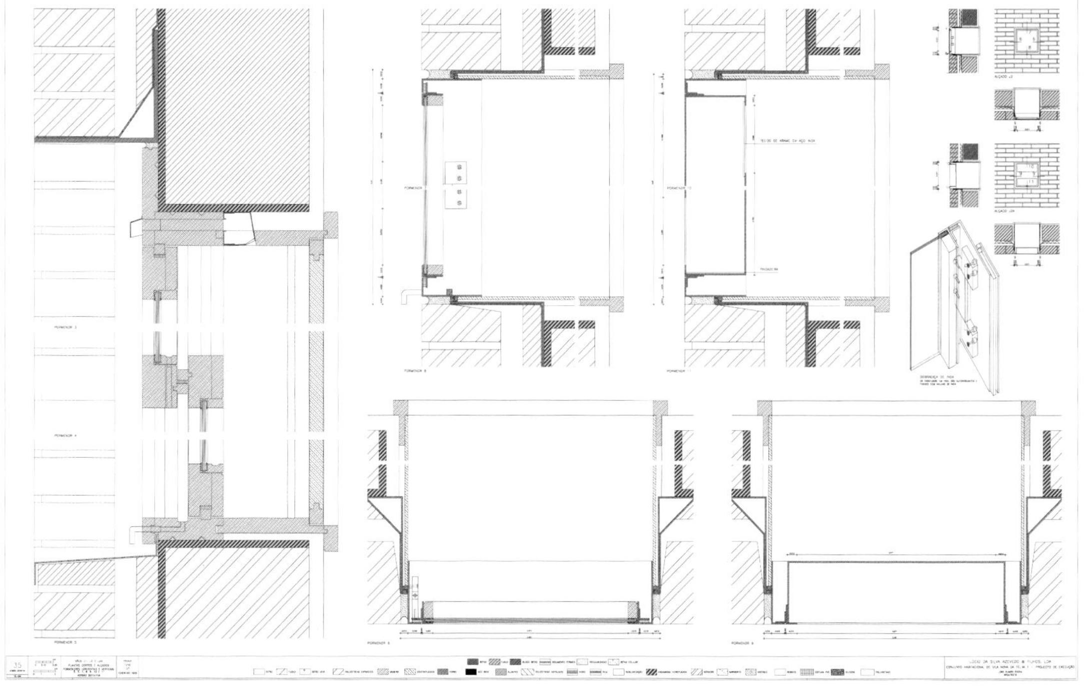

Courtyard façade windows, vertical details.

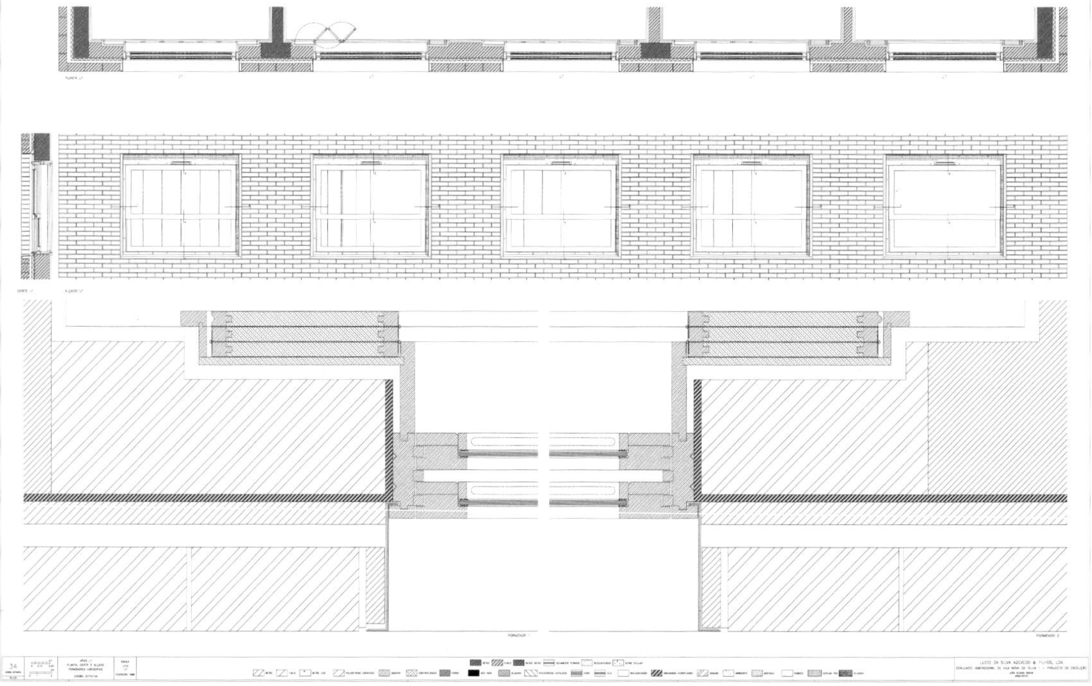

Courtyard façade windows, horizontal details.

Living room, view towards
the courtyard.

11. Social Housing Gemunde PER - Special Housing Program Gemunde - Maia

Design
João Álvaro Rocha, Architect
1997

Construction
1998

Collaborators
Francisco Portugal e Gomes, Architect
António Luís Neves, Architect
Carla Garrido de Oliveira, Architect
Pedro Tiago Pimentel, Architect
Sónia Campos Neves, Practice Architect

The land where this housing complex is located is set in a predominantly rural territory, punctuated by urban centres among wide areas of agricultural fields. It is a place where the mountain prevails over the plain – the last place where construction seems possible.

The general topography of the spot, which resembles a valley, is softened by terraces sustained by granite walls, perspectivally open towards the landscape.

The complex should consequently be conceived as a non interfering element, a structure perfectly harmonized with the characteristics of the territory.

In this context the design should be capable, in its whole, of defining a system of relations that, without disregarding the complex's actual size, are capable of diluting its presence, controlling the articulative scale that it wants to keep with the landscape.

That is why the residential buildings are placed in line with the land's longitudinal axis, and substitute one of the terraces; in this way they don't alter the characteristics of the existing topography, and at the same time do explore the multiplicity of views over the landscape through the various paths that should be established to reach the complex.

The association of the courtyards that give access to the car parkings with the building's volume guarantees a separation between public and private, because the adjoining exterior space is intended to be an open public park; moreover, it results in a number of platforms that allow to resolve the connection of the building with the soil, by securing and articulating levels, and also as a way of dividing and relating the two more extensive sides. It is, after all, a way of using the volume ot the building as if it were a thickness capable of separating and simultaneously relating that wide open space with another, located northward on the opposite side, also of collective use but directly related to the inhabiting area.

The project also explores the movement offered by the linearity of the many paths of access to the buildings as opposed to the sinuosity of the existing trails, in search of a connection between the two as a possibility of continuity between the different times in which the territory has been arranged.

Independently of its functional and aesthetic value, the project should be translated into an urban gesture less related to the territory and more intended as a simple but real support to people's lives. Only in this way, can it aim to have a place in that territory.

This is the sense of transformation that has historically characterized all Great Architecture, and that the project, in its modesty, wants to grasp as its own.

Porto, March 2002

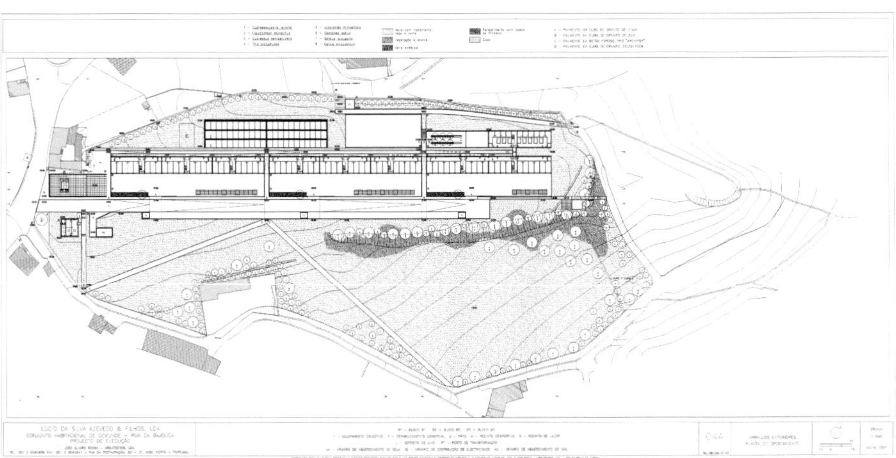

Site plan.

General view from the south side.

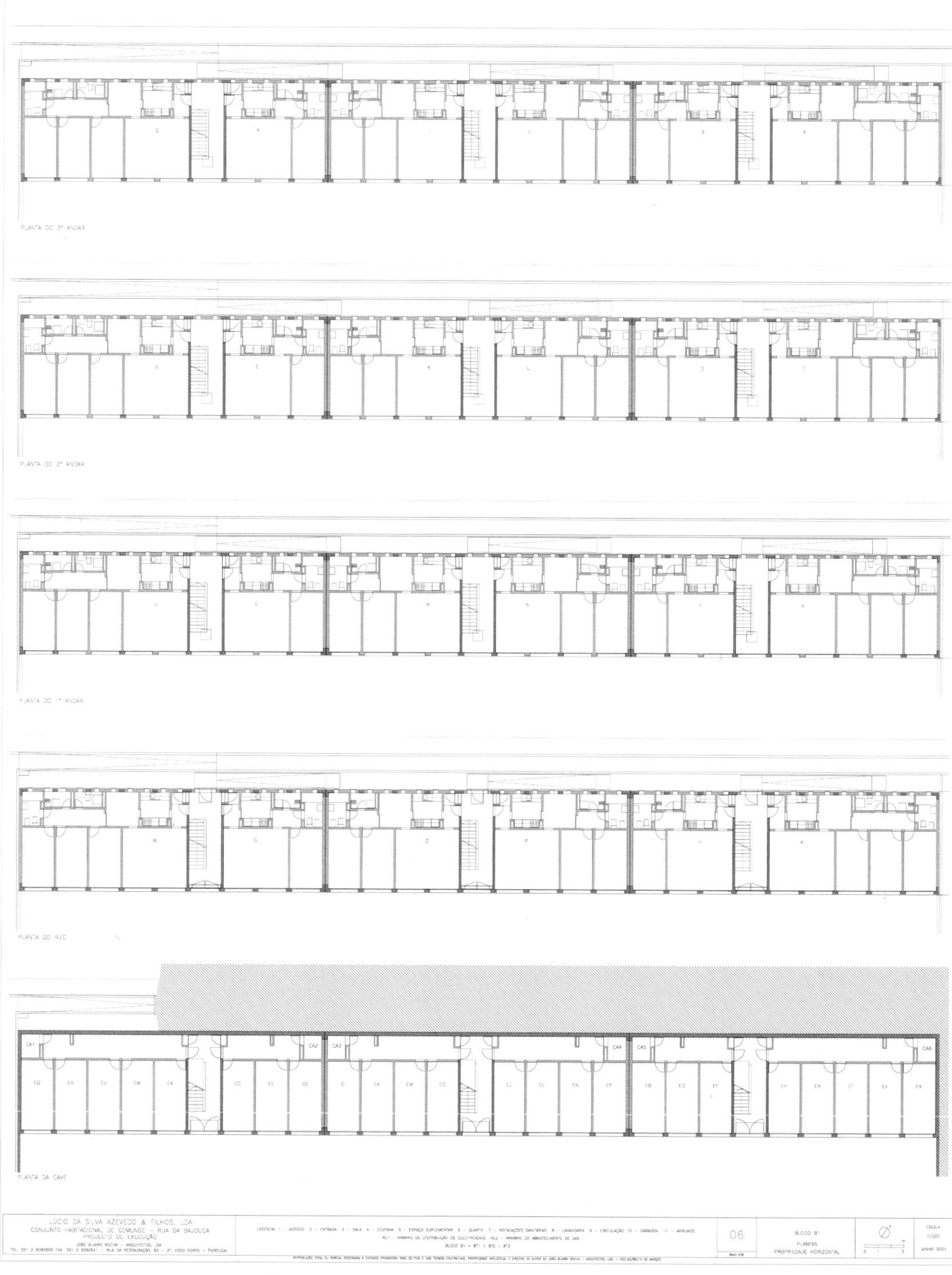

A1 & A2 blocks, basement, general 1st, 2nd and 3rd floor plans.

A3 block, basement, ground, 1st and 2nd floor plans.

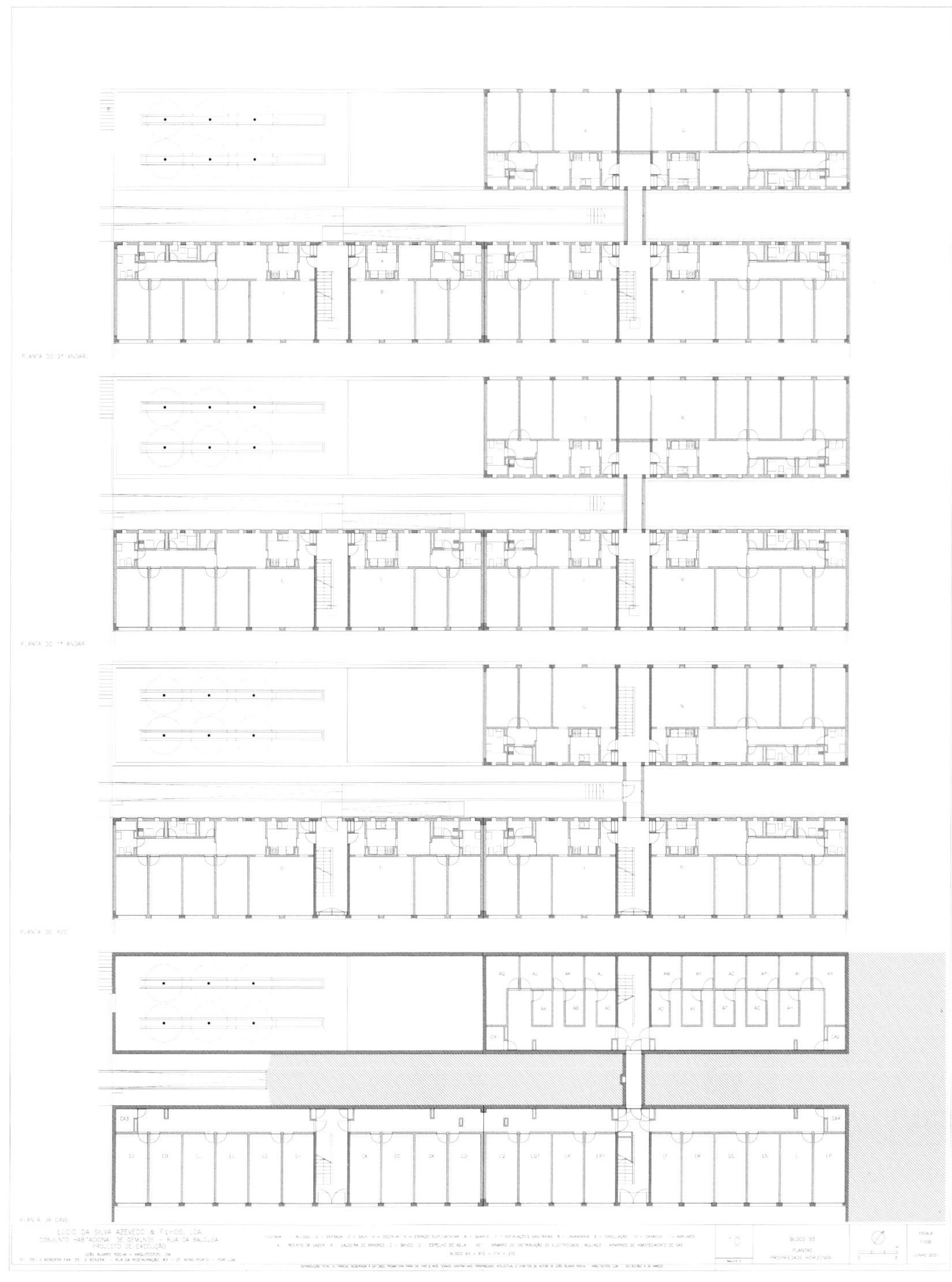

South façade, partial view with the front courtyards.

South façade, partial view
with the car entrance.

North façade, general view.

North façade, partial view with passage between the two ends of the complex, and the vegetable garden in the foreground.

North side, with the walkway to the entrances and service facilities on the left.

Inner garden with block A3 in the background.

Entry of block A3.

12. Portofino Apartment Building
Rua de Quires, Vila Nova da Telha - Maia

Design
João Álvaro Rocha, Architect
1999-2000

Construction
In adjudication phase

Collaborators
João Ventura Lopes, Architect
Tiago Macedo Correia, Architect

Models
Armando Lopes Teixeira, Architect

The building is located in a position apparently marginal to the complex of which it is part. Owing to this spatial condition, the building has been conceived both as a moment of decompression, and as a landmark, in the way it relates to the dwelling forms that characterize this part of the territory.

The regularity of form, the neutrality of the treatment with which surfaces are defined, the absence of a dominant direction, and its location apparently out of the alignments to the complex confirm the building's decompressive nature, but also its predominance.

Its dual character is evidenced by the uncommon cylindrical form, and the apparent protection it offers; by occupying the most inside part of the land, it acts as a summarizer and organizer of an urban image still in the process of affirmation.

The composition is consequently organized on the pretexts which determine the geometry of the actual form chosen. The rigorous planning and the spatial clarity that characterize the design of the dwelling unit, and which are repeated throughout the whole building, are expressed in an image whose neutrality is somehow compensated by the movement intrinsic to the elements used in the exterior "surface" (metallic blinds).

The variety that results from this movement does not necessarily mean that the structure has to be repetitive or monotonous, redundant or expressionless.

Indeed, it is in space that life happens. And that's all.

Porto, April 2000

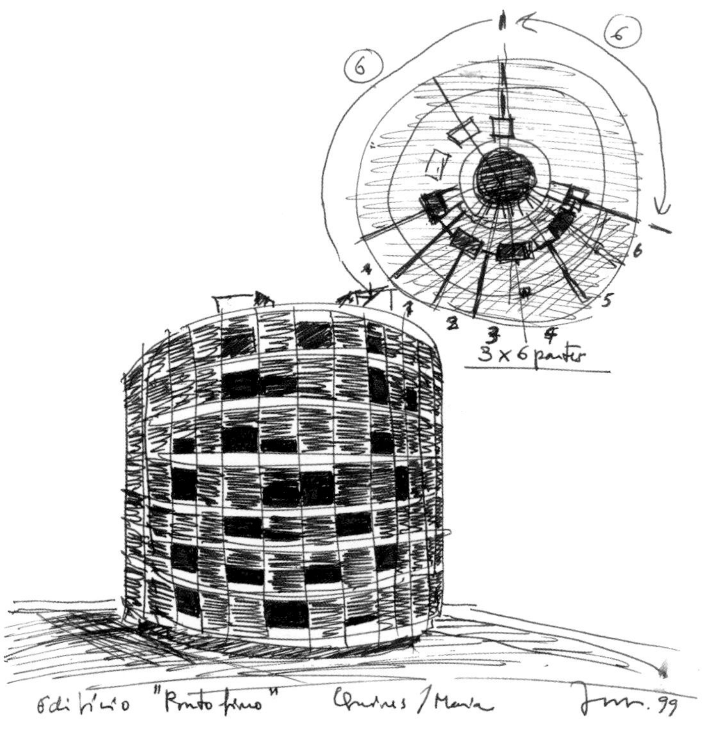

Study sketch, general view and scheme plan.

Facing page:
Site plan.

Model, view from the north side.

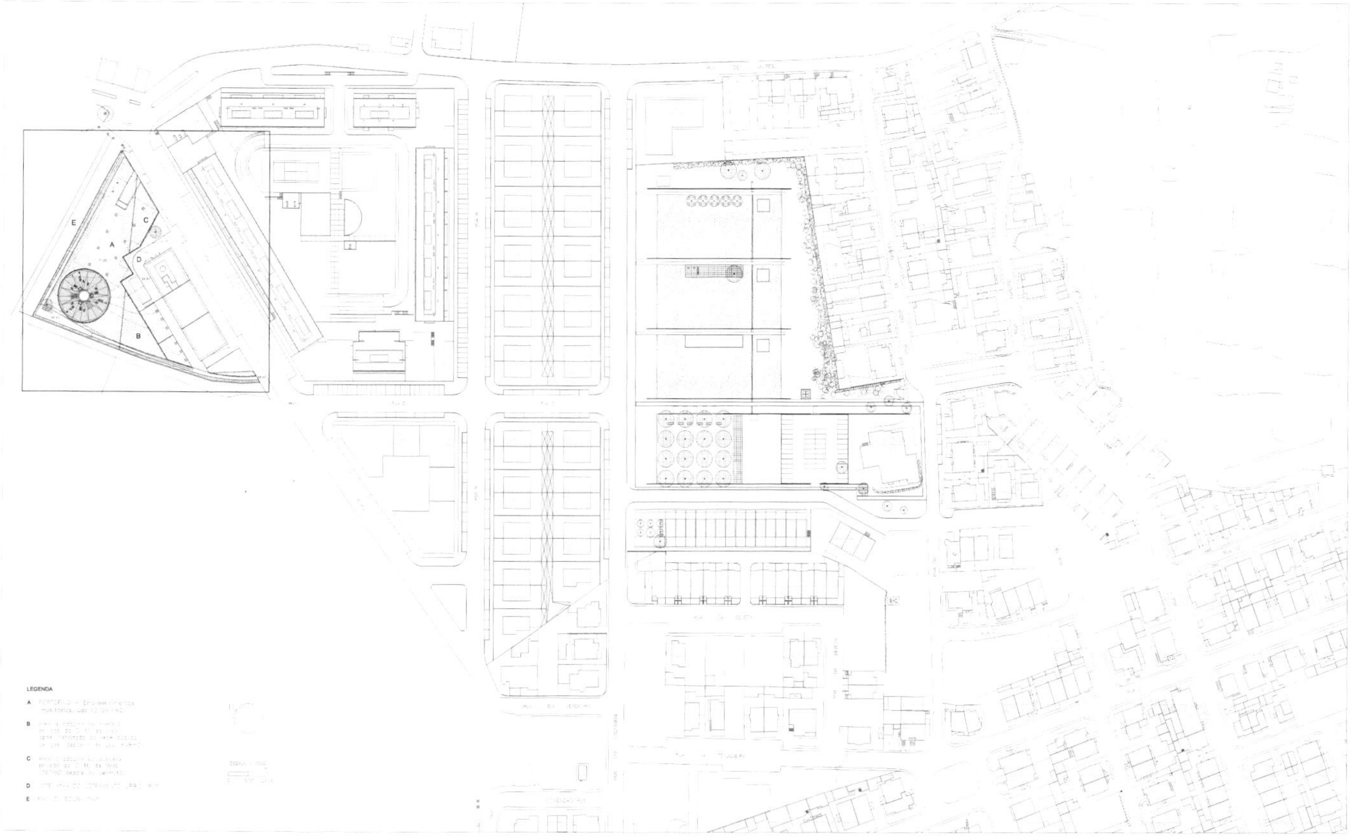

LEGENDA

A

B

C

D

E

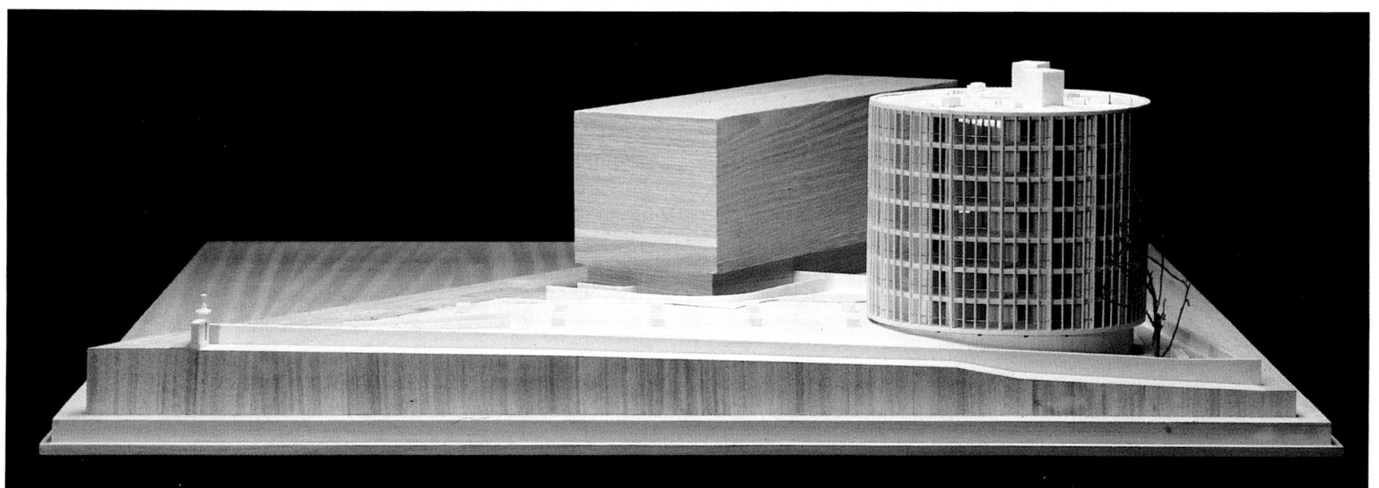

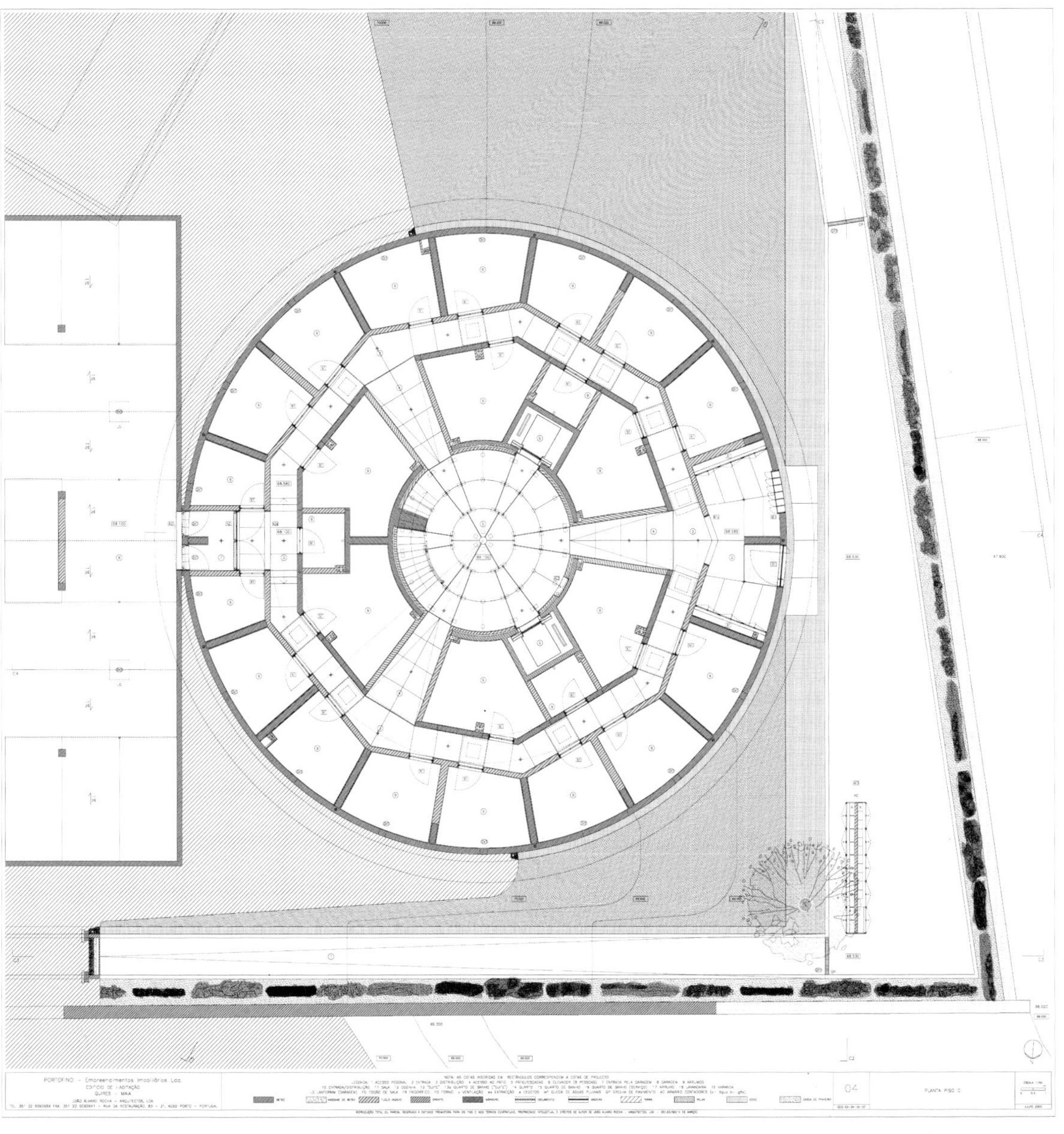

Basement plan.

Type floor plan.

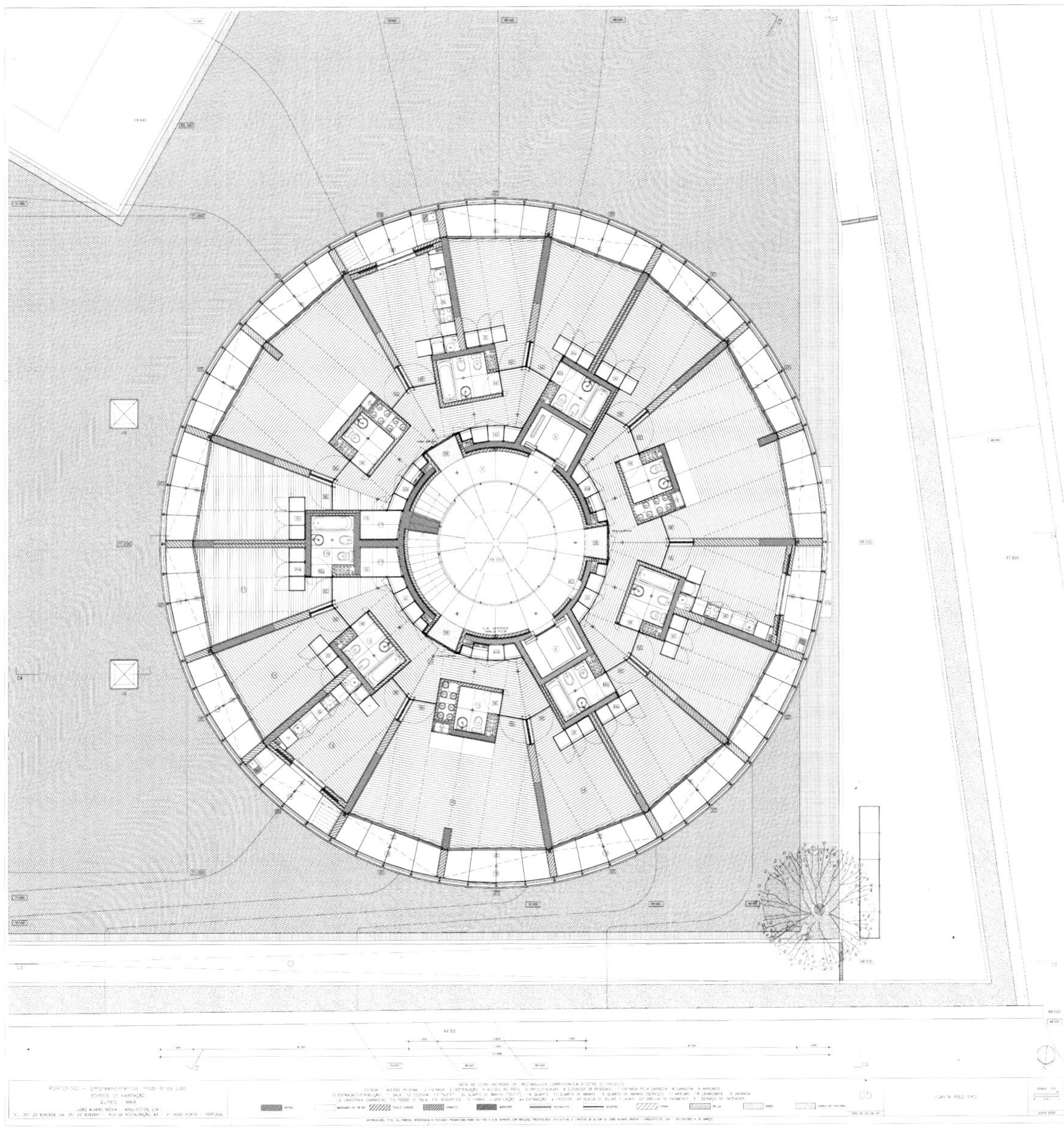

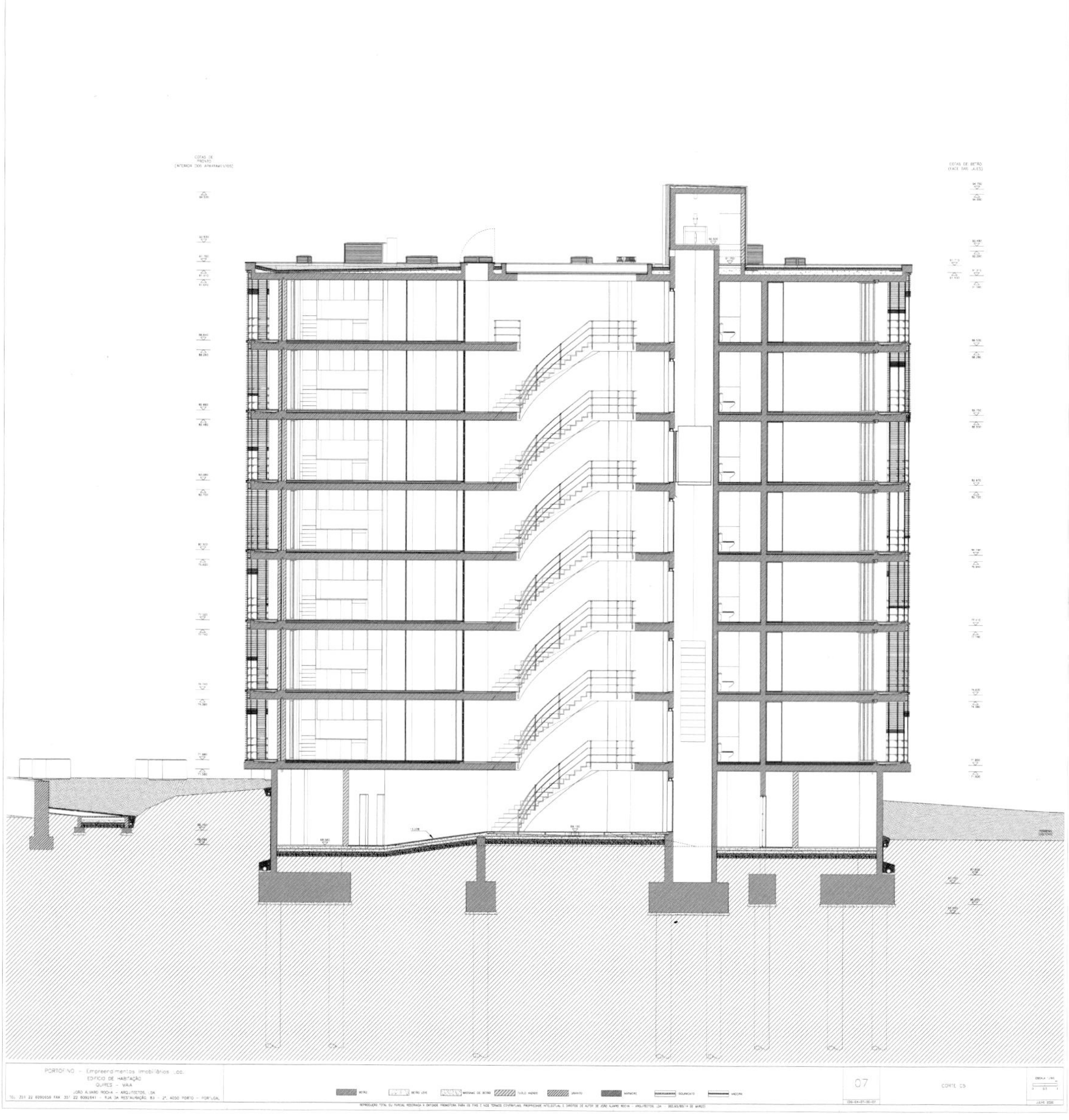

Section through stairs.

South elevation.

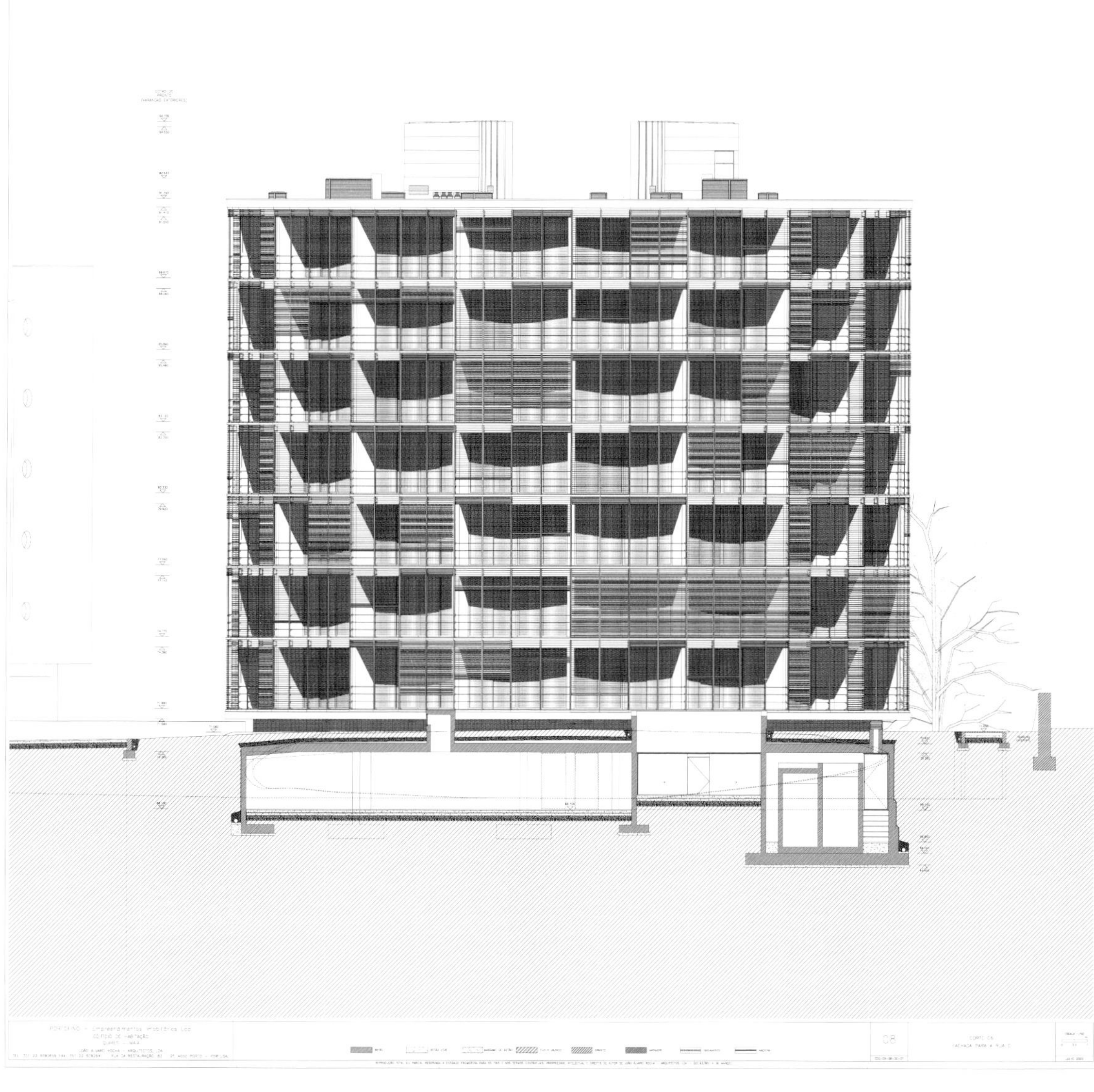

PUBLIC AND SERVICE BUILDINGS

Specific circumstances represent the opportunity of any project, not simply the cause or pretext for its creation. Therefore, if considered as the field of action, landscape is an ethical reality, inherent to the world of the "possible", not of the "necessary". Its own identity is built by starting with the rigorous definition of the relations between the elements that compose it; form and material are to be understood as essential components of substance, and not as instruments of decoration: in the ability to absorb and abstract the essence of things we communicate the logic of the solutions. Clarity expresses disinterest for the incomprehensible, liberating ourselves from the superfluous. *(F.C.)*

13. LNIV - National Veterinary Investigation Laboratory

14. ICP - Portugal's Communication Institute

15. Moutidos Leisure Park

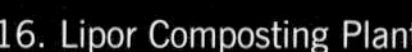

16. Lipor Composting Plant

17. Medical Office

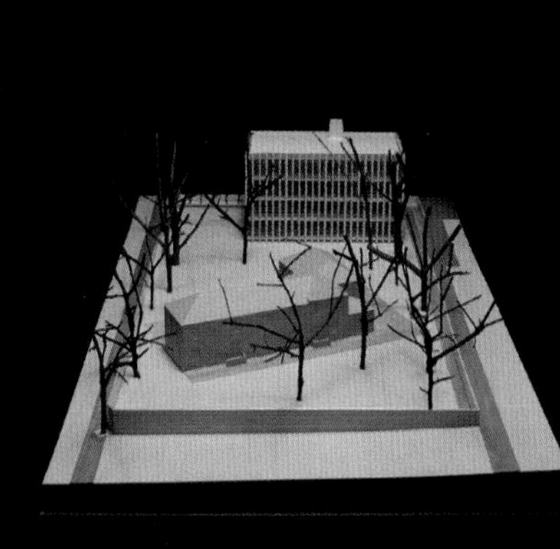

18. Espaço Viso: Office Building

13. LNIV - National Veterinary Investigation Laboratory
Vairão - Vila do Conde

Design
João Álvaro Rocha, Architect
José Manuel Gigante, Architect
1991-93

Construction
1994-98

Collaborators
Francisco Portugal e Gomes, Architect
Ana Sousa da Costa, Architect
Maria João Lima, Architect
Luís Tavares Pereira, Architect
Roberta Albiero, Architect
Jorge Pereira Esteves, Practice Architect
Pedro Ruano de Castro, Practice Architect

Model
Francisco Portugal e Gomes, Architect
Maria João Lima, Architect
Ana Sousa da Costa, Architect
Jorge Pereira Esteves, Practice Architect

Located on a territory of wide horizons, outlined by large agricultural fields and by scattered housing centres, this articulated and massive project is intended to recreate the harmonic balance already existing between those centres and the landscape.

The guidelines of the project are founded on the relation between place and landscape, and the various scales it proposes: the single unit, the whole complex, the entire territory.

The bodies are fragmented in an attempt to create an equilibrium between the building and the landscape – in the way they come into contact, they support each other, and can be read.

Notwithstanding the building size, this same equilibrium should find expression in the identity of each individual segment, whose formal result is inseparable from the reason that gives sense to the whole.

The project's formal order results from the capacity to standardize the elements and to set a rule that allows both repetition and exception.

The repetition is a means of identifying the unit correctly, of revealing its capacity to vary within the same rule and to integrate future expansions. The unit design principles result from the need to mould the land, and its pattern reflects that of the land itself, in the aim to match the scale of the place with the scale of the territory.

The exception is used to confirm the identity of each unit, and to fix their scale with reference to a multifaceted approach to the place.

The spatial composition of the building precisely results from this interaction of repetition and exception played on the different scales.

Structure and infrastructure give life to one space whose design is obtained by the convergence of the various levels of information. Such space becomes the protagonist – and its essence transcends the meaning of the parts that shape it.

The formal concept is not constrained by any pre-figured images potentially evoked by the nature of the research relating to this project; on the contrary, its formal synthesis is a creative result of the balanced manipulation of all the specific elements underlying the program.

The form is, after all, the way of architecturally expressing all these conditions.

Porto, May 1995

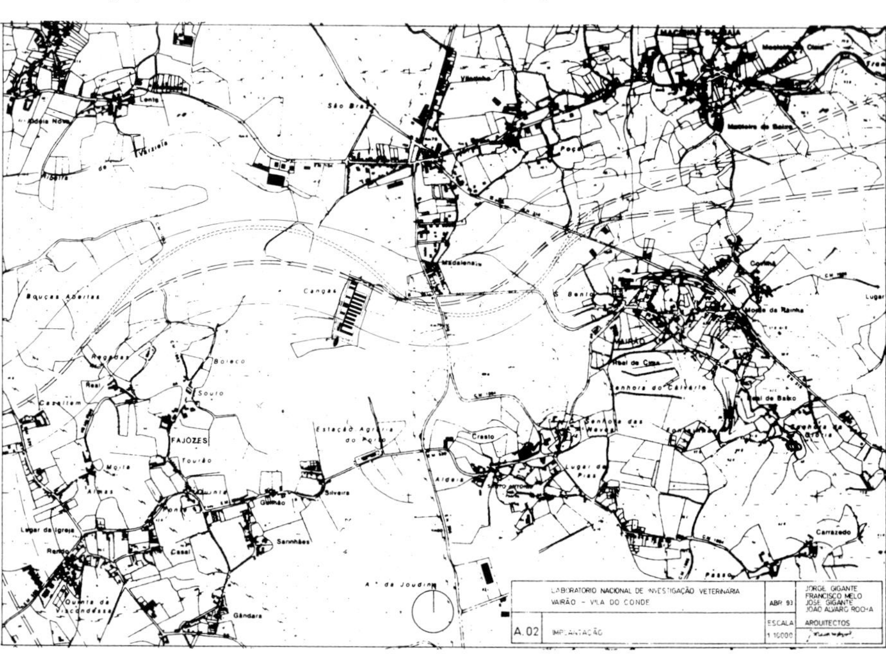

Localization plan.

East side, general view.

General plan
and longitudinal sections.

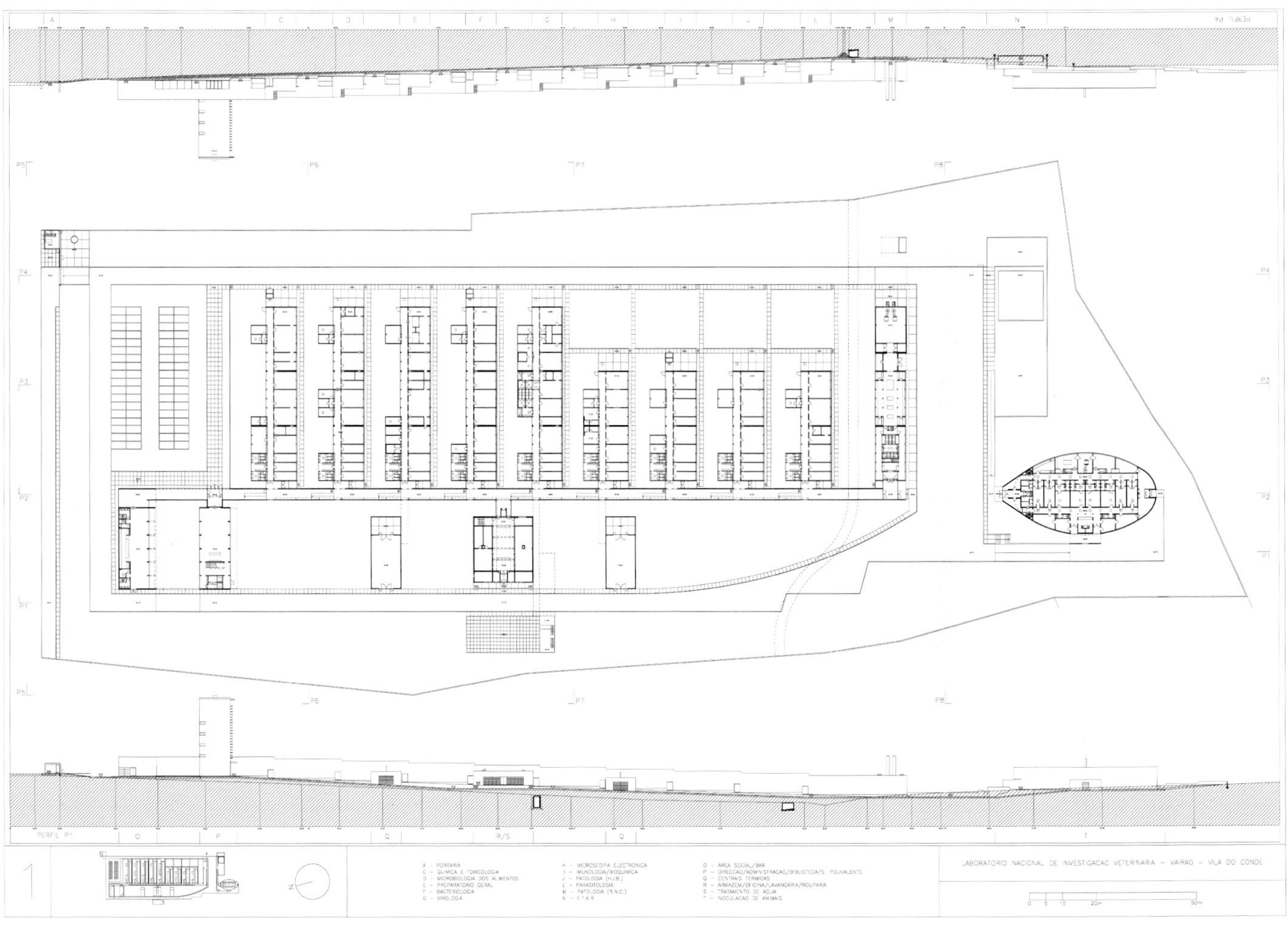

East side, partial view
from the south.

Laboratory pavilions,
partial view from the east.

Facing page:
Administrative building, view from the south side with the laboratory pavilions in the foreground.

Water courtyard with the reception area of the administrative building.

Water courtyard with the canteen building to the left.

Facing page:
Distribution gallery, general view from the south to the north sides.

Library, on the upper floors of the administrative building.

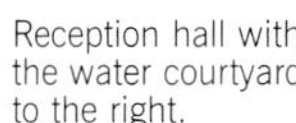

Reception hall with the water courtyard to the right.

14. ICP - Portugal's Communication Institute Northern Headquarters Porto

Design
João Álvaro Rocha, Architect
José Manuel Gigante, Architect
1993-94

Construction
1994-95

Collaborators
Francisco Portugal e Gomes, Architect
Ana Sousa da Costa, Architect
Jorge Pereira Esteves, Architect
Manuel Fernando Santos, Draughtsman

Model
Francisco Portugal e Gomes, Architect
Jorge Pereira Esteves, Architect

The site is in the city outskirts, in an area subject to quick transformation processes. The urban layout is irregular, and characterized by disarticulated elements that define its heterogeneous allotment (agriculture, industry, service and residences). Few spaces, usually devoid of any design strategy, show architectural quality.

The land, adjacent to a small rural nucleus, stretches between a social housing complex and some agricultural fields.

The building is aligned with the street, and has a reduced size, similar to that of the neighbouring construction; its design makes it inseparable from the land on which it stands, as if they merge one into the other.

The building is placed on the land in a way that accentuates the perception of its own limits. Therefore, its design also results from the act of (re)designing the land: breathing proportions are established that, by measuring the distances, help secure the scale of the complex.

The organic relation between building and land is essentially drawn from their mutual interaction: a horizontal interaction between the inside and the outside, so that work spaces have the best solar exposure and view of the garden; a vertical interaction between the ground (basement) and the upper level (accessible roof), through the elevation volumes (work areas/services).

Such ordered arrangement of forms and spaces strengthens the unified character of the complex. The external façades are also the internal façades – the thin metallic membrane which forms and separates them is also the element that defines their continuity. The image of the exterior will therefore be present in the interior, when walking through the vertical access and the corridors that lead to the rooms, and where the cycle closes, in the visual return to the garden.

The building scale transcends the meaning of its strict physical dimension.

The idea of a pavilion inside a garden emphsizes a modular conception aimed at clarifying the relations between space and structure – and between space and the surfaces that shape it.

The image of the building resides in the way it is built.

To modulate the space involves a writing skill whose objective is immediate communication – the language is strictly architectural, adjectives or quotes are removed.

The apparent formal abstraction fades into the compromise with the idea of architecture that informs it, scourged inside the relation between Place, Program, and Construction.

Porto, July 1995

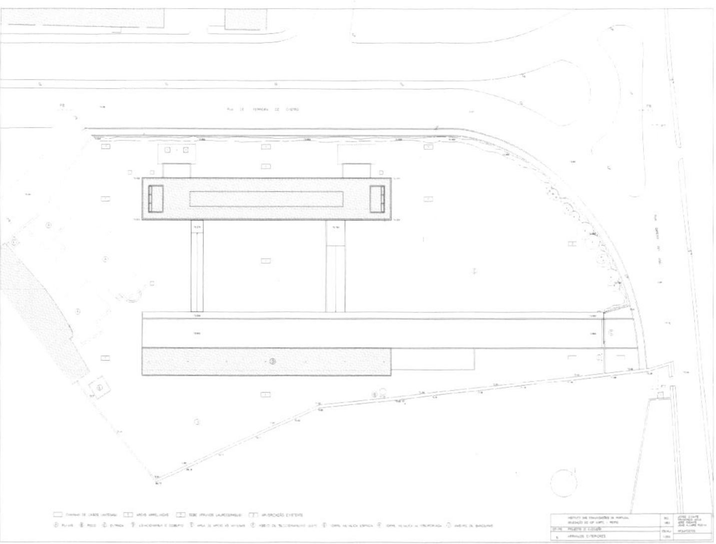

Site plan.

Facing page:
General view with the surroundings.

Ground floor plan.

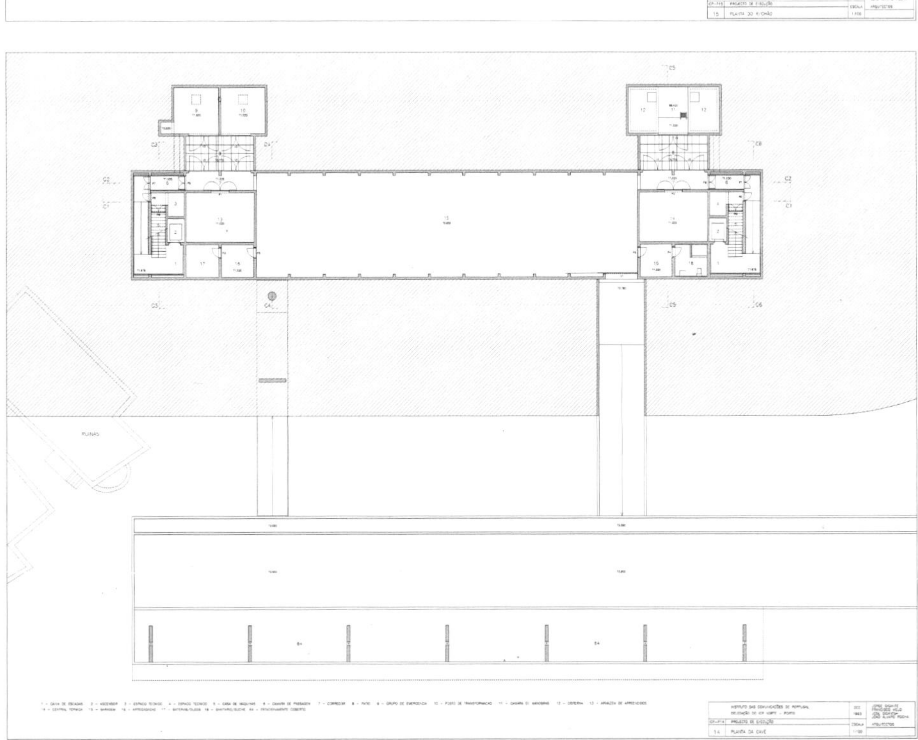

Basement plan.

South façade, view from the public entrance with the carport in the foreground.

North façade, view from the street.

Transverse sections.

Facing page:
South façade, general view.

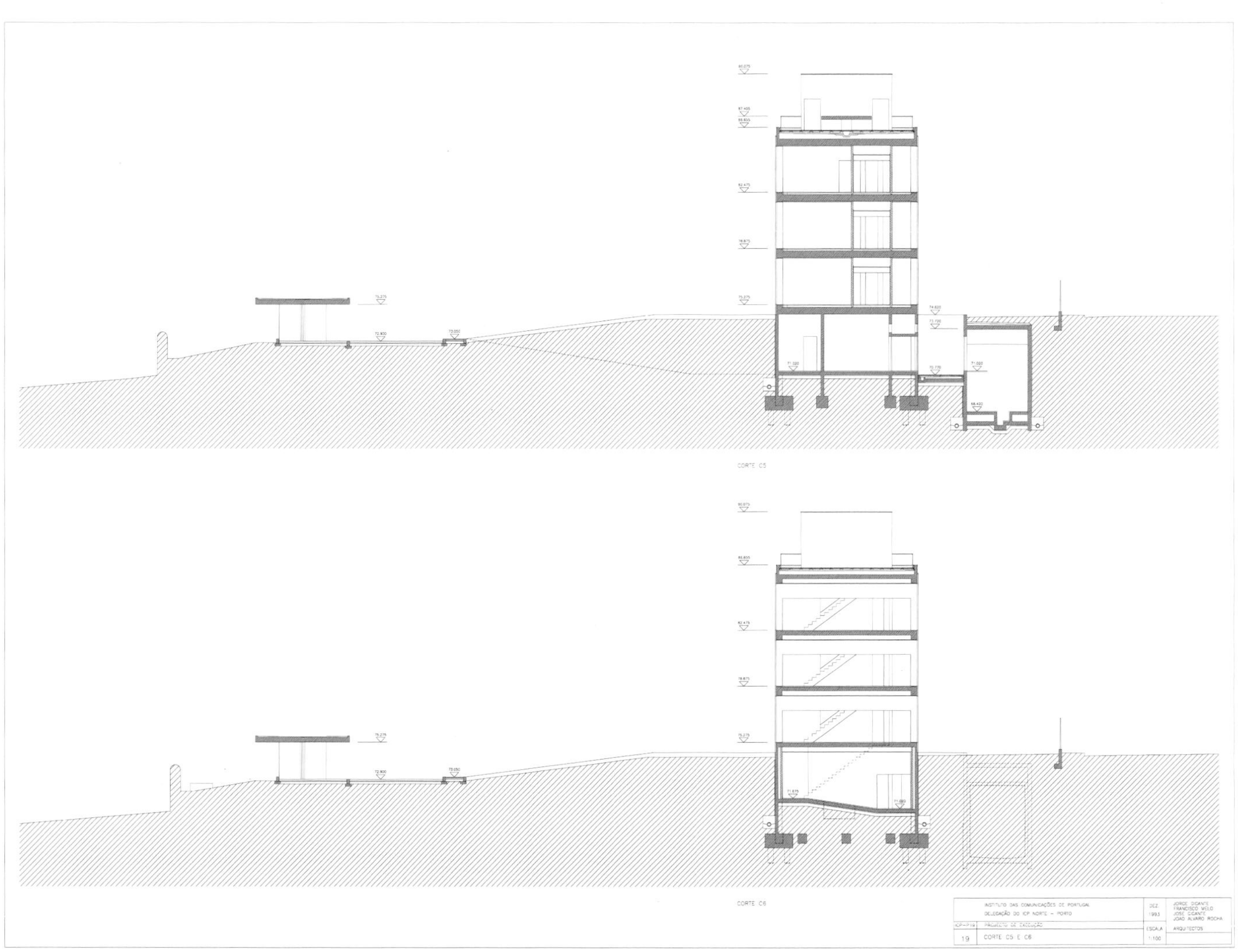

Entry hall, general view.

A meeting room in the office areas.

The corridor along the north façade.

Stairs, general view towards the south façade.

15. Moutidos Leisure Park
Águas Santas - Maia

Design
João Álvaro Rocha, Architect
1997

Construction
1999-2001

Collaborators
Francisco Portugal e Gomes, Architect
Ana Sousa da Costa, Architect
Jorge Pereira Esteves, Architect
José Eurico Salgado dos Santos, Practice Architect
Ana Sofia Ribeiro, Practice Architect
Carla Garrido de Oliveira, Practice Architect
Pedro Tiago Pimentel, Practice Architect

Furniture Design
João Álvaro Rocha, Architect

Model
Carla Garrido de Oliveira, Practice Architect
Ana Sofia Ribeiro, Practice Architect

The park is located on a territory marked by strong tensions between recently constructed complexes, small tree-lined areas, and fields for agricultural use; it should be able to create an equilibrium between these very different situations, which apparently can't produce any structural cohesion of the layout.

This situation is common to territories that are expanding: rural areas are slowly being substituted by structures that spread along the main roads, without any order and attention to the arrangement of public space.

Facing this scenario, the project should find the right place for its peculiar character, both through the acknowledgement of its different constructive features, and the way it occupies the land.

The meaning of the architectural intervention can be established only in the relation between land and territory, in the dialogue between constructed forms, between open and closed, between big and small – between man and nature.

Object and place are not contradictory, but the dual expression of unquestionable realities. The awareness of this duality coincides with the deep perception of the actual place.

To draw the different scales of proximity between object and place, to establish the right proportions necessary to dimension space: these are the steps to unmistakably affirm the degree of exposure that one wishes to attain.

The design results from the fact that the project relates to a physically enclosed park, in this case a vital condition of the urban character that the project would like to grant.

The physical boundaries of this large precinct are defined through the use of two distinctive materials, their respective construction techniques, and consequent sensorial perception. They are organized in two categories corresponding to the two realities that coexist on the territory: one residential, with schools, houses, and the strip built along the street that the park faces; the other rural, including small agricultural properties and a large estate to the east.

Two articulated "frames" define the precinct: to the west, along the street, it takes a more urban character, as if it were a façade, a solid and static expression, richly textured in the form of what could be defined as a "mineral wall"; to the east, the boundary element is softer, equally uniform, but organic in its extension and landscape continuity, a sort of "vegetable wall".

The way objects are placed inside this precinct is based on the repetition of a simple element that unfolds to meet different uses: sometimes elements are grouped, sometimes aligned. Their placement is not random, but organized in an order that tries to characterize the territory, appealing to the memory of urban images. This because cities are always built by exploiting repetition more than exception, and repetition is not necessarily a synonym of monotony.

The plainness of the design disguises its multifaced organization; as in nature, simplicity conceals the true complexity of the ordered matter.

This is the condition of the design.

"It is enough to find one of those happy coincidences when the world asks to be watched, and watches in the one same instant."[1]

Porto, December 1997

[1] Italo Calvino, *Invisible Cities*, 1974.

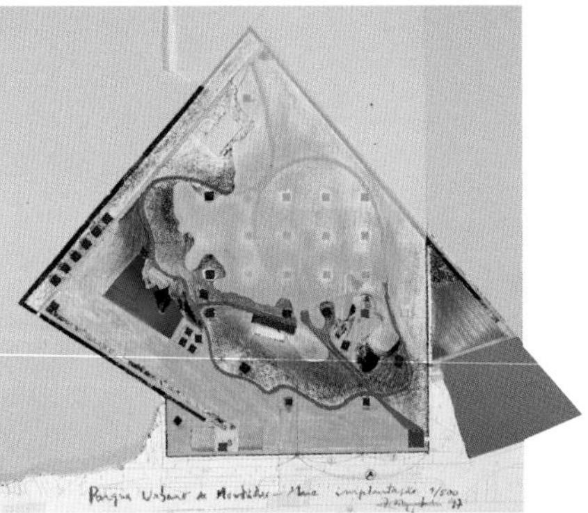

Collage study of the general composition.

Facing page:
General plan (1st phase).

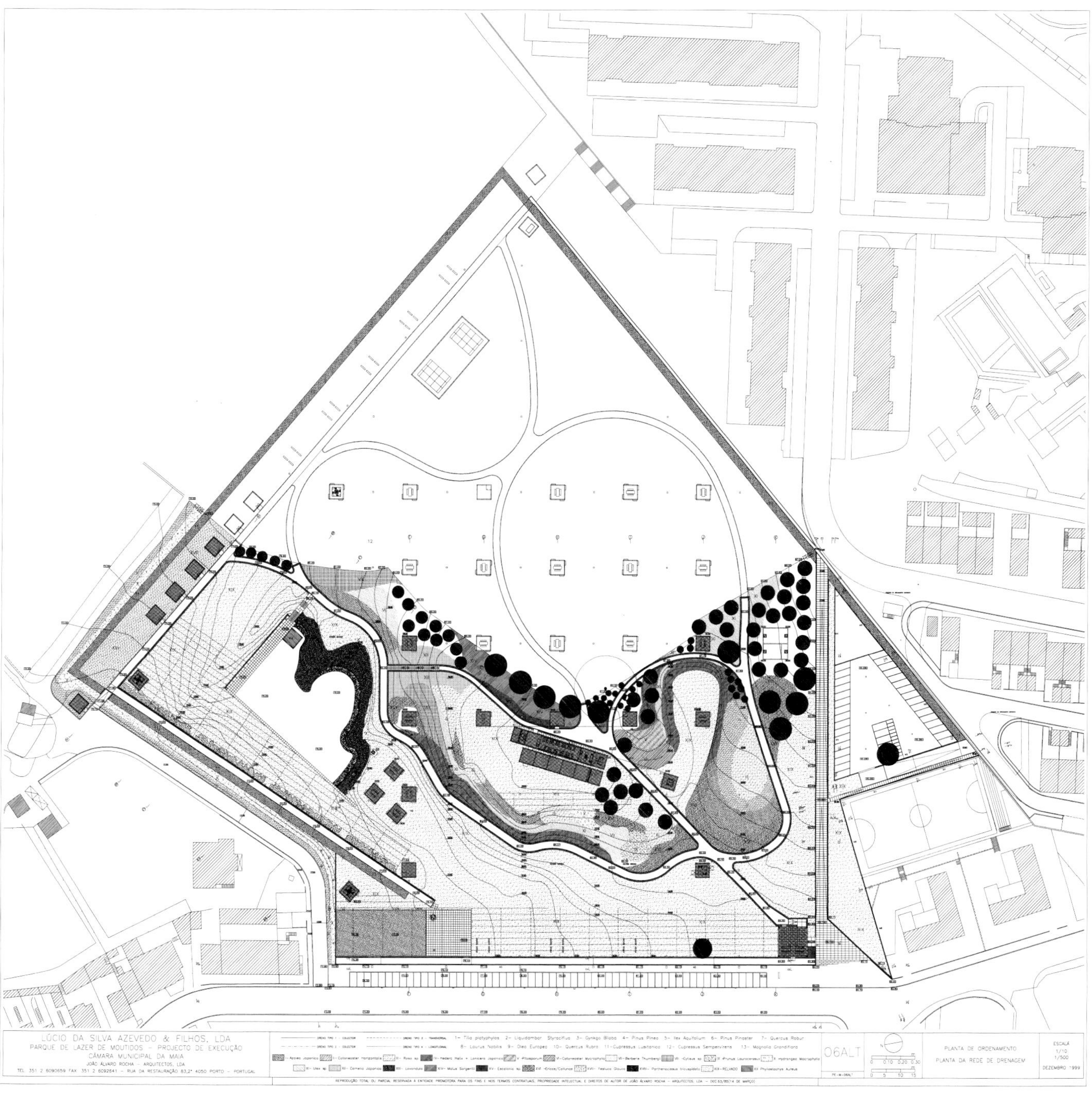
LÚCIO DA SILVA AZEVEDO & FILHOS, LDA
PARQUE DE LAZER DE MOUTIDOS – PROJECTO DE EXECUÇÃO
CÂMARA MUNICIPAL DA MAIA
JOÃO ÁLVARO ROCHA – ARQUITECTOS, LDA
TEL. 351 2 6090659 FAX. 351 2 6092641 – RUA DA RESTAURAÇÃO 83,2° 4050 PORTO – PORTUGAL
1– Tilia platyphylos 2– Liquidambar Styraciflua 3– Gynkgo Biloba 4– Pinus Pinea 5– Ilex Aquifolium 6– Pinus Pinaster 7– Quercus Robur
8– Laurus Nobilis 9– Olea Europea 10– Quercus Rubra 11– Cupressus Lusitanica 12– Cupressus Sempervirens 13– Magnolia Grandiflora
06ALT
PE-M-06ALT
N
0 0.10 0.20 0.30
0 5 10 15
PLANTA DE ORDENAMENTO
PLANTA DA REDE DE DRENAGEM
ESCALA
1/10
1/500
DEZEMBRO 1999

Public entrance on the south side with exterior walkway.

General view with
the tea house on the left.

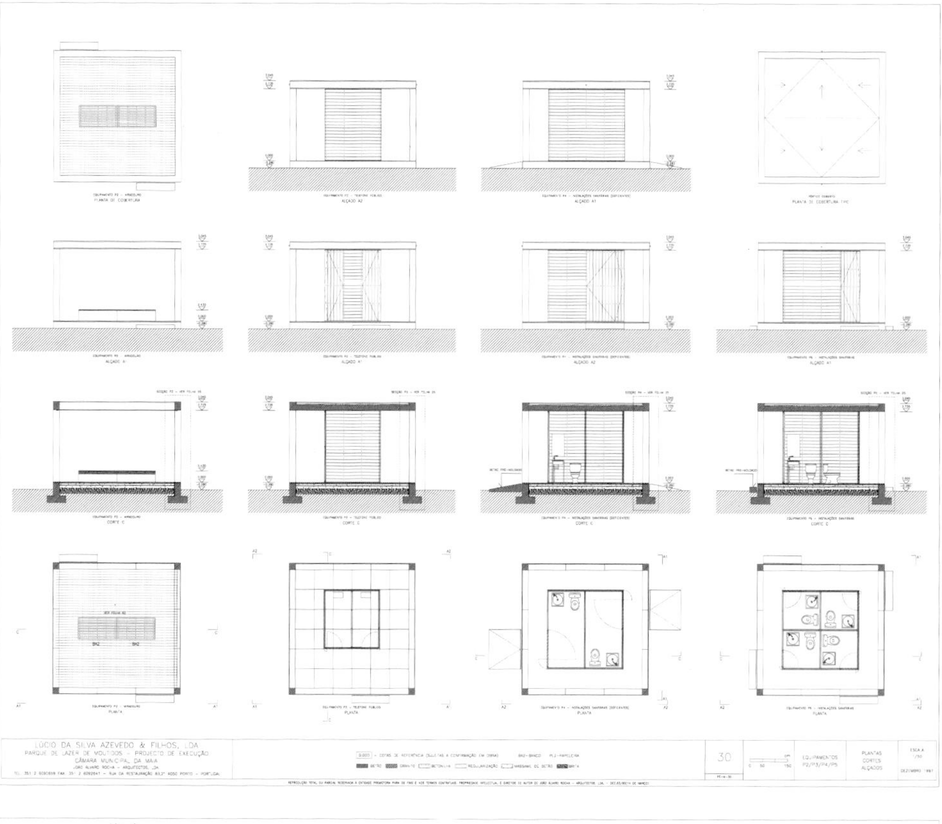

"Portico" elements, plans, sections and elevations.

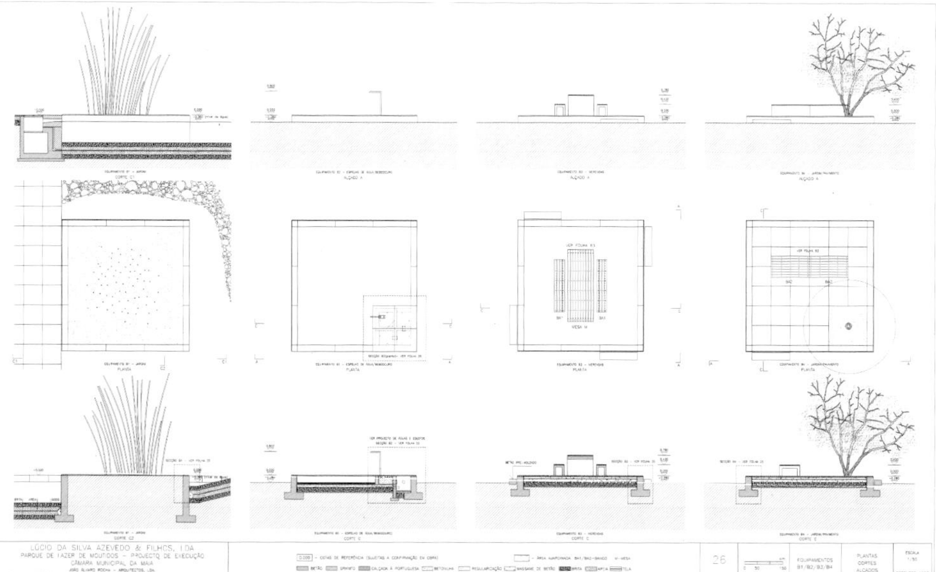

"Horizontal" elements, plans, sections and elevations.

"Portico" elements (public bathrooms) with tea house in the background.

Relation between "porticos" and the surroundings with the lake in the middle.

"Portico" element inside the old stone quarry.

A group of "portico" elements with a "horizontal" element in the foreground.

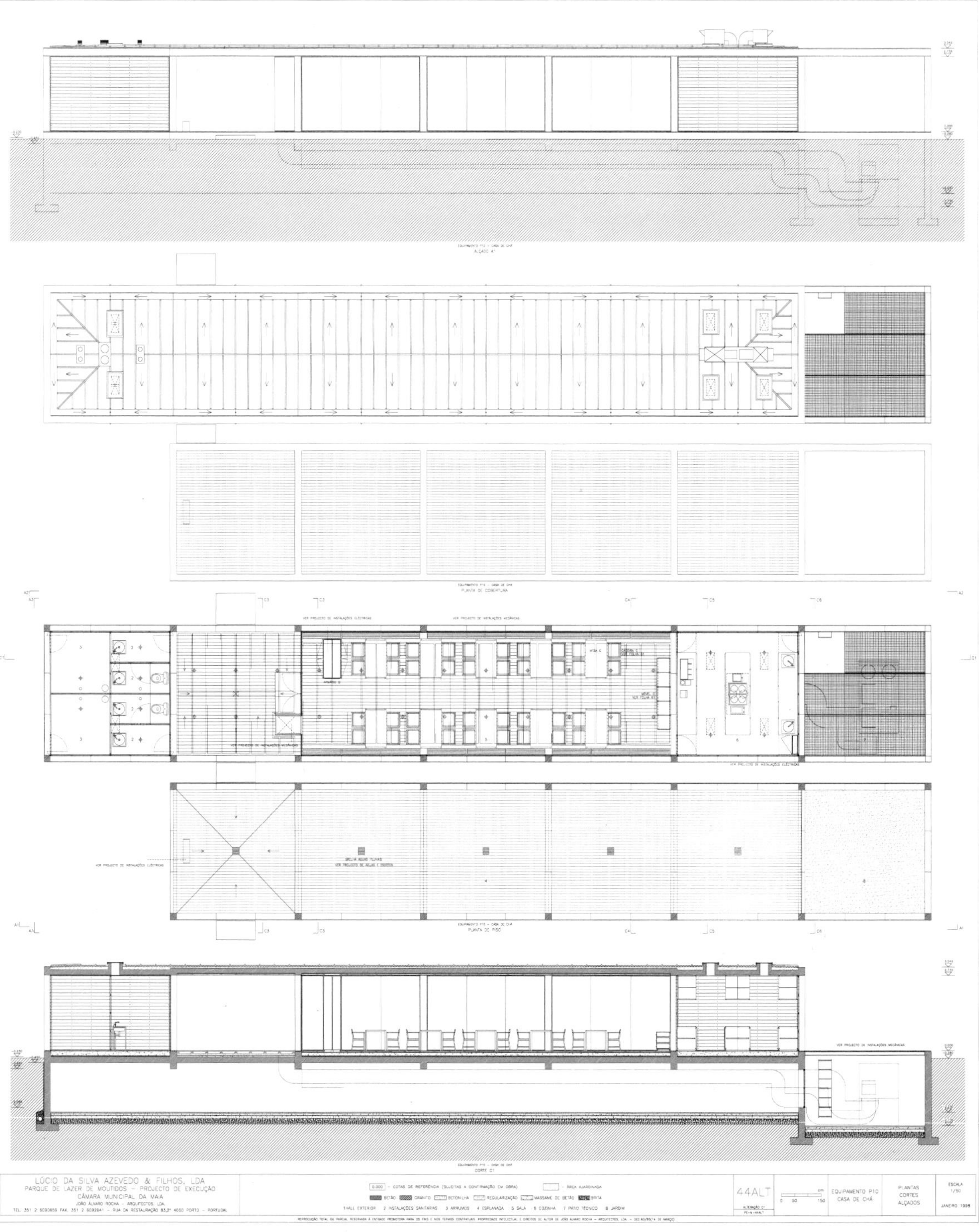

Tea house, plans and sections.

The esplanade with
the tearoom along it.

The tearoom, view from
the entry.

The lake, general view with some "portico" elements in the background.

The lake and the old stone quarry.

Some pavement textures.

Lake, view of the angle walkway.

"Steel garden", walkway protection.

Lake, the relation between the water and the granite of the old stone quarry.

The granite of the walkway and the old stone quarry.

16. Lipor Composting Plant
International Public Competition for Design, Construction, Supply and Exploration of a Composting Plant
Baguim do Monte - Gondomar

Competition Design
2000

Design
João Álvaro Rocha, Architect
Francisco Portugal e Gomes, Architect

Collaborators
Alberto Barbosa Vieira, Architect
António Luís Neves, Architect
João Ventura Lopes, Architect
Pedro Tiago Pimentel, Architect
Sónia Campos Neves, Practice Architect
Tiago Macedo Correia, Practice Architect

Model
Alberto Laje, Architect

The building complex of the composting plant should comply with the new environmental directives, enforced in Portugal and the European Community, in matter of security in the treatment and final destination of wastes.

Many noted examples of such complexes testify to the divergence between technological needs and coherent and intelligible architectural solutions.

It is precisely this divergence that this project tries conceptually to avoid, by taking the technological aspects into account, and by merging them with those that characterize the building location on a specific territory.

The building, which is inscribed in a large-scale precinct, is conceived as a sort of box capable of housing technological equipment whose arrangement in the different spaces exclusively responds to functional needs.

The larger body is then articulated with smaller ones, and the scale is defined both through the relationship between the various elements, and that between the complex and other existing buildings.

It is this articulation that helps to determine the "location" of the complex in the place and define its "framing" on the territory.

The rigour followed to locate the buildings, to define their final impact, and to arrange the surrounding spaces, represents an effort to improve the scenery.

The constructive method has been chosen both to establish the right scale relations, and to stress on the industrial nature of the complex, a nature that should be also sensed in the rationalization of processes and economy of means.

The building's final image should reflect its constructive process.

The construction, just like the image, is organized on juxtaposed layers that not only correspond to a building sequence, but also allow multiple readings while approaching the different elements.

The three-dimensional metallic structure, the white cement panels, and the copper threads on which the surrounding greenery grows – as an element of constant evolution throughout the year – participate in the creation of a sort of "industrial nave", with all the sobriety and simplicity that this image communicates.

The buildings that complete the complex are all in plywood in order to meet their specific program, and to keep the same design strategy. They are articulated elements between the main body and the nearby surroundings.

Porto, March 2000

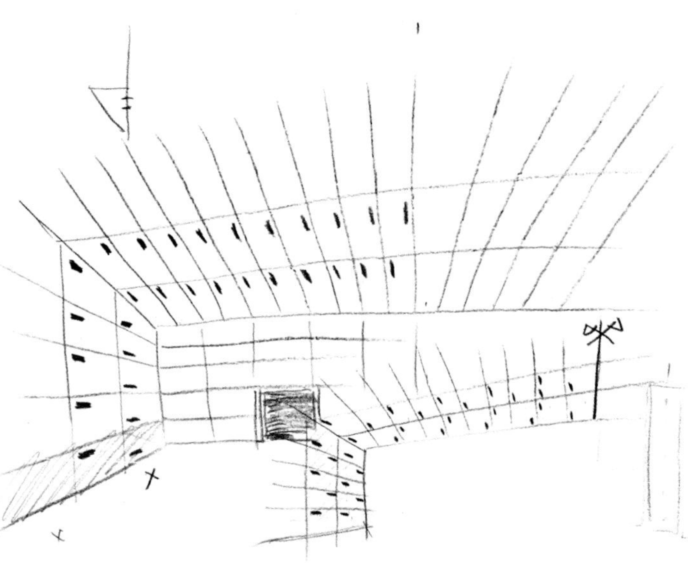

Study sketch, inner space.

Facing page:
Site plan.

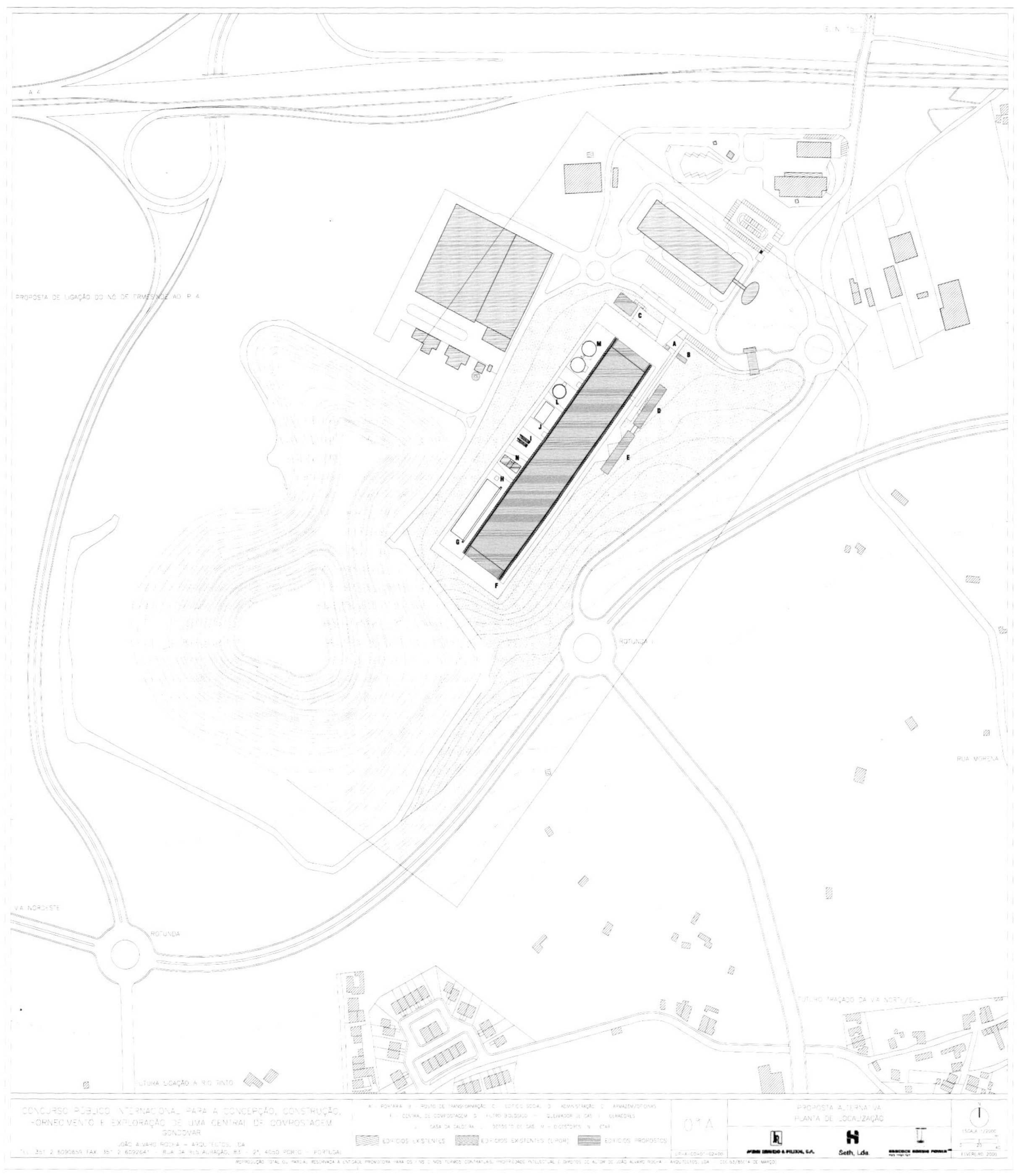
ROTUNDA
VIA NOROESTE
CONCURSO PÚBLICO INTERNACIONAL PARA A CONCEPÇÃO, CONSTRUÇÃO, FORNECIMENTO E EXPLORAÇÃO DE UMA CENTRAL DE COMPOSTAGEM
GONDOVAR
JOÃO ÁLVARO ROCHA – ARQUITECTOS, LDA
EDIFÍCIOS EXISTENTES
EDIFÍCIOS PROPOSTOS
01A
PROPOSTA ALTERNATIVA
PLANTA DE LOCALIZAÇÃO
Seth, Lda.
ESCALA 1/2000
0
20
40
FEVEREIRO 2000

Sections and elevations.

Ground floor plan.

Facing page:
Model, general view from the southwest.

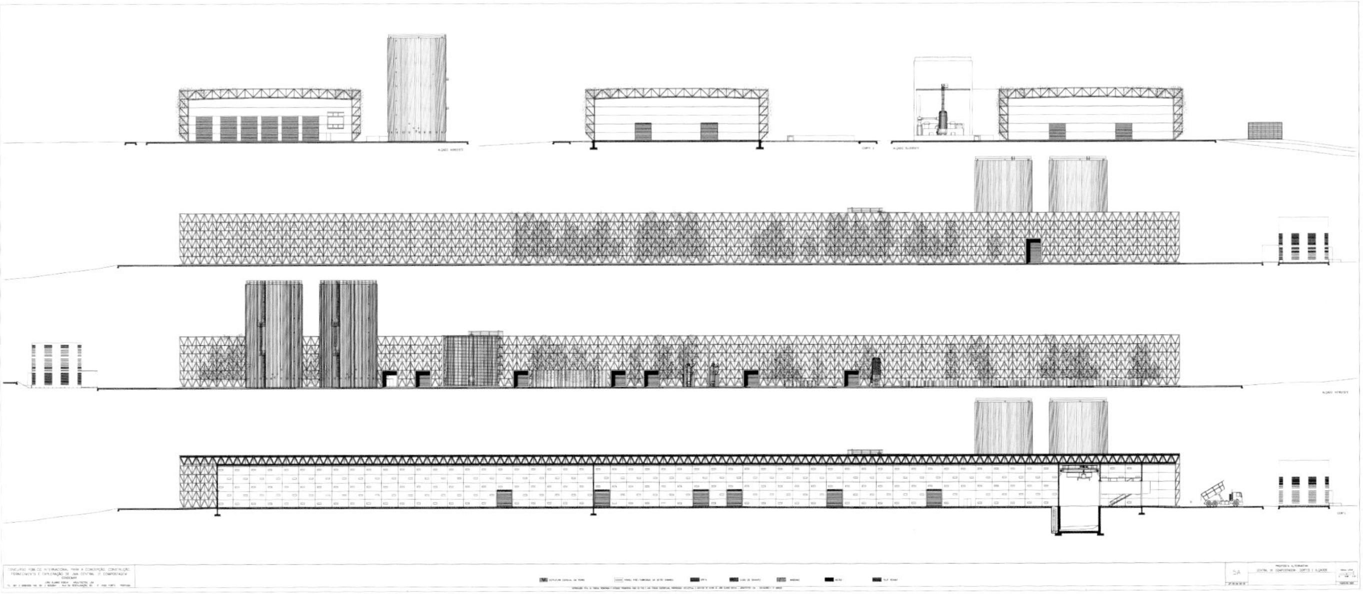

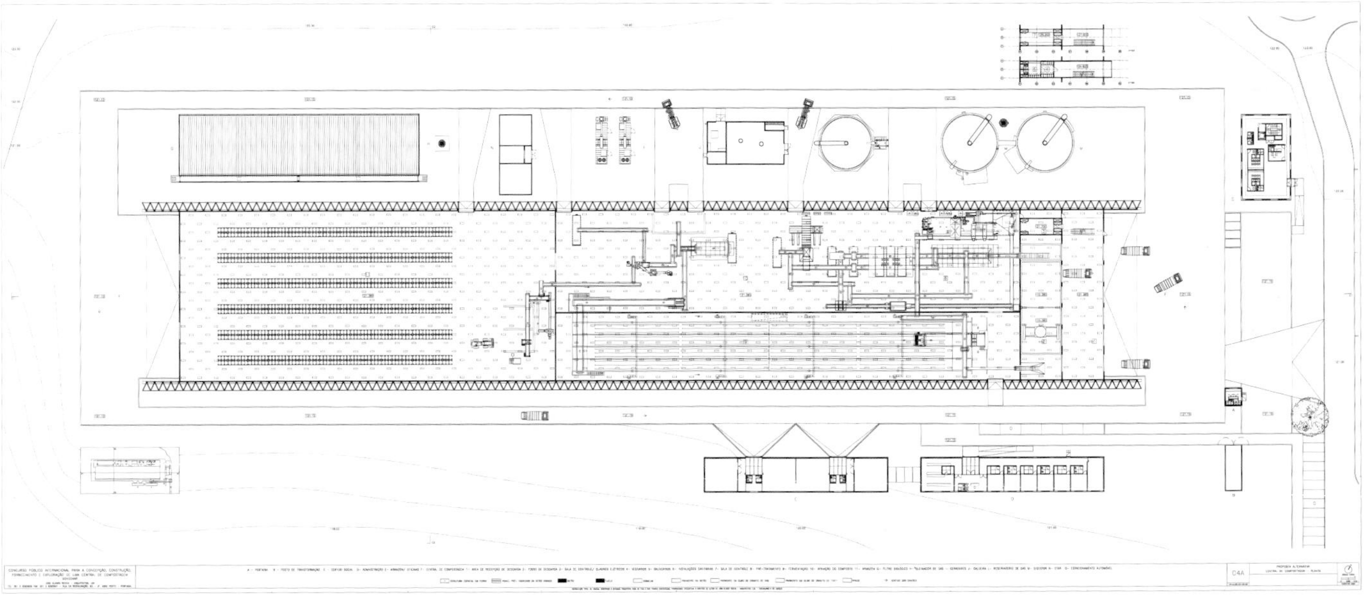

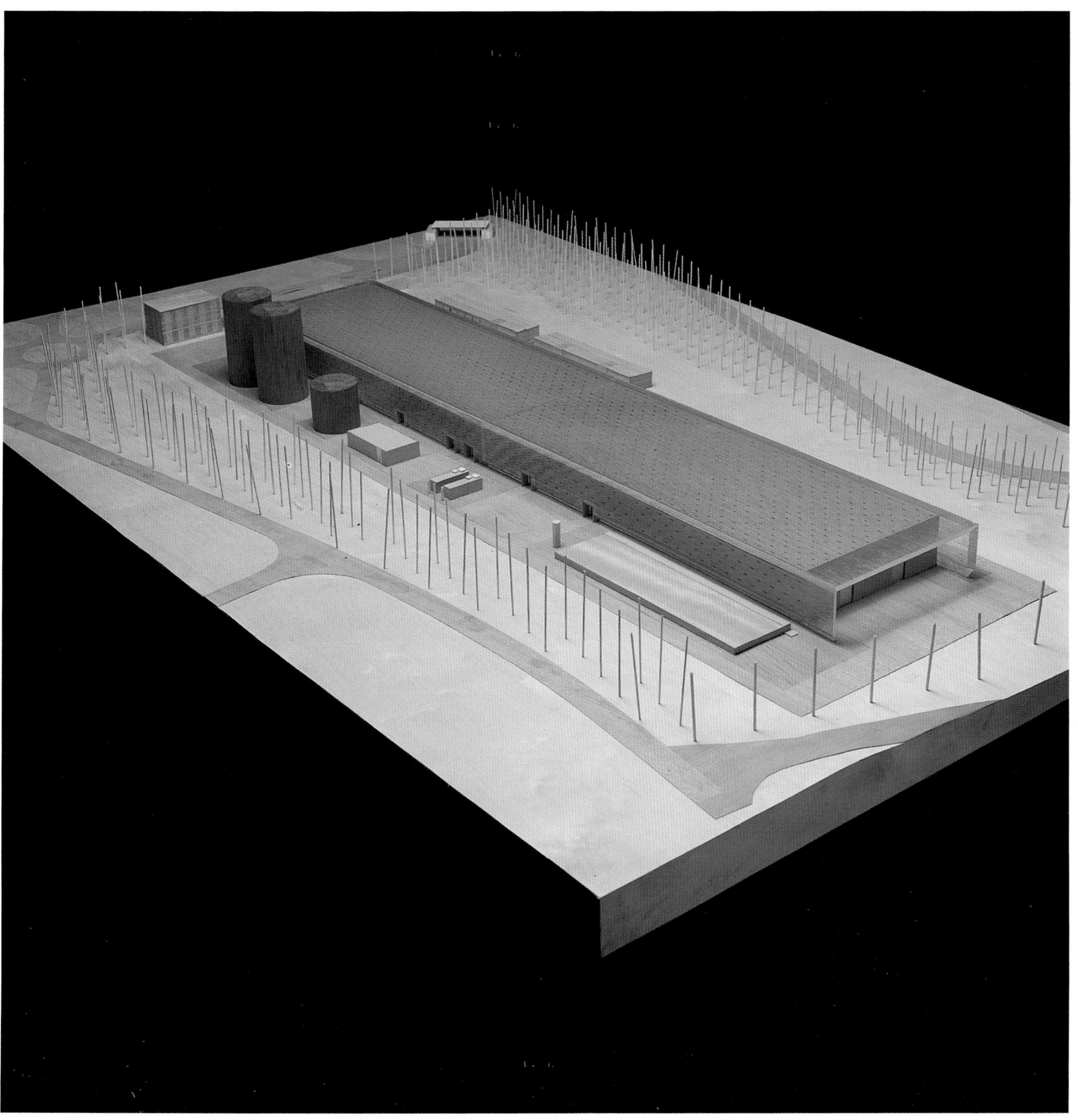

17. Medical Office
Central Plaza Building - Maia

Design
João Álvaro Rocha, Architect
2000

Construction
2000-01

Collaborators
António Luís Neves, Architect
Sónia Campos Neves, Practice Architect

Model
Sónia Campos Neves, Practice Architect

The medical offices are going to be placed inside a building. This does neither mean that they have any "place", nor that this place should coincide with the building.

To define the "nature" of this place and its relation with the pre-existent elements is one of the first tasks of the project. Its unavoidable foundation should be the connection with the exterior, with a dimension that transcends the building itself and takes the city as its reference.

All efforts consequently focus on space and its definition, but also on its significance – everything happens more by summoning than by affirming.

The detail should be discrete, almost imperceptible, until it dissolves, so that silence is obtained.

Only in this way can space be a unique and indivisible whole, as well as an evoking plurality of elements.

Light unites all, but also vibrates like silence.

Porto, 2000

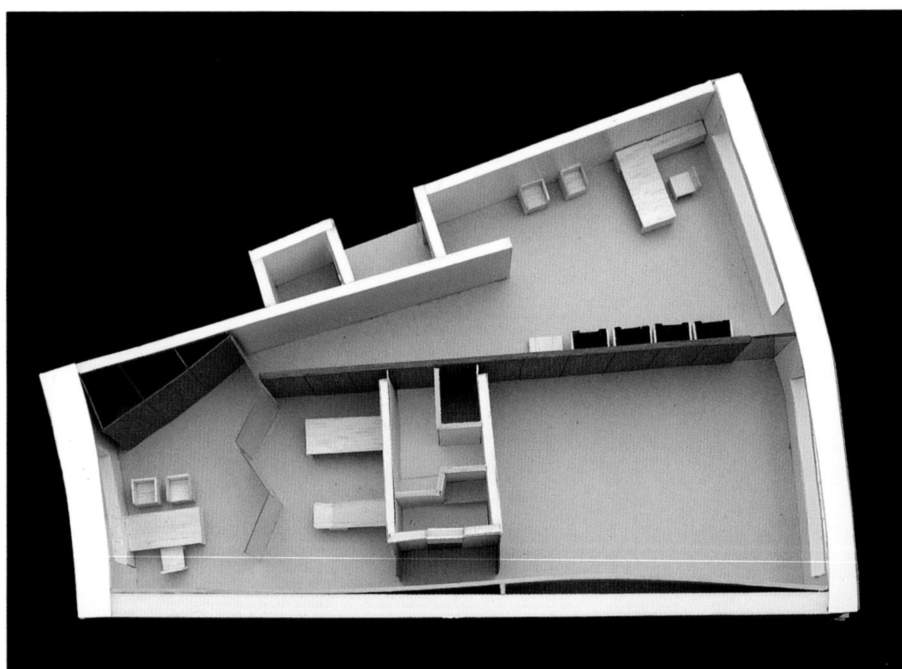

Model, general view.

Plan, space and furniture.

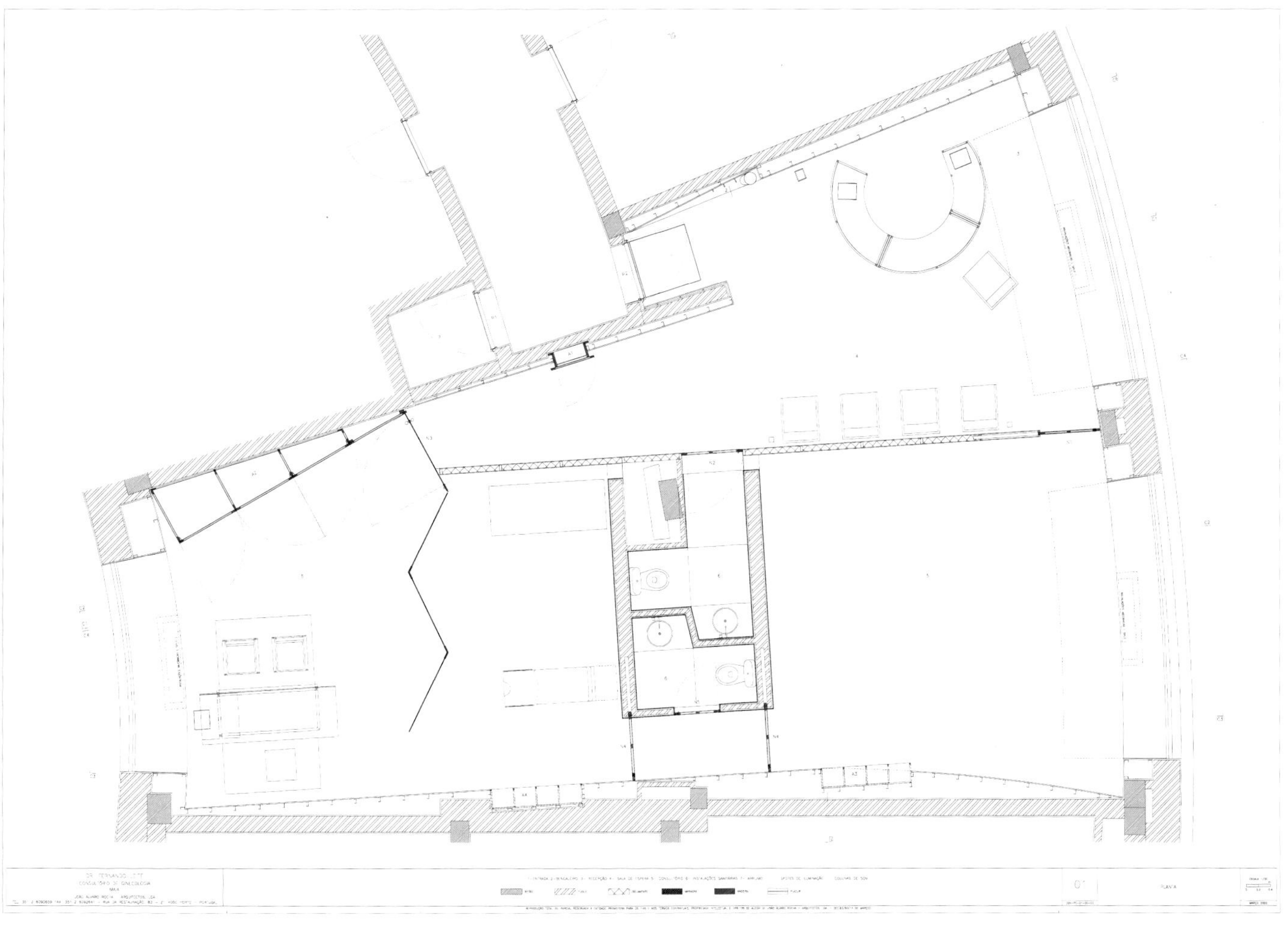

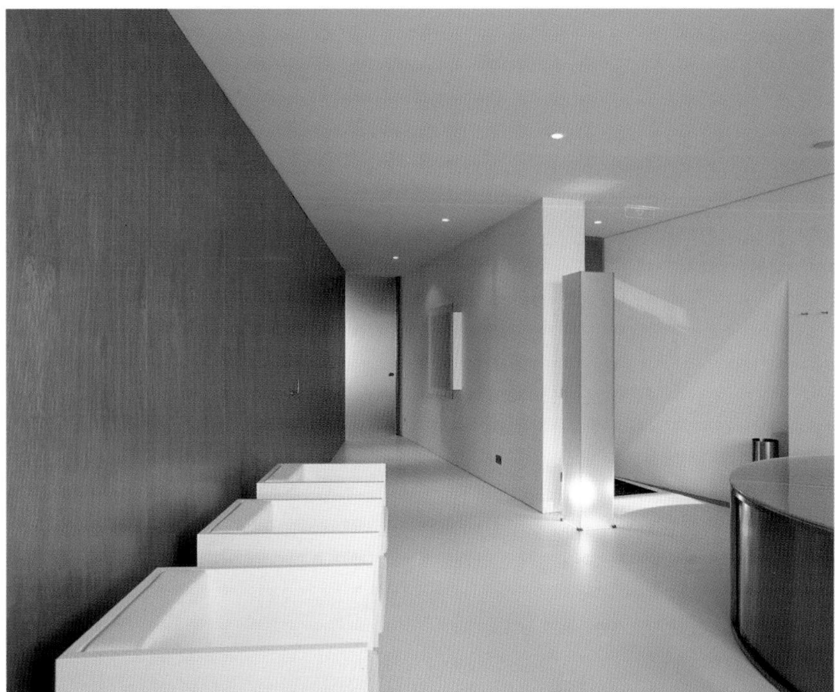

Waiting room, general view towards the office, on the left, and the entry, on the right.

The office, view towards consulting room.

The reception area.

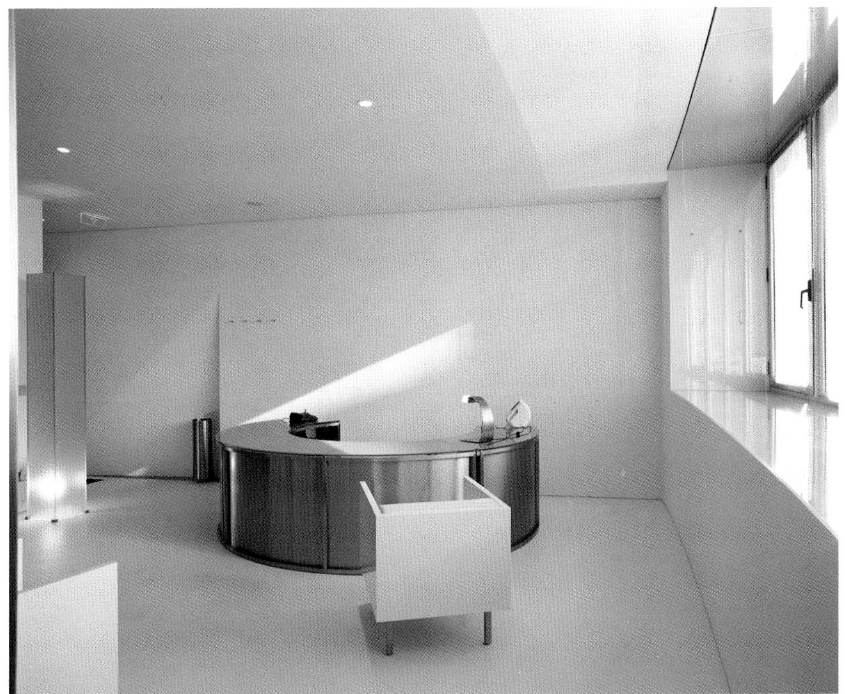

The office.

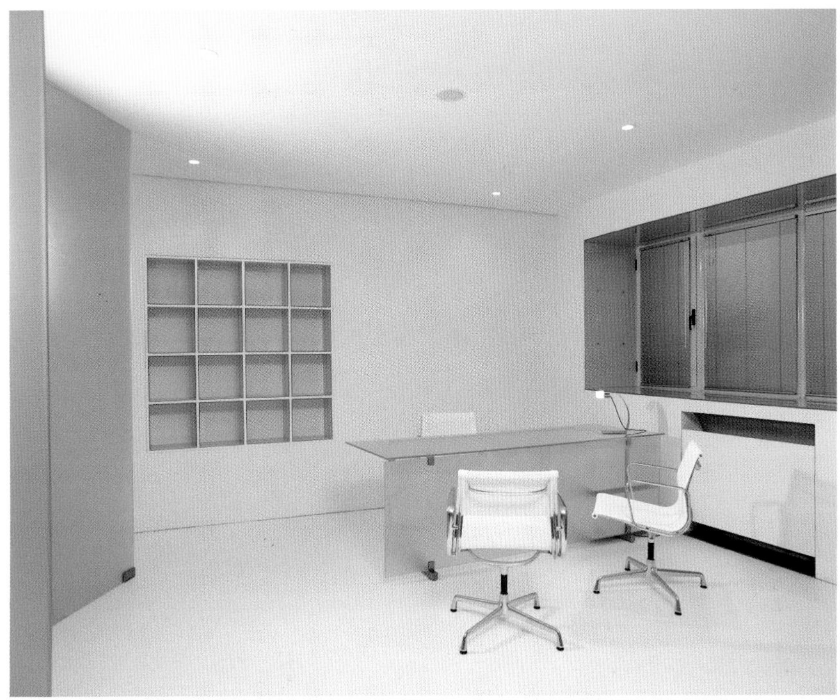

The consulting room.

The access corridor
to the office.

Window detail.

Detail of the articulation between window and cupboard.

18. Espaço Viso: Office Building
Senhora da Hora - Matosinhos

Design
João Álvaro Rocha, Architect
2001

Collaborator
Pedro Tiago Pimentel, Architect

Model
Alberto Laje, Architect

The house and the land are what remains of a vast territory that has been extensively exploited for quarrying purposes. Today this vast territory has been converted into a large urban allotment clearly weak and uncharacteristic in its morphology. The old house and the little land that surrounds it are like a memory of that time.

The urban planning regulations for this part of the city prevent the demolition of the house; the project consequently proposes to reconvert it – by attributing it a use different to its present day one (service facility) – and to construct a new building, not only as a way of making the reconversion economically viable, but also as a possibility to recreate its nearby surroundings in the aim to re-frame and give them new value.

This re-framing of the existing situation, which the project claims to be an essential aspect of the approach it proposes, is achieved through the redefinition of the land's limits, the quality treatment of the exterior spaces adjacent to the old house, and the establishment of the new background offered by the new building.

The repositioning of the entrances, now located at the extremities of the northern summit of the land and established by both streets, generates new (other) ways of approach to the place, allowing a more amplified and diverse reading of the existing building as well as a more intense perception of the presence of the large trees that still subside and evolve it.

The location of the new building at the northern summit of the land – on an orthogonal axis with the streets that surround it and in alignment with the construction situated to the north – gives it a character of neutrality that is essential to the affirmation of exceptionality that today marks the existing house.

This neutrality is obtained through the architectural language of the regular mesh, and defines a homogenic and abstract volume that functions "simultaneously" as a background to the building to restore and as a way to make it seem more present.

But this homogeneity is much more apparent than real, because the surfaces that characterize the new building present slight differences that, according to the conditions of light, make its expressive presence differ from time to time.

This is how sensations are generated, moments of relation, but also accomplices in the way one wishes to see and simultaneously be seen.

Porto, November 2001

Study sketch, general view.

General plan and
sections.

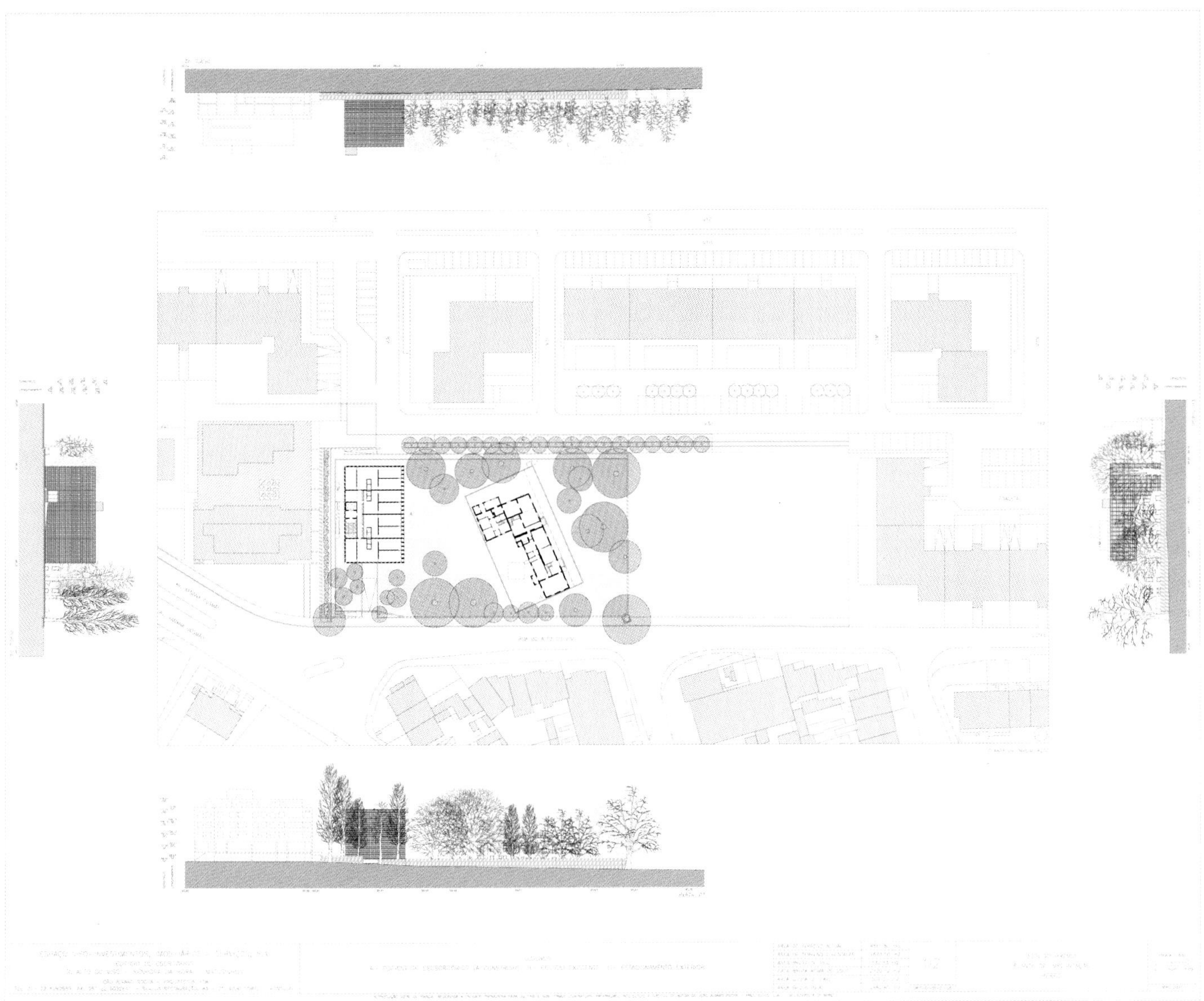

Basement, ground and floor plans.

Model, general view with the old house in the foreground.

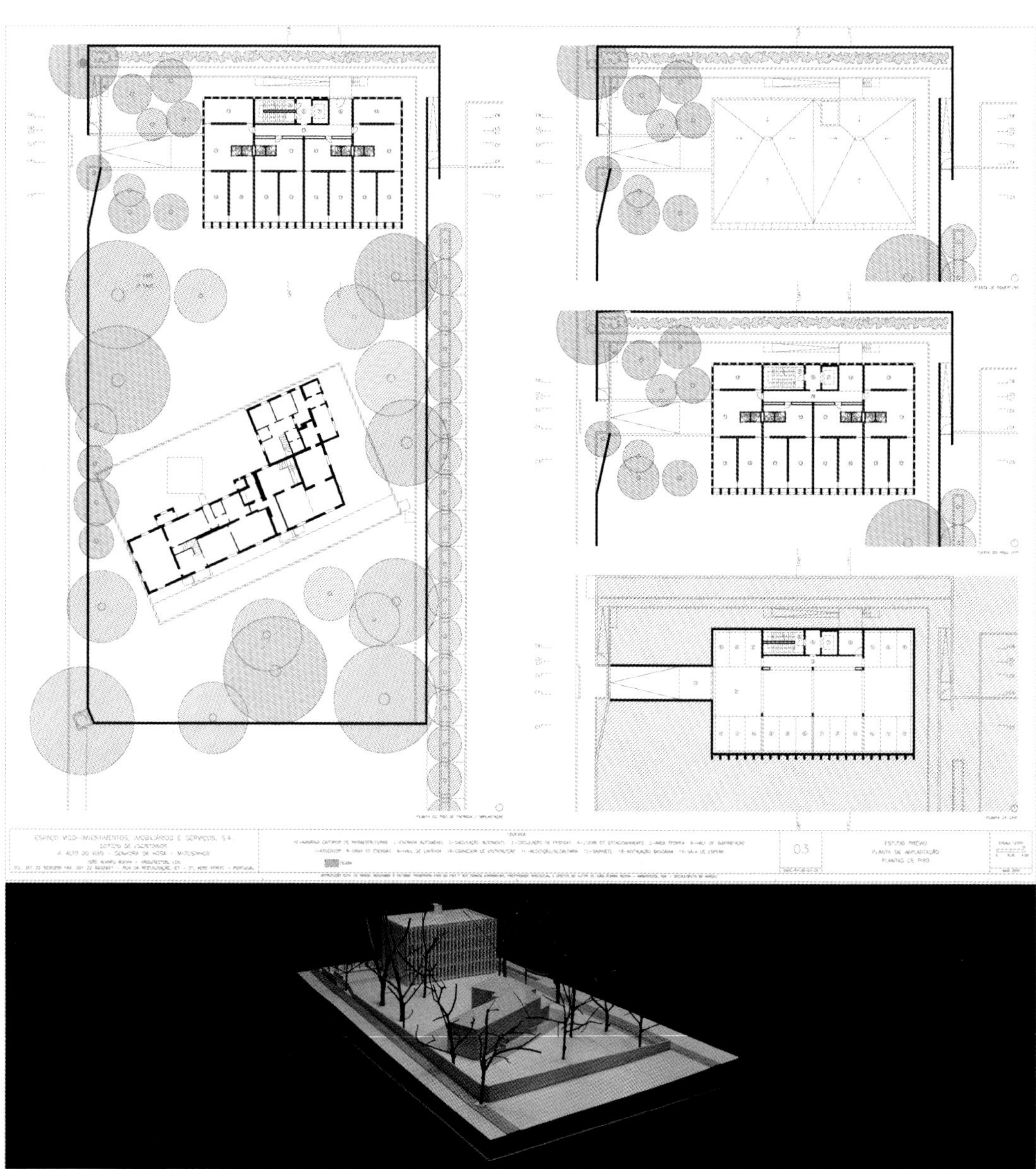

Sections and elevations.

Model, general view with the old house in the background.

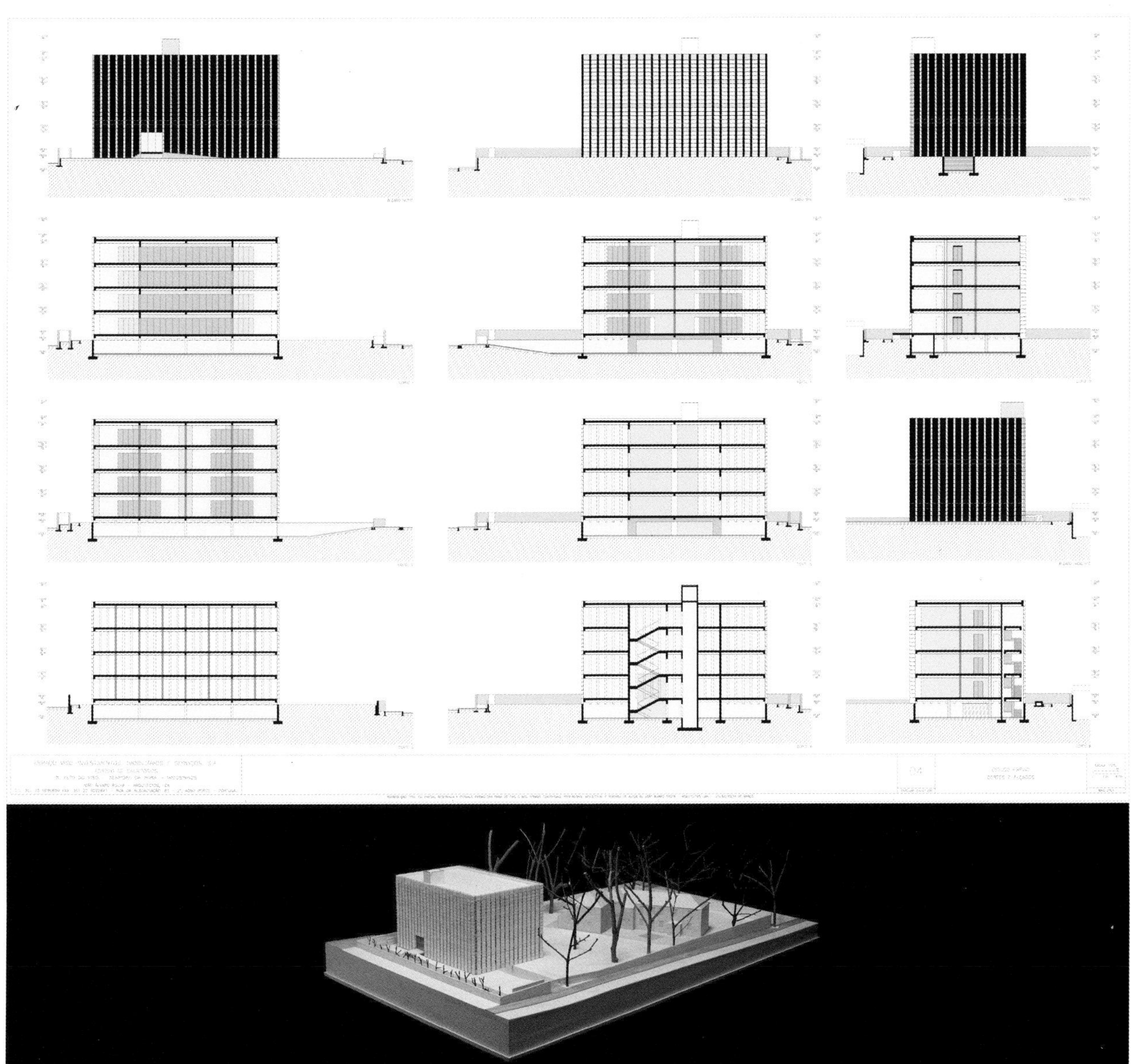

URBAN PROJECTS

Any action on the city implies the comprehension of its natural conditions as a heterogeneous entity in permanent transformation. Any action on it must thus be considered as a single moment, one of a series of episodes that transform it by means of the ethical consciousness of its problems, and the dignity of each solution. By individuating hierarchies and revaluating differences and exceptions, a project searches and prepares the necessary structure which allows the city to grow and transform itself in space and time: by organizing, it determines function, by ordering, it applies significance, thus adopting simplicity as a way of communicating the profound complexity of reality. *(F.C.)*

19. Quinta dos Cónegos: Urban Study

20. Vila do Castelo: Detail Plan

21. Vila do Castelo: Urban Park - Garden Renovation

22. Vila do Castelo: Urban Park - Homestead Remodelling

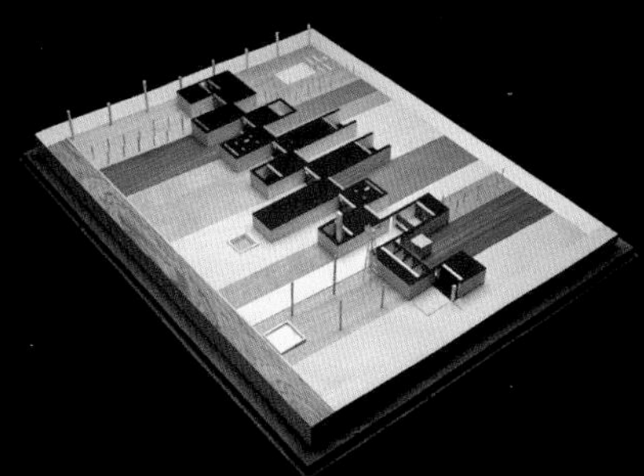

23. Vila do Castelo: Urban Park - Environment Education School

24. Museo de Sanfermines, Pamplona

19. Quinta dos Cónegos: Urban Study
Maia

Design
João Álvaro Rocha, Architect
1998

Collaborators
António Luís Neves, Architect
Francisco Portugal e Gomes, Architect
Jorge Pereira Esteves, Architect
João Ventura Lopes, Architect

Model
Pedro Valentim, Practice Architect
Carla Garrido de Oliveira, Practice Architect

Inexplicably and contrary to speculative tendencies that have characterized the development and construction of this territory, the land where this intervention is meant to occur, although very close to the city centre, has remained free from any occupation – it's like a memory of a time where man's relation with nature depended more on his capacity to adapt rather than on the prevailing of the former on the latter.

The land is vast, with dense and wide tree areas, characterized by a soft topography and defined by a waterline, circumscribed by a system of access ways established by a logic of a road system with no structural capacity.

Unfortunately every territory in the city has a owner, and this site is no exception. It ought to belong to the city, and to all its inhabitants, but a recurrent process of easy profit, based on uncontextual models, populist and of doubtful taste, is here once again the case, to the detriment of the collective interest and well being.

This is the present inevitable reality of our cities; in this context, the privileged field of an architect's activity – far from any moral judgement and false aesthetic speculations – should be capable of producing an architecture that is truly changeable, because it is established on that same reality.

It may have been the awareness of this situation that has motivated the city council to look for alternatives to strong real-estate pressures on this part of the city, in a moment when also large urban interventions in matters of infrastructures, transport and communication are in sight and will largely change the city's existing configuration.

In this context, the operation should possess an eminent urban character, one that wants to be an example, a somewhat didactic evidence in the way forms and spaces are defined.

All action is conducted as if it were the last opportunity to make this portion of the territory significant: such action should not only find sense in the city's morphology and hierarchy, but also simultaneously redefine it, thus providing relations or articulating some of its parts in a scale that cannot and should not limit itself to the physical dimension of the intervention.

We are, after all, attempting to reach an always difficult equilibrium between public and private interests, of which the city will always benefit.

Will this be an impossible compromise because of the short-sightedness of the great majority of the building firms, which only conceive easy and immediate profit, even when that can cause an enormous collective loss?

I don't believe it will necessarily be so, in spite of the rejection of the various studies that were drawn up, of which only the first is presented, the one which seems to illustrate the contrary.

Time, because it is wise, will not forgive and will place judgement on the validity of the convictions.

What city will we have then?...

Porto, 1998

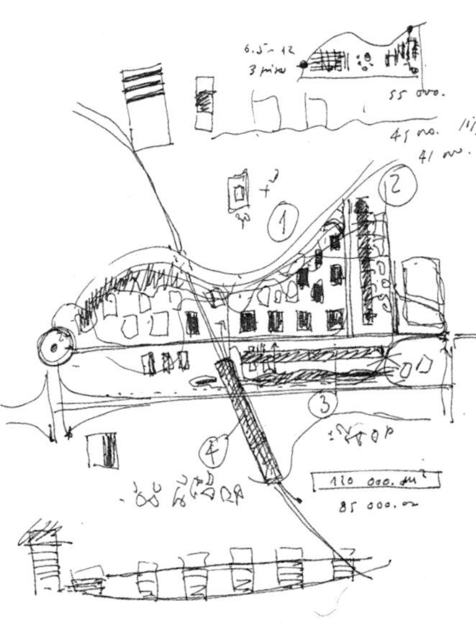

Study sketch.

Facing page:
General plan.

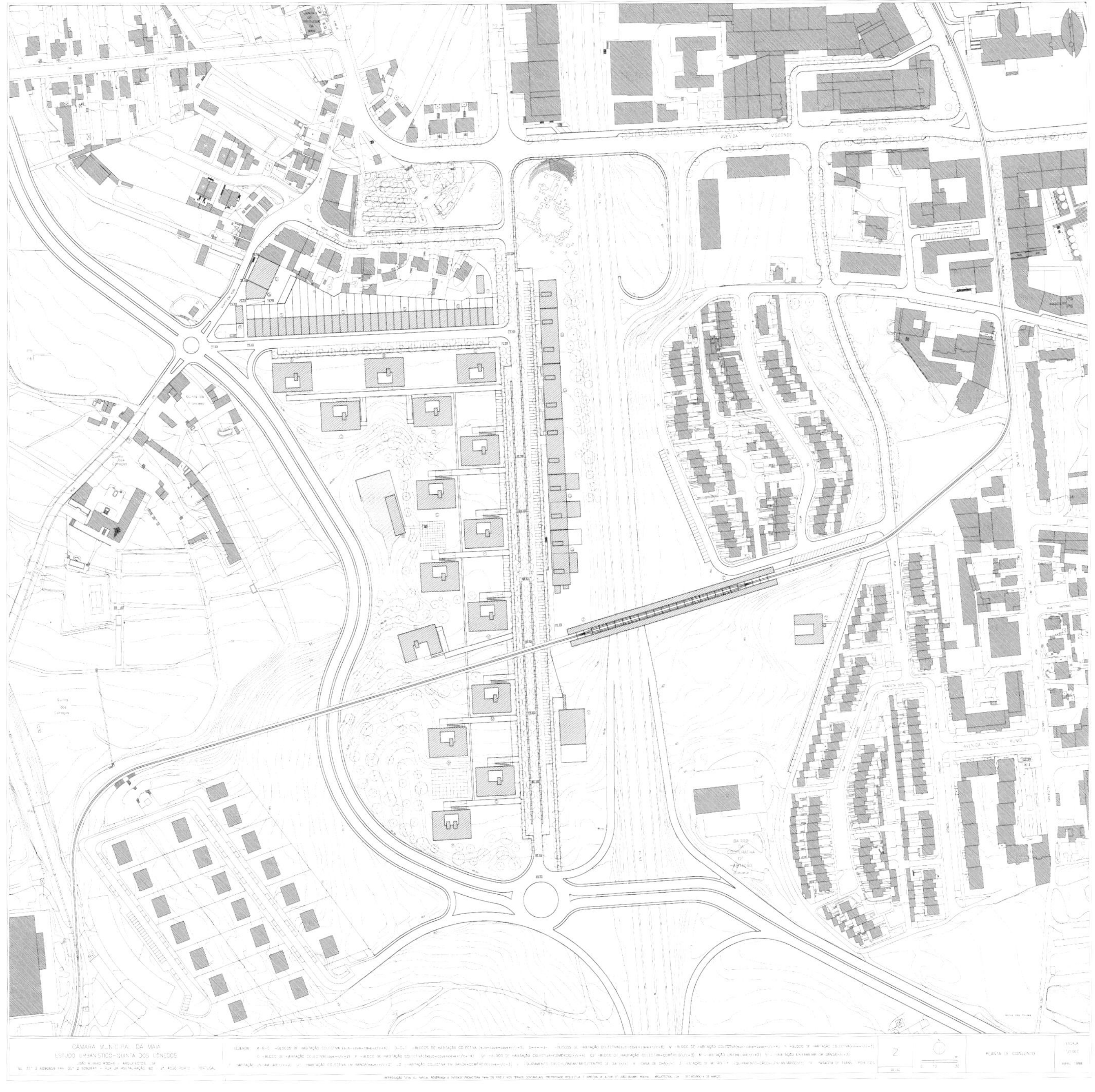
AVENIDA VISCONDE DE BARREIROS
CÂMARA MUNICIPAL DA MAIA
ESTUDO URBANÍSTICO – QUINTA DOS CÓNEGOS
LEGENDA
PLANTA DO CONJUNTO
AVENIDA NOVO RUMO

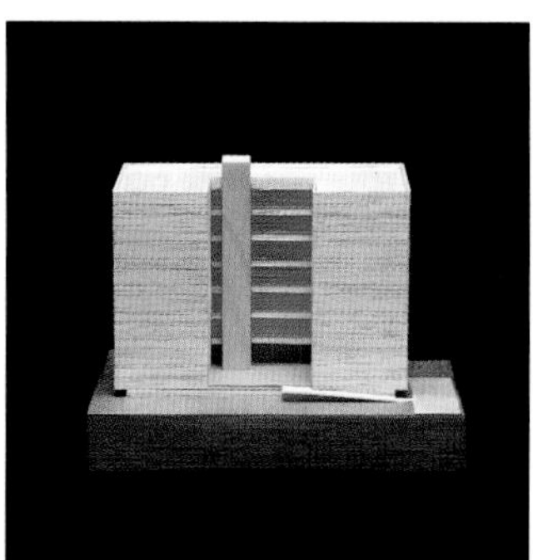

Model, view of the south side.

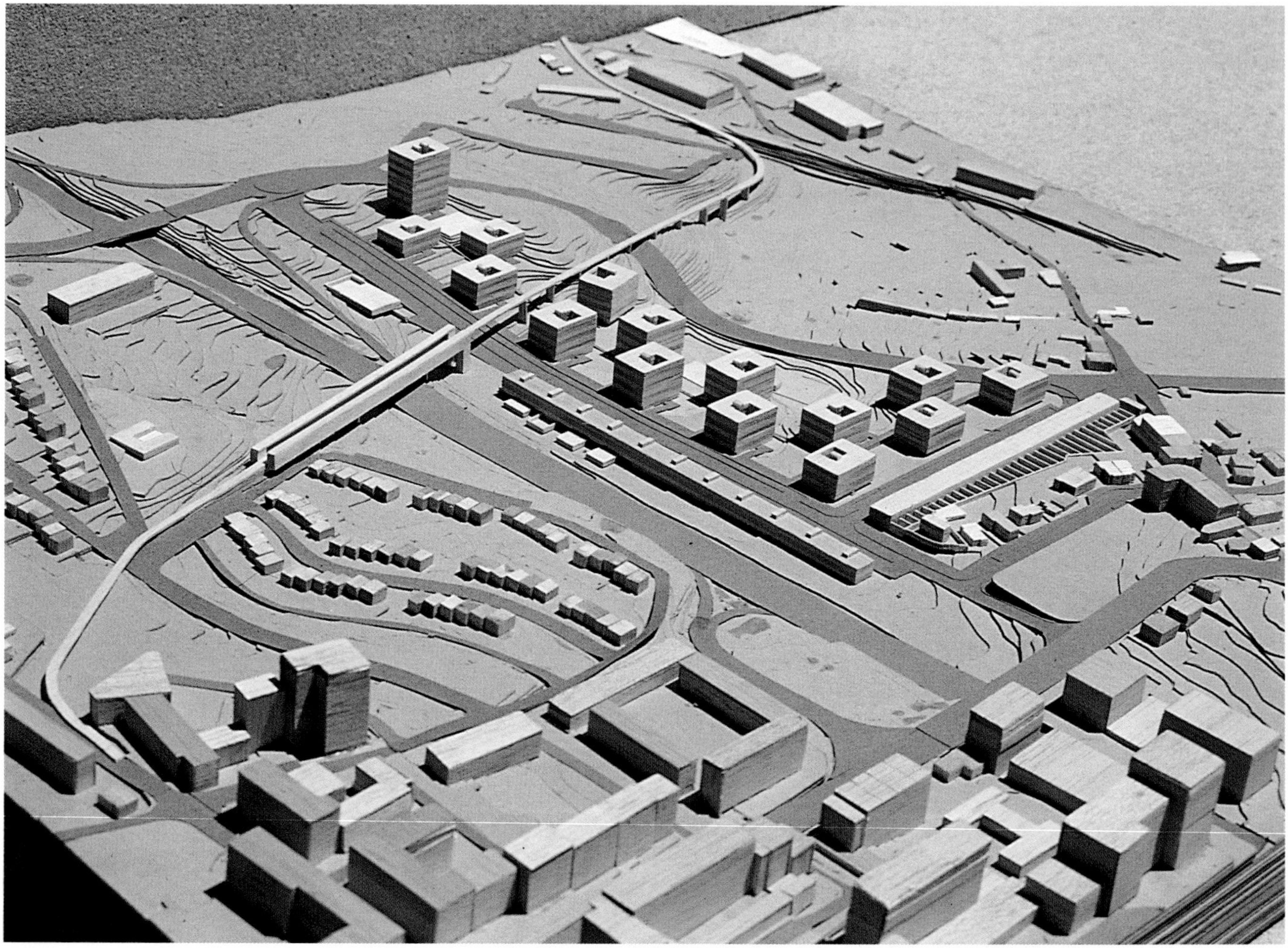

Model, general view from the northeast.

Model, view of the north side.

Model, general view from the southeast.

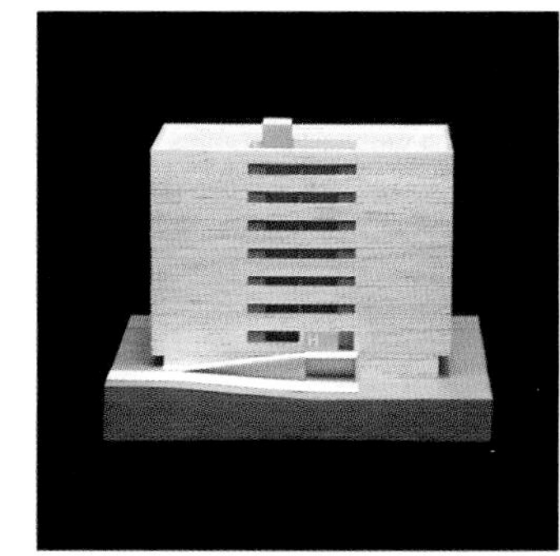

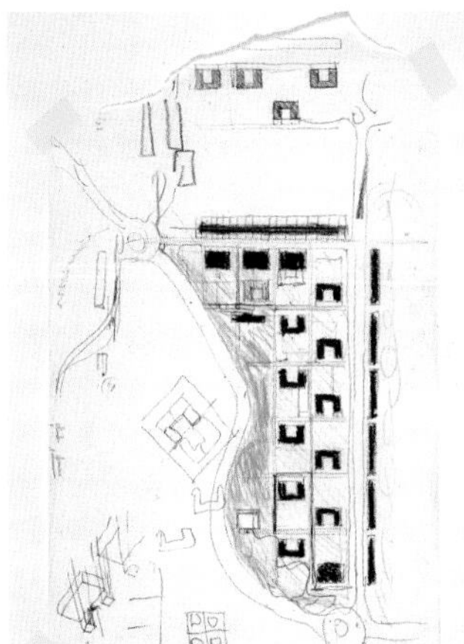

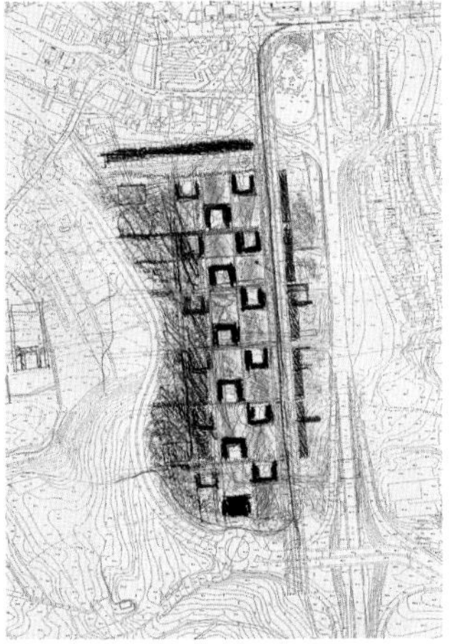

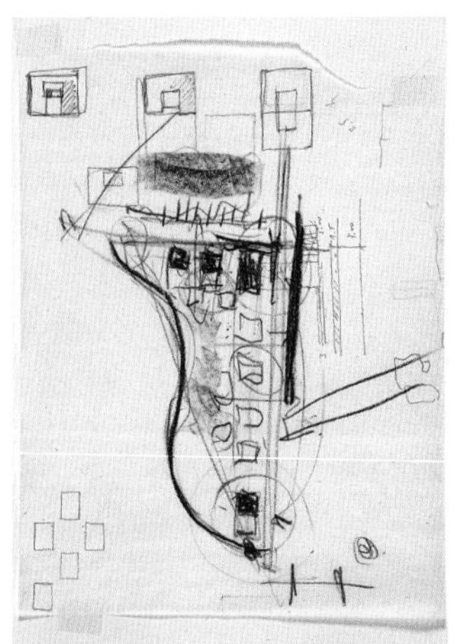

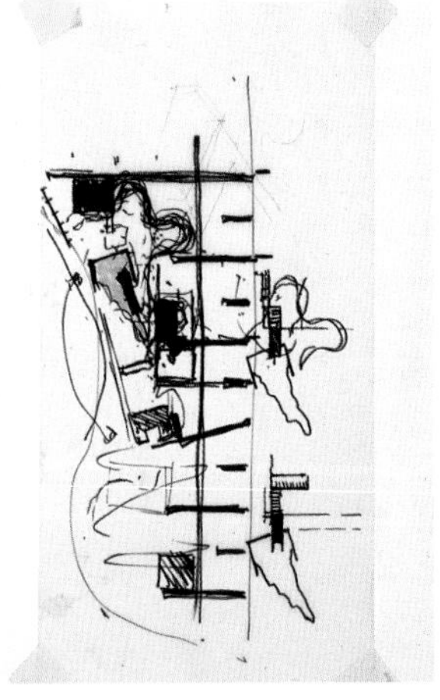

Study sketches, development of the solution in different stages.

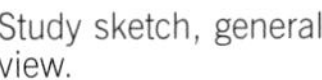

Study sketch, general view.

Facing page: Sections.

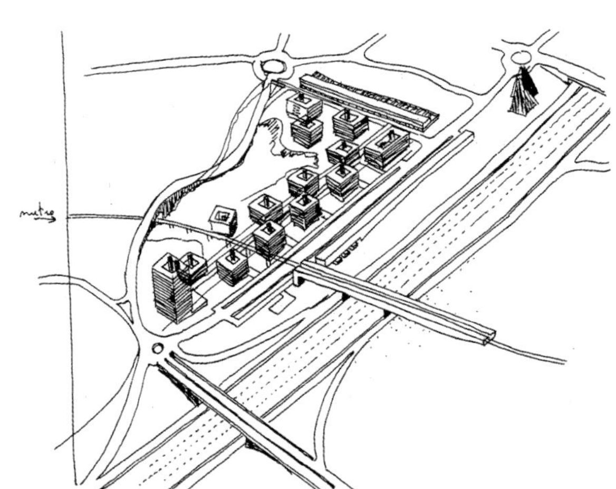

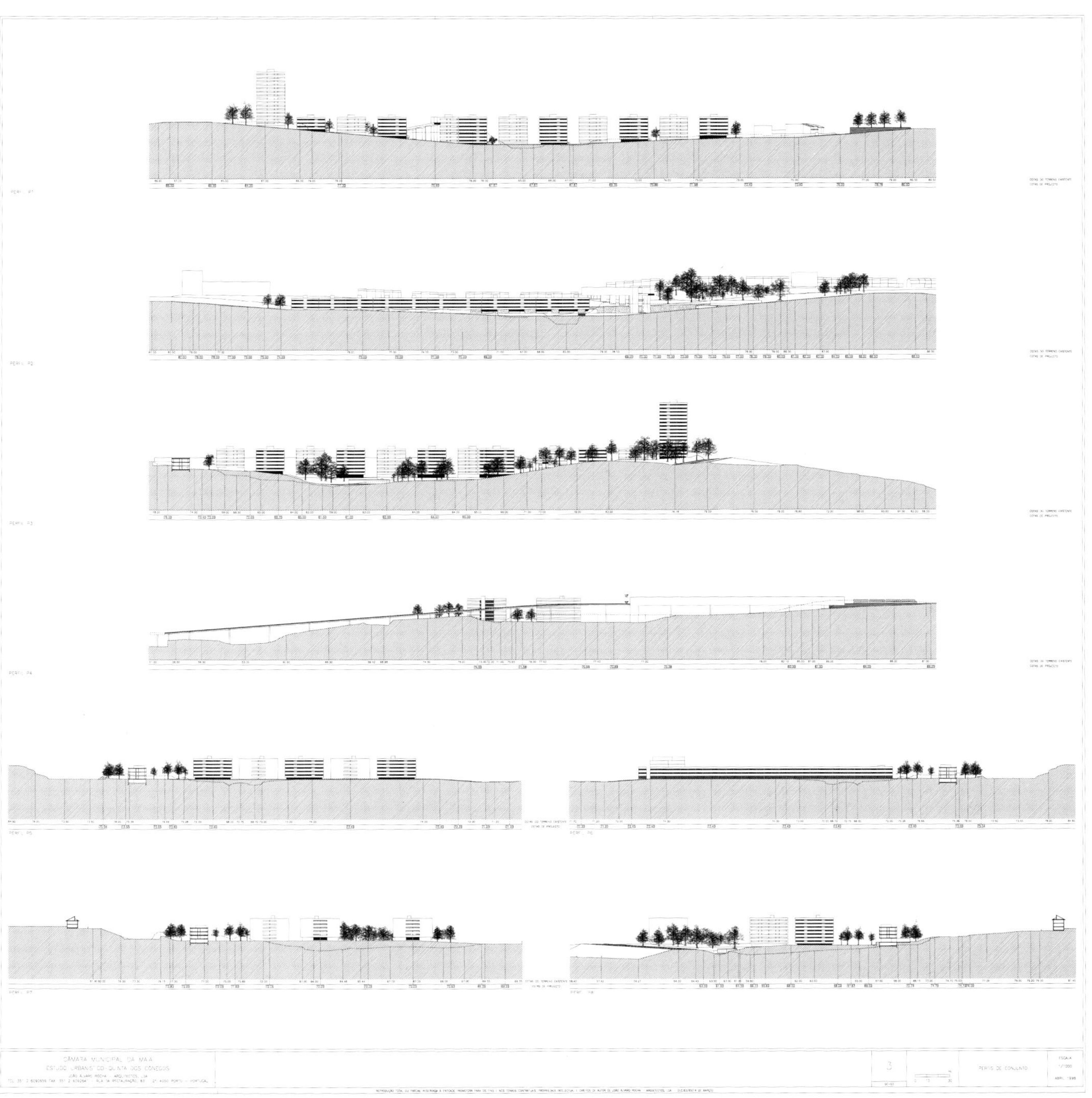

Basement, ground and floor plans.

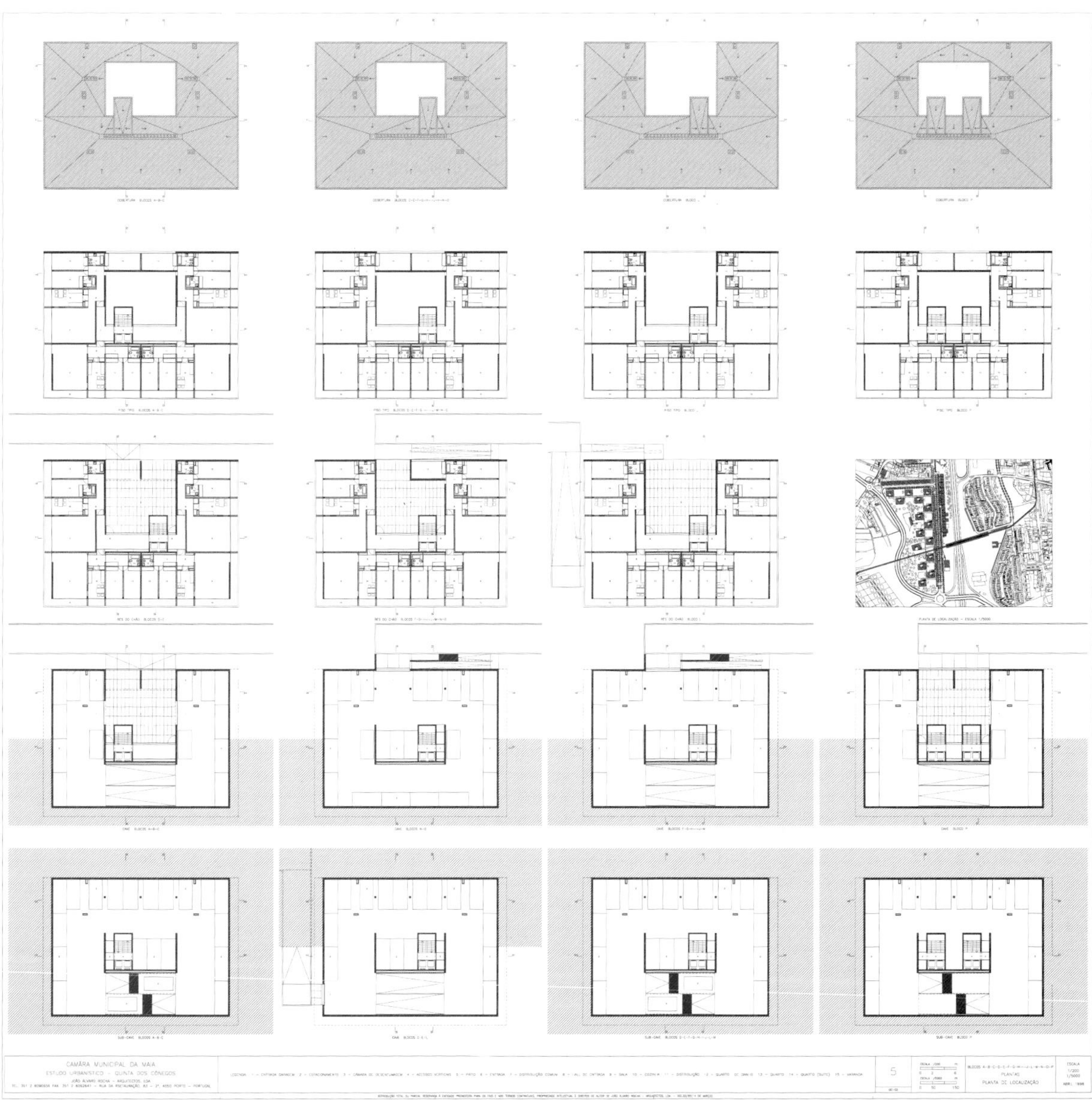

Sections and elevations.

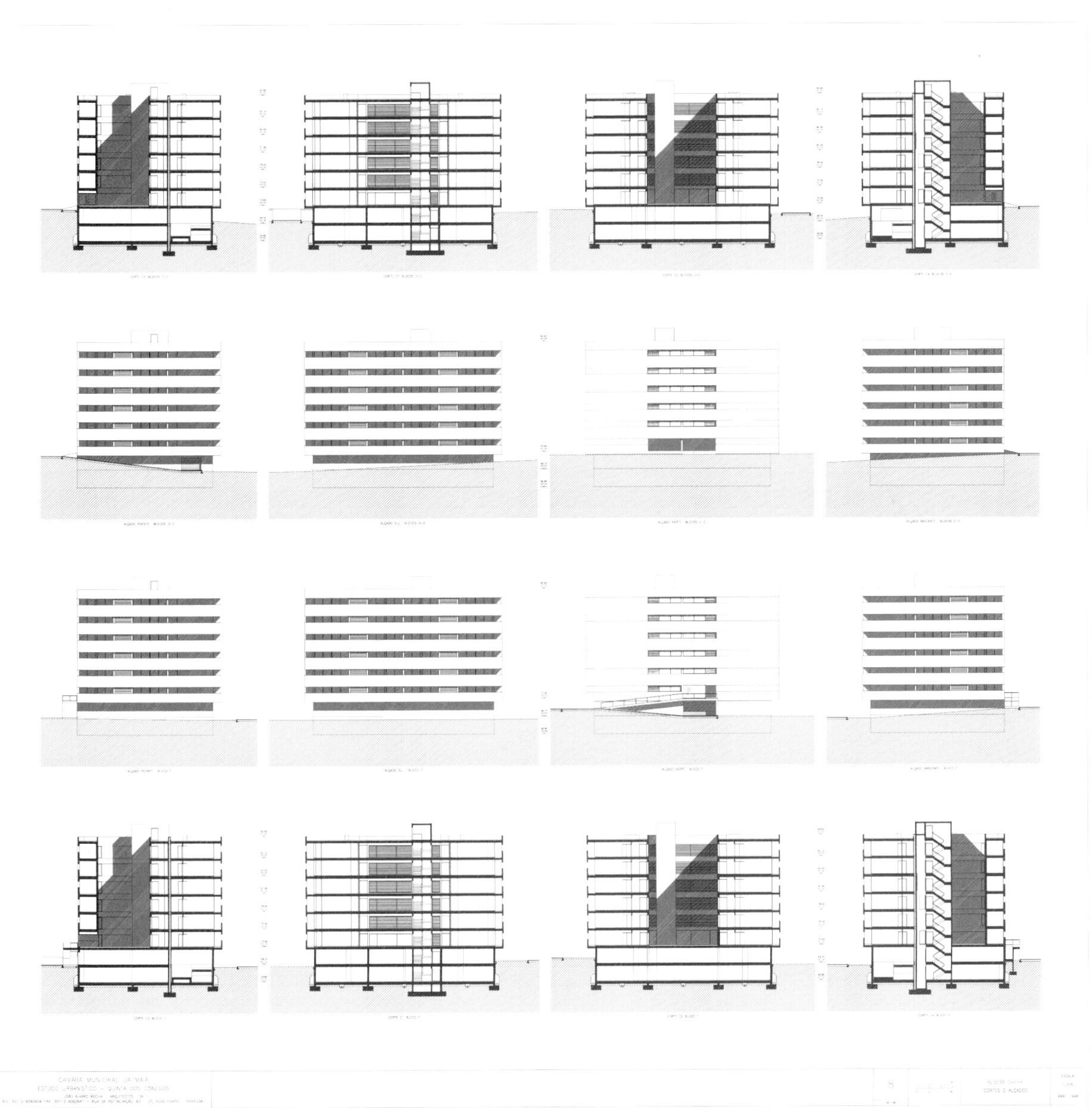

20. Vila do Castelo: Detail Plan Castelo da Maia - Maia

Detail Plan
1998-2001

Design
João Álvaro Rocha, Architect

Collaborators
António Luís Neves, Architect
Victor Oliveira, Architect

Model
Armando Lopes Teixeira, Architect

The part of territory on which the Quinta da Gruta estate is located – correctly defined as the centre of the village of Castelo da Maia – has been characterized, until relatively recent times, by the centralizing presence of the national road (E.N. 14) and the railway, both axis of national importance that cross it in the north-south direction, and by the many arteries in the east-west direction which link it to the municipal area.

Consequently, many service facilities and municipal buildings have been located in this area, contributing to accentuate its central, although unwisely arranged, character.

These last decades have been marked by deep and accelerated transformation processes. But in this area, these processes have led to indiscriminate urban expansion to the detriment of preexisting rural settlements, and the linear residential pattern resulting from the presence of communication arteries.

Little by little, the lack of cohesion between old and new complexes, and even between the newly built ones, has led to a disarticulated reality in which public spaces are reduced and the centrality of the area is lost.

The aim of this project is that of rediscovering this centrality, and of endowing the area with an urban sense which would become the instrument of its affirmation on the territory.

The pretext, on its turn, is the reformulation of the estate as a space of leisure.

It should be transformed into what could be defined as an "almost building", whose scale overcomes its physical limits and finds its way into a wider territory, so as to reveal its true public dimension as a potentially structured element of this same territory.

The area's centrality is going to become a present, contemporary feature, with no need to get rid of its rural memory; it should be able to reinterpret those aspects that still survive and deserve to be maintained.

This is not nostalgia; quite the opposite, this is the search for an equilibrium that allows transformation – a dialogue between different construction periods, between new and old, between big and small, between public and private.

The strategical approach should not impose itself, it should not be exterior to the territory, but should spring out from it.

Porto, July 2000

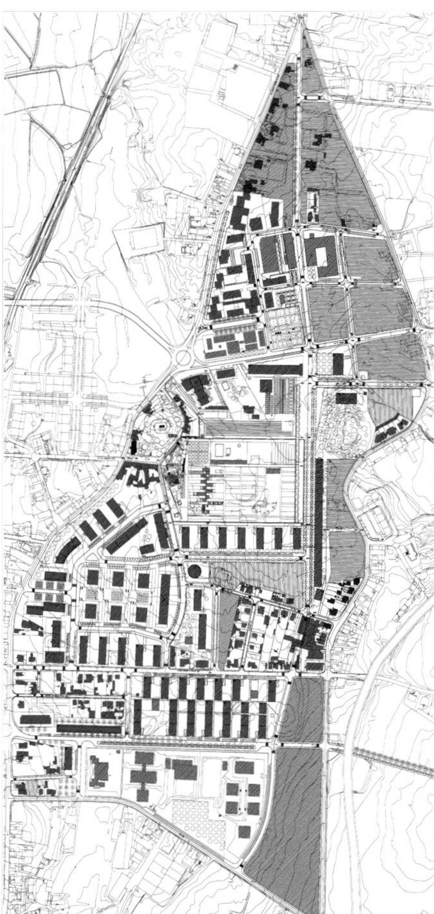

Master plan.

Model, general view
of the central area.

21. Vila do Castelo: Urban Park - Garden Areas Renovation Castelo da Maia - Maia

Design
João Álvaro Rocha, Architect
1998-2001-(underway)

Construction
1998-2001-(underway)

Collaborators
Alberto Barbosa Vieira, Architect
Carla Garrido de Oliveira, Architect

Model
Armando Lopes Teixeira, Architect

The Quinta da Gruta estate has always been a unique place in the territory, not because of its historical significance, but because of its "geographical" centrality.

This is a condition that should be preserved, not for mere traditional reasons, but as an opportunity of an urban rearrangement capable of setting rules and order among recent unqualified building interventions.

The adaptation and the extension of the estate's physical space into an urban park is an attempt both to maintain its links with the existing farming fields, and to strategically define its role in the transformation process of the territory it is a part of, so that it can grow and change according to social dynamics, meet people's needs, and take a more urban character.

The estate re-invented as a space for leisure and education, as a green area endowed with facilities for present and future activities, becomes an instrument of promoting the citizens environmental awareness, and their participation in urban life.

The facilities relating to the different activities will develop in successive projects to allow the subdivision of the respective works. The sum of all these projects – which will be conceived within a more general organizational plan – will give the territory its final consistent character.

A sort of "non-project", or a "project under construction", which means it is open, permanently available and attentive to all the changes that social development will suggest.

Porto, July 2000

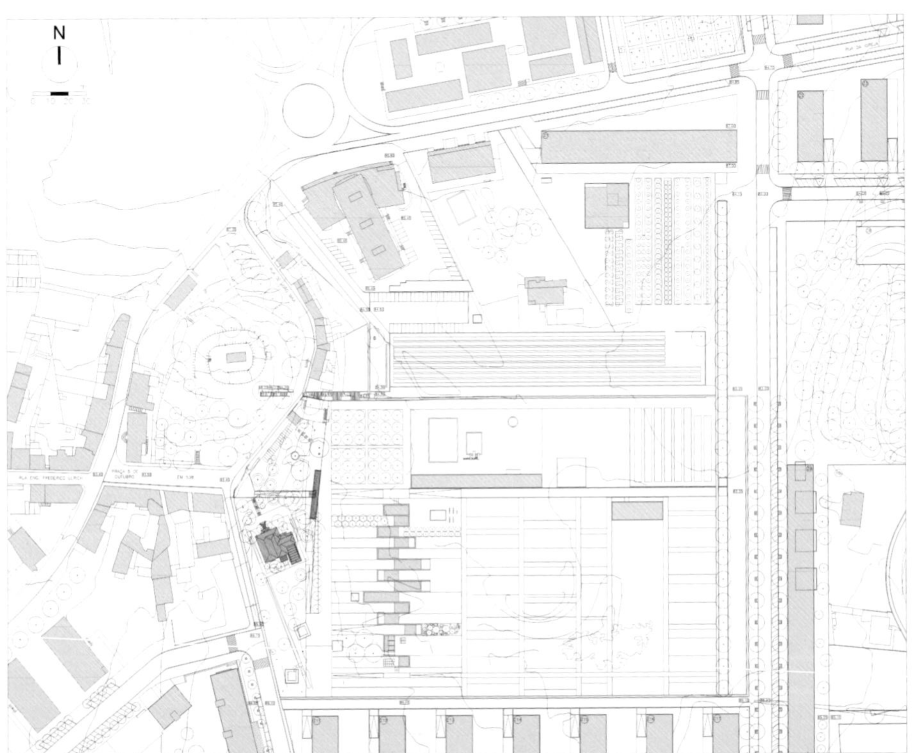

General plan.

General layout
(1st phase).

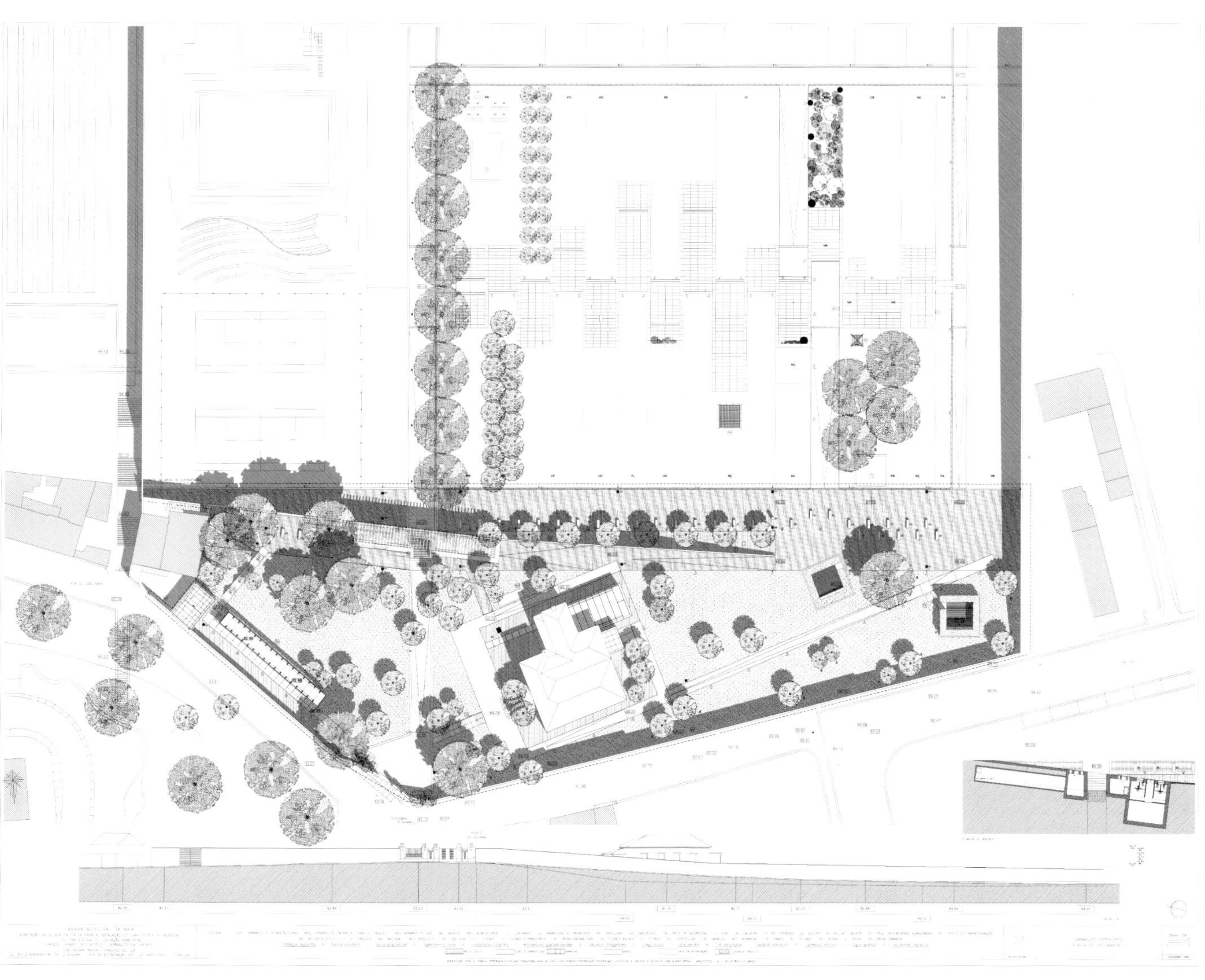

Facing page:
General view of the garden with the existing house reconversion in the background.

Winter garden greenhouse in the existing garden.

General view of the existing garden with the greenhouse in the background.

The existing garden, the new paths and the greenhouse in the background.

The greenhouse, westside view (entry) along the path.

The greenhouse, eastside view from the existing garden.

An old tree in the existing garden and a path.

Facing page:
Densities: diverse articulations between materials and "landscape".

22. Vila do Castelo: Urban Park - Homestead Remodelling
Castelo da Maia - Maia

Design
João Álvaro Rocha, Architect
1998-99

Construction
1998-2001

Collaborator
Alberto Barbosa Vieira, Architect

Furniture Design
João Álvaro Rocha, Architect

The intervention on this structure of the Quinta da Gruta estate is not one of restoration or refurbishing. The idea is to find a new role for a building which, on other occasions, would probably be excluded or re-located, and at the same time to erase the marks of successive interventions which bear no cohesion or relationship between them.

The projects are consequently founded on an almost archaeological study of the site, in the aim not to restore the past, but to recognize the place past essence, to rediscover its relations, and use them to establish a conceptual plan capable of converting the other spaces and buildings into "matter".

The subjects of this study are not the individual sections of the estate, but their unifying factors, and the relationships between them – all should be rearranged into one indivisible whole, the building and the garden converted into one unique entity.

This is necessary because transformation – even the most violent – only occurs when it does not break, interrupt or create gaps, and when it is able to express itself in continuity.

In this case, to transform means to go back to the original essence of the work, and to follow its development along the path of memory.

And it is memory that confirms contemporaniety and becomes an unmistakable sign of the connection between past and present.

Beyond this... only a beautiful garden with tall trees, even more... a surprise.

Porto, July 2000

General view of the existing house reconversion from the new garden.

General view of
the existing house
reconversion with
the small auditorium.

Ground and first floor plans.

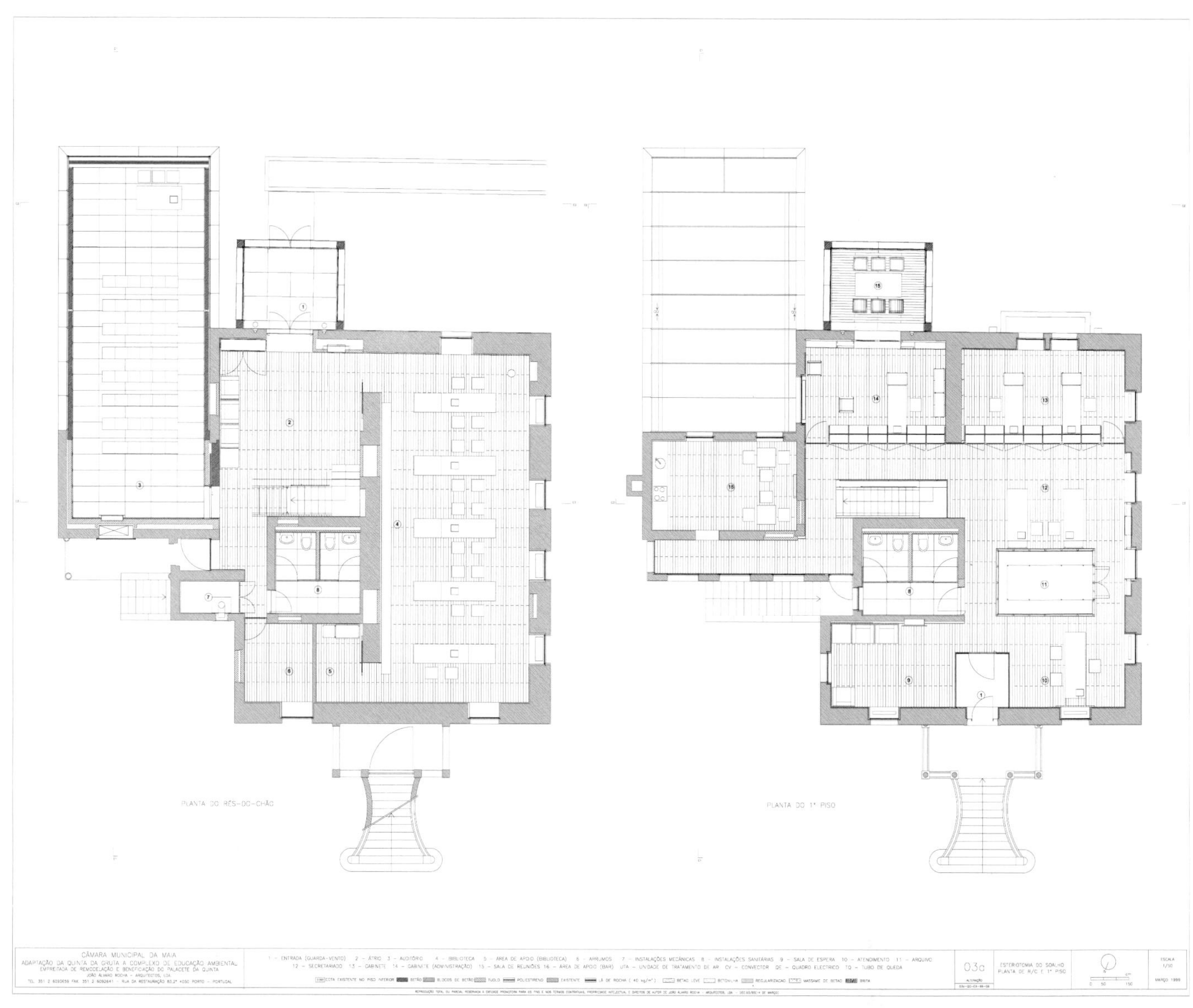

Public entry on the first floor, view from the waiting room.

Waiting room with the entry on the left.

View from the office area with entry at the far end.

Administrative offices meeting room.

General view of the office area.

Stairs in the ground floor entry hall.

Library, general view.

Sections.

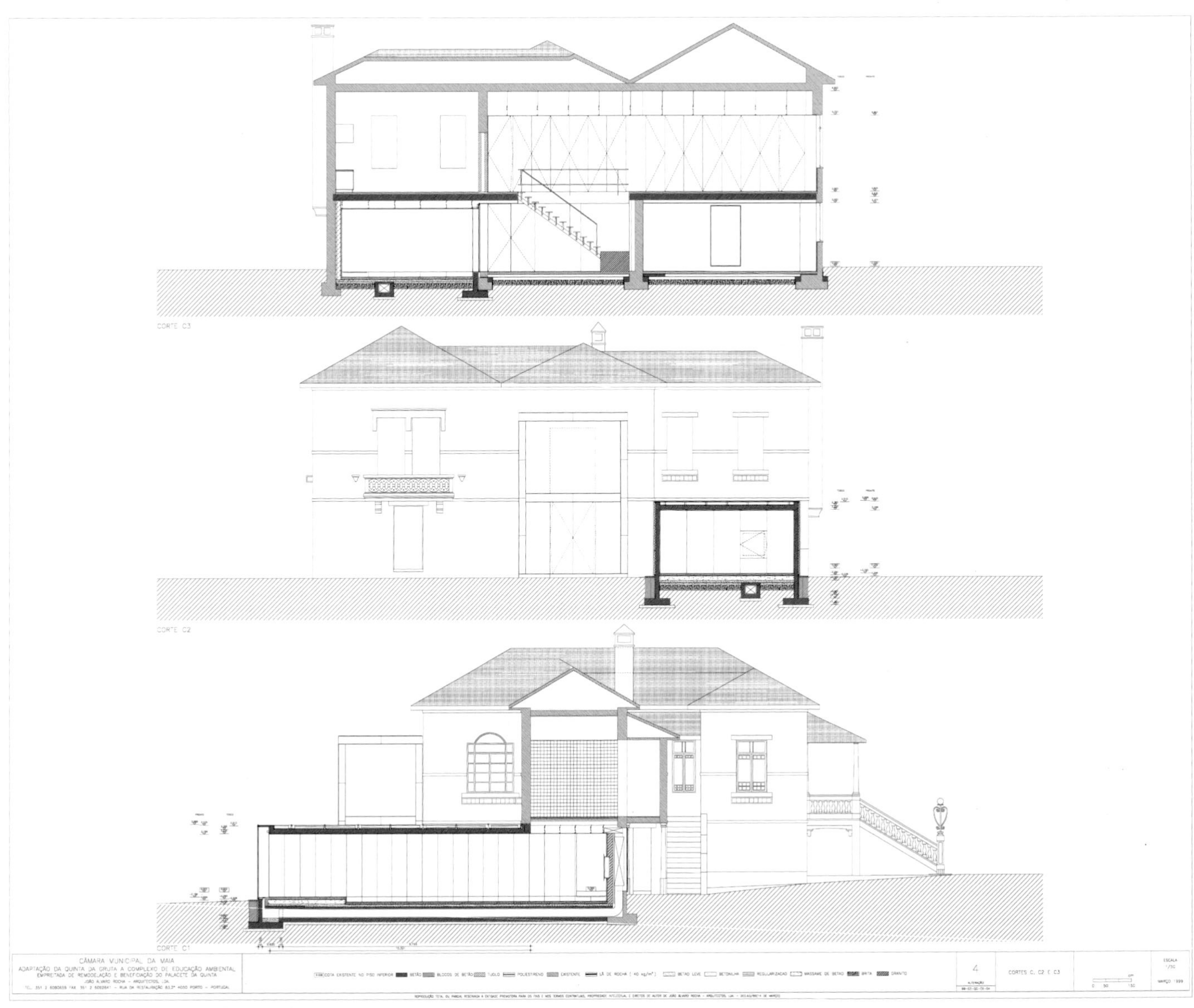

CORTE C3
CORTE C2
CORTE C1
CÂMARA MUNICIPAL DA MAIA
ADAPTAÇÃO DA QUINTA DA GRUTA A COMPLEXO DE EDUCAÇÃO AMBIENTAL
EMPREITADA DE REMODELAÇÃO E BENEFICIAÇÃO DO PALACETE DA QUINTA
JOÃO ÁLVARO ROCHA – ARQUITECTOS, LDA.
4
ALTERAÇÃO
CORTES C1 C2 E C3
0 50 150
ESCALA
1/50
MARÇO 1999

Auditorium, view from the stage.

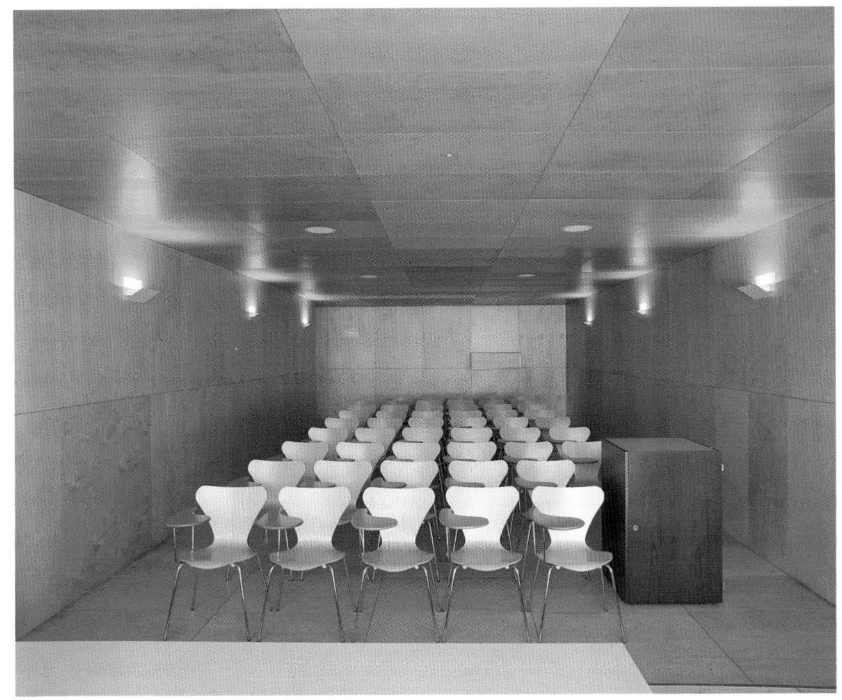

Auditorium, view towards the garden (the building in the background will be demolished with the construction of the 2nd phase of the park).

23. Vila do Castelo: Urban Park - Environment Education School
Vila do Castelo - Maia

Design
João Álvaro Rocha, Architect
1999

Construction
2001-(underway)

Collaborators
Alberto Barbosa Vieira, Architect
Francisco Portugal e Gomes, Architect
António Luís Neves, Architect
João Ventura Lopes, Architect
Pedro Tiago Pimentel, Architect
Sónia Campos Neves, Practice Architect
Tiago Macedo Correia, Practice Architect

Model
Armando Lopes Teixeira, Architect

The Quinta da Gruta estate already possesses its own "house". It is the school which, as a building, should be *a* house without being *the* house – an unassuming presence rather than an imposing one.

With reference to the existing and now transformed house, the school should be seen as a secondary element, a sort of supplementary building, whose form results from the interdependence between the two buildings.

Everything should be simple and direct as it has always been in rural constructive tradition.

This because a house is always, merely and only, a house...

"Art is not in decadence, on the contrary it's slowly penetrating the new evolution of the artistic environment.

"Stone, bronze, inexorably surrender to new technologies, in the same way that in architecture cement, glass and metal originated a new architectural style.

"In art, it is not possible for an evolution to take place with only stone or colour, but a new art form can be made with light and television – only the creative artist can and should transform these techniques into Art.

"The material is static, human intelligence defines it, finds its sense, dominates it in figures and art, makes it a heritage of humanity."[1]

Porto, 1999

[1] Lucio Fontana, 1968

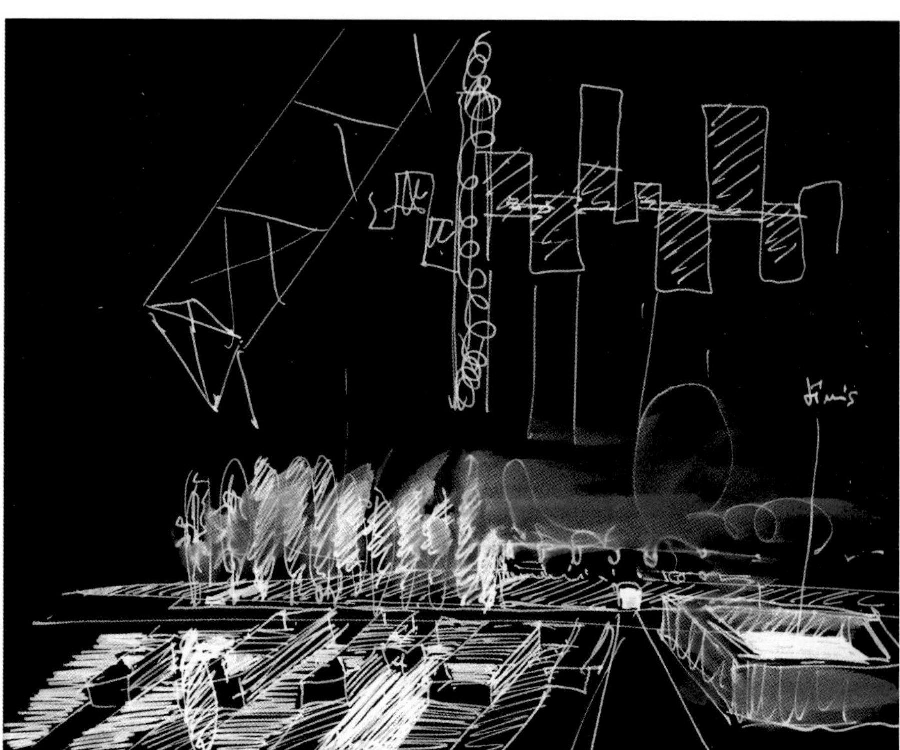

Study sketch.

General plan (2nd phase: school and new garden).

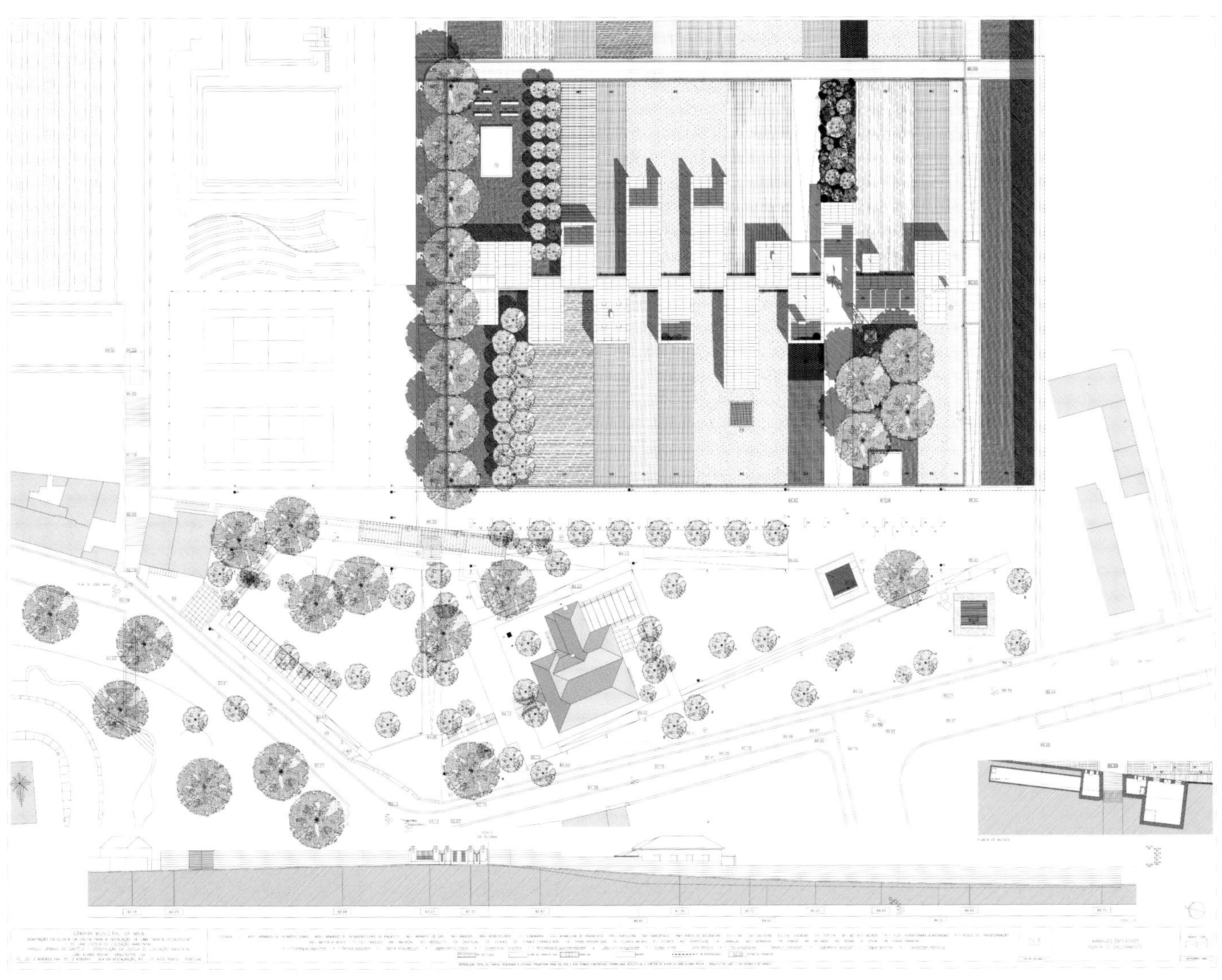

Ground floor plan.

Model, general view from the west.

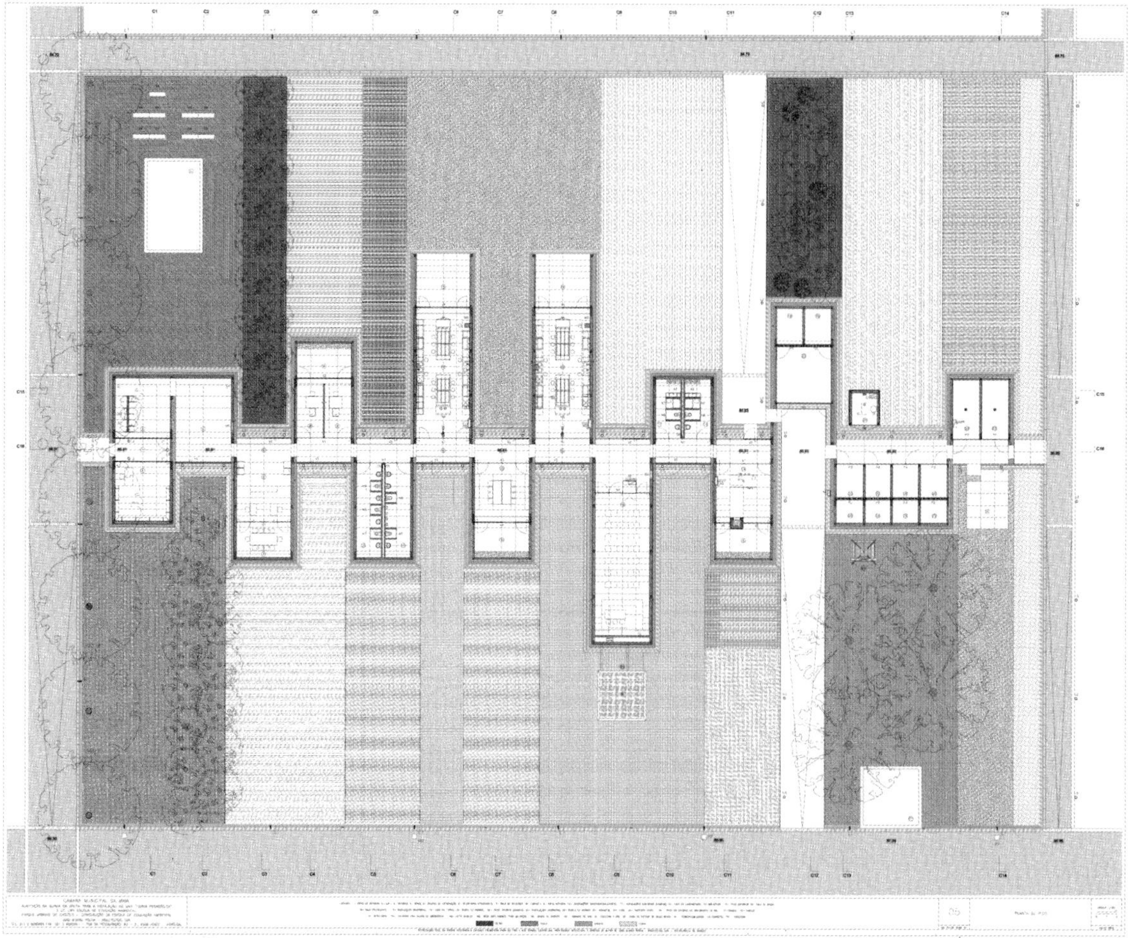

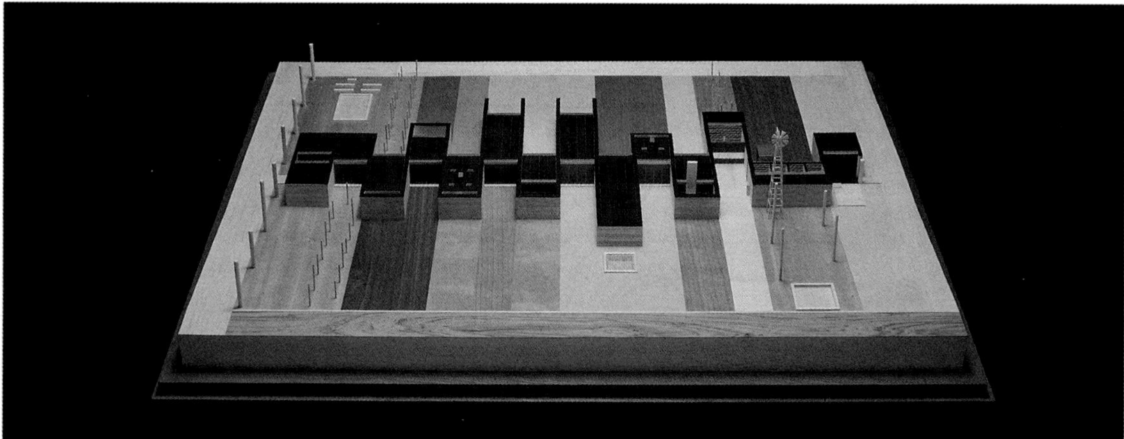

Sections.

Study sketch, east side view.

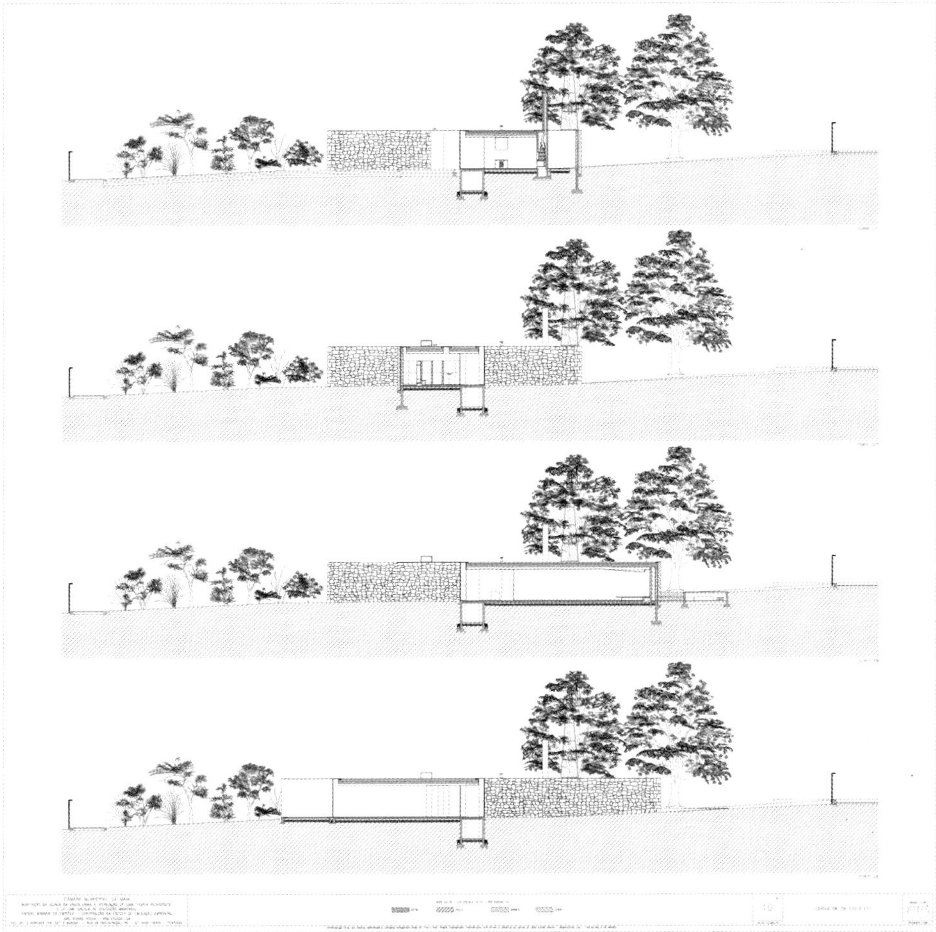

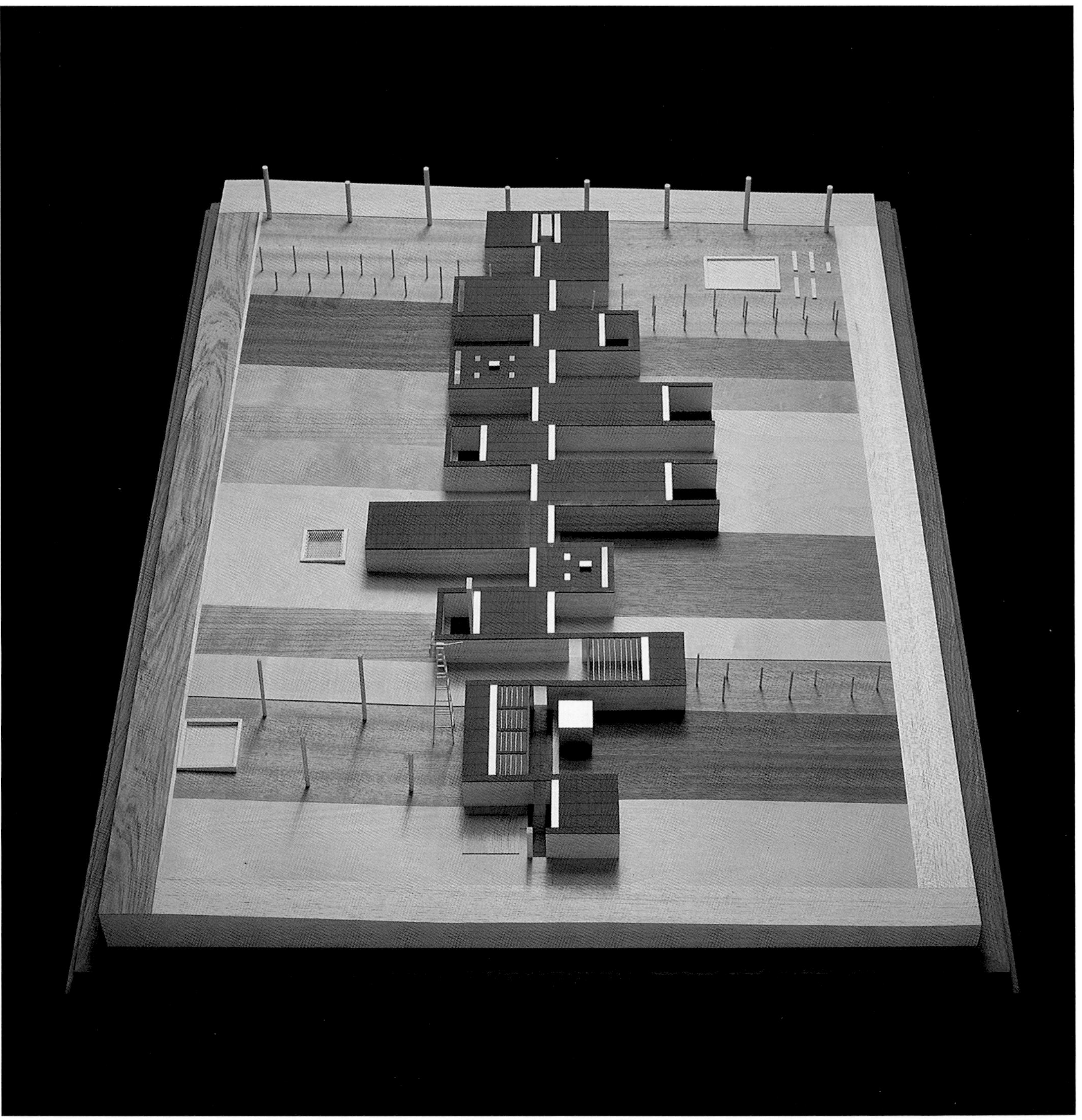

Facing page:
Model, general view
from the south.

Longitudinal sections
and elevations.

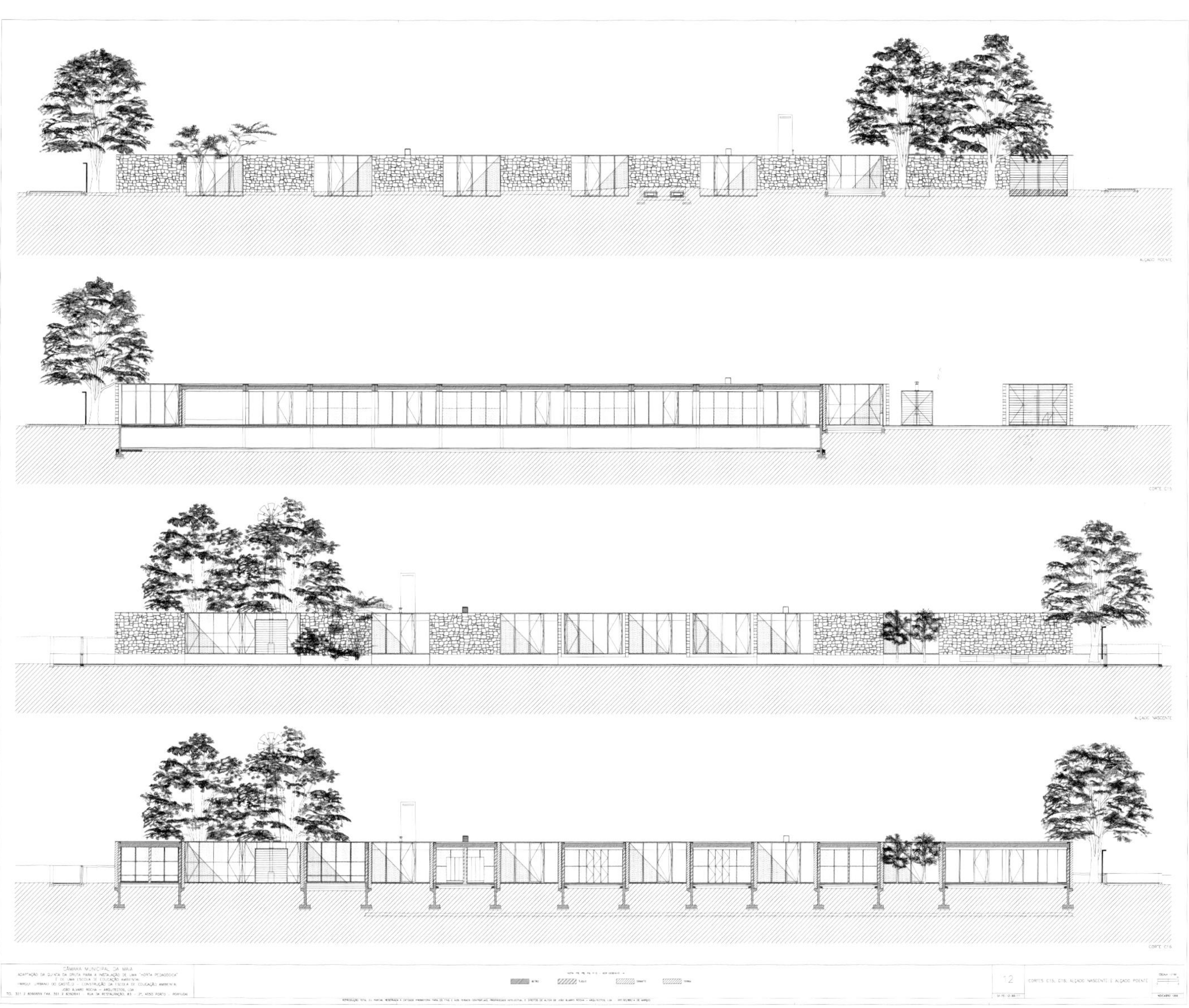

24. Museo de Sanfermines, Pamplona
Encierro

Design
João Álvaro Rocha, Architect
2001

Collaborators
Camilo Rebelo, Architect
Alberto Barbosa Vieira, Architect
António Luís Neves, Architect
João Ventura Lopes, Architect
Pedro Tiago Pimentel, Architect
Rosana Caro, Architect
Sónia Campos Neves, Practice Architect
Tiago Carvalho, Practice Architect
Susana Vilela, Practice Architect
Ricardo Cruz, Practice Architect
Ana Luisa Teixeira, Practice Architect

Models
Manuel André Gaspar, Model Maker
Ana Luisa Teixeira, Practice Architect

The choice of the site destined to the museum building seems somewhat contradictory with the development of a natural park along the river. That was the objective at the origin of the earlier urban plan, in which the city front should retreat to allow the setting of a park of an appreciable size. Thus the location of a building of museum dimensions precisely in the place where the available land is the narrowest could compromise the natural richness of this area and its relieving role between two "cities".

On the other hand, the Rochapea fortress constitutes, in its present form, a kind of gap in the city urban structure, a fact that the opportunity of intervention can't ignore; the project should promote the articulation between two parts of the city without forgetting their individual autonomy; it should create a place both of separation and continuity, in which the museum building represents the physical connection between the upper level (historic centre) and the lower level (river, park and new city).

The excavation of the bulwark, more than constituting a memory of an earlier topography, recreates a new "square" at the lower level, allowing the walls to become façades, and making the physical limit they represent obvious.

The building and the excavated area are independent and should be read separately, even if the building is also itself an excavation. Parts of its base were in fact removed to articulate internal spaces and evoke the city – the squares, the streets, the gates...

But if the museum building has been conceived as a new doorway into the historic centre of Pamplona, it will also be an exit way to the park, a tunneled passage towards the new city to be built at a sufficiently low level to avoid any physical interference with the fortress wall.

The internal organization of the museum matches the conceptual program of its exterior areas; the exhibits will be arranged from the upper to the lower level, suggesting a continuity with the the park and the city, an ideal path which from the inside will lead to the outside, beyond the walls.

Our project for the park is founded on this connection between inner and outer, upper and lower, and also suggests changes to the Rochapea urban plan. The public park will be a connecting space between "cities" (the historical city, on one side, and the new city still under construction, on the other); it will be a territory with an identity, not a mixture of two ways of being a city, but one of the individual parts of a whole that wishes to be coherent.

More than a museum, the space to be conceived is going to be a house, because the house embodies the notion of shelter and human sympathy, in a truly popular dimension.

In its genesis, the spaces should be articulated in order to generate movement, to reproduce city spaces. Visitors to the museum should begin their tour outside, by gathering images and sensations that will be reinforced and contextualized inside, and end it once again outside; thematic spaces will take them on a rediscovery of the city with different eyes.

The Sanfermines museum is not meant to be a monument on its own, bearing its peculiar image. On the contrary, it will reflect itself in the city, in the complexity of the urban plan.

This, because any part of the city is a reproduction of the whole. As in the *encierro*, the spaces translate movement, but also flexibility and multiplicity.

The interior layout will be completely free, allowing various possible combinations. Each department will be like a home, where furniture will become accessories (displays) that recreate space.

The challenge is that visitors could feel the emotion and the intensity of the *encierro*, and recognize themselves, at the end of each visit, as true citizens of Pamplona.

Porto, November 2001

A general view of the city of Pamplona with a simulation of the project.

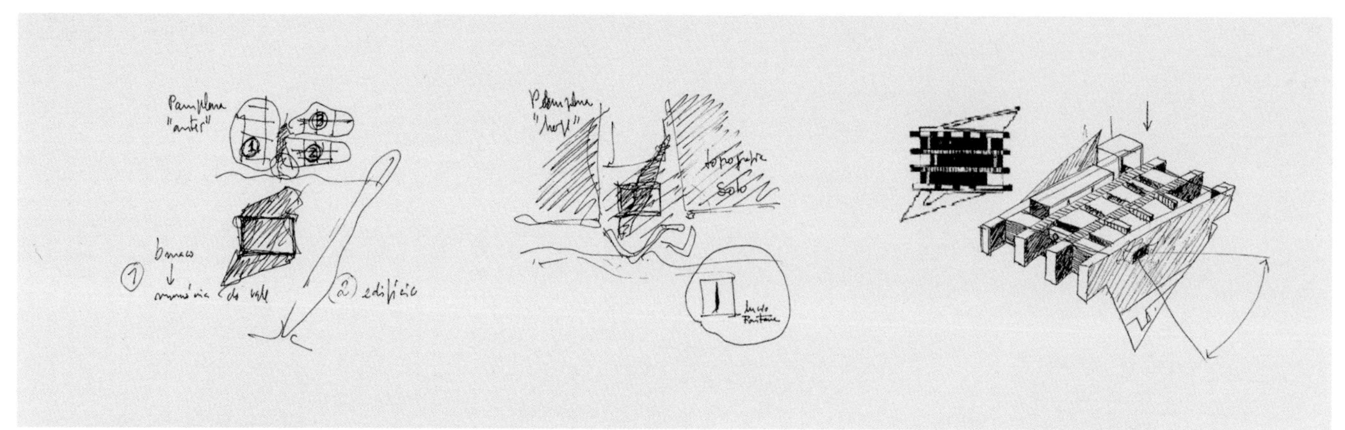

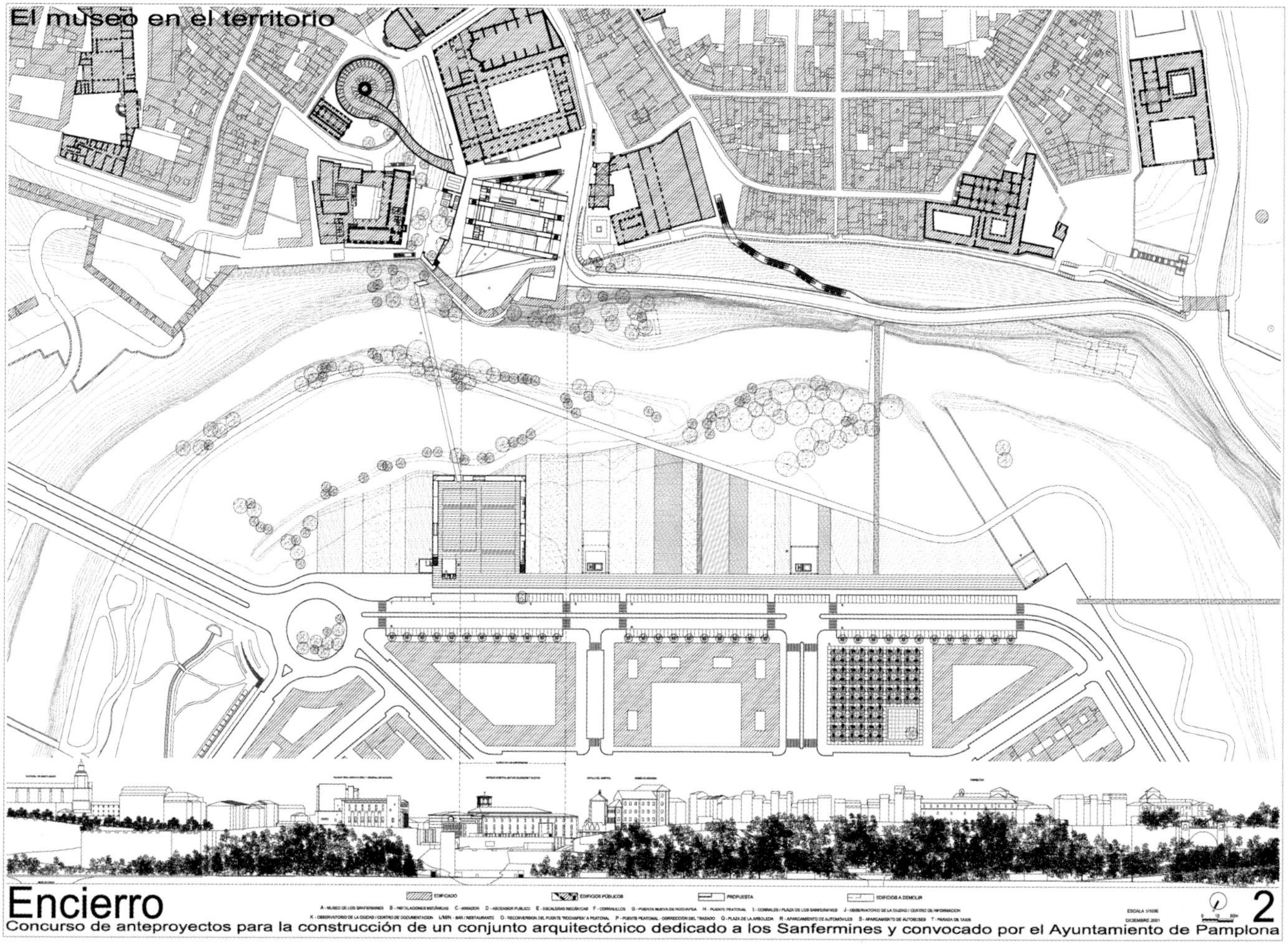

El museo en el territorio

Encierro

2

Concurso de anteproyectos para la construcción de un conjunto arquitectónico dedicado a los Sanfermines y convocado por el Ayuntamiento de Pamplona

Facing page:
Study sketches, concept design: site relations.

General plan.

Partial site plan, upper level plan and longitudinal sections.

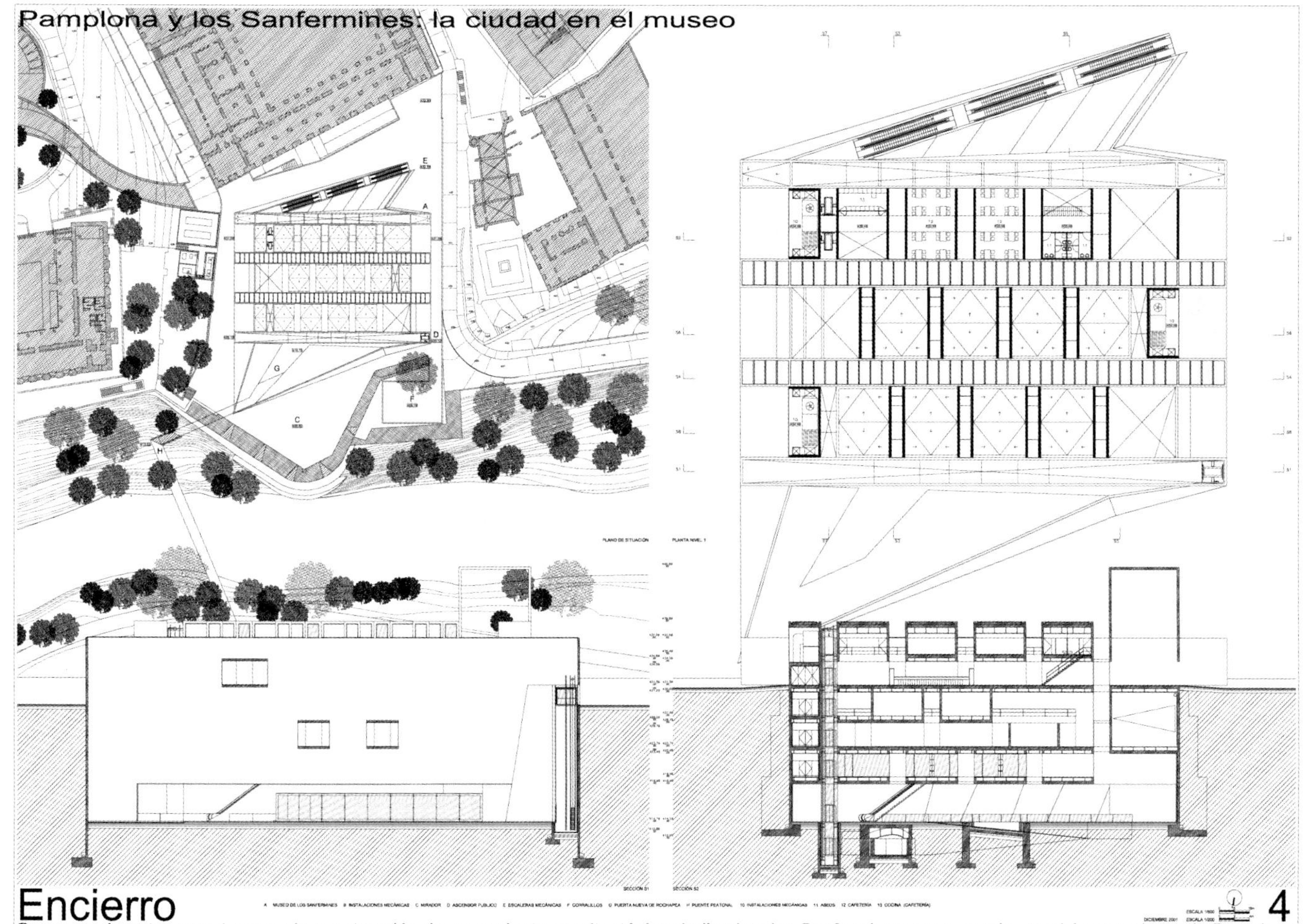

Ground and 1st level plan, longitudinal and transversal sections.

Facing page:
Study sketches, concept design: sections.

2nd and 3rd level plans, longitudinal and transversal sections.

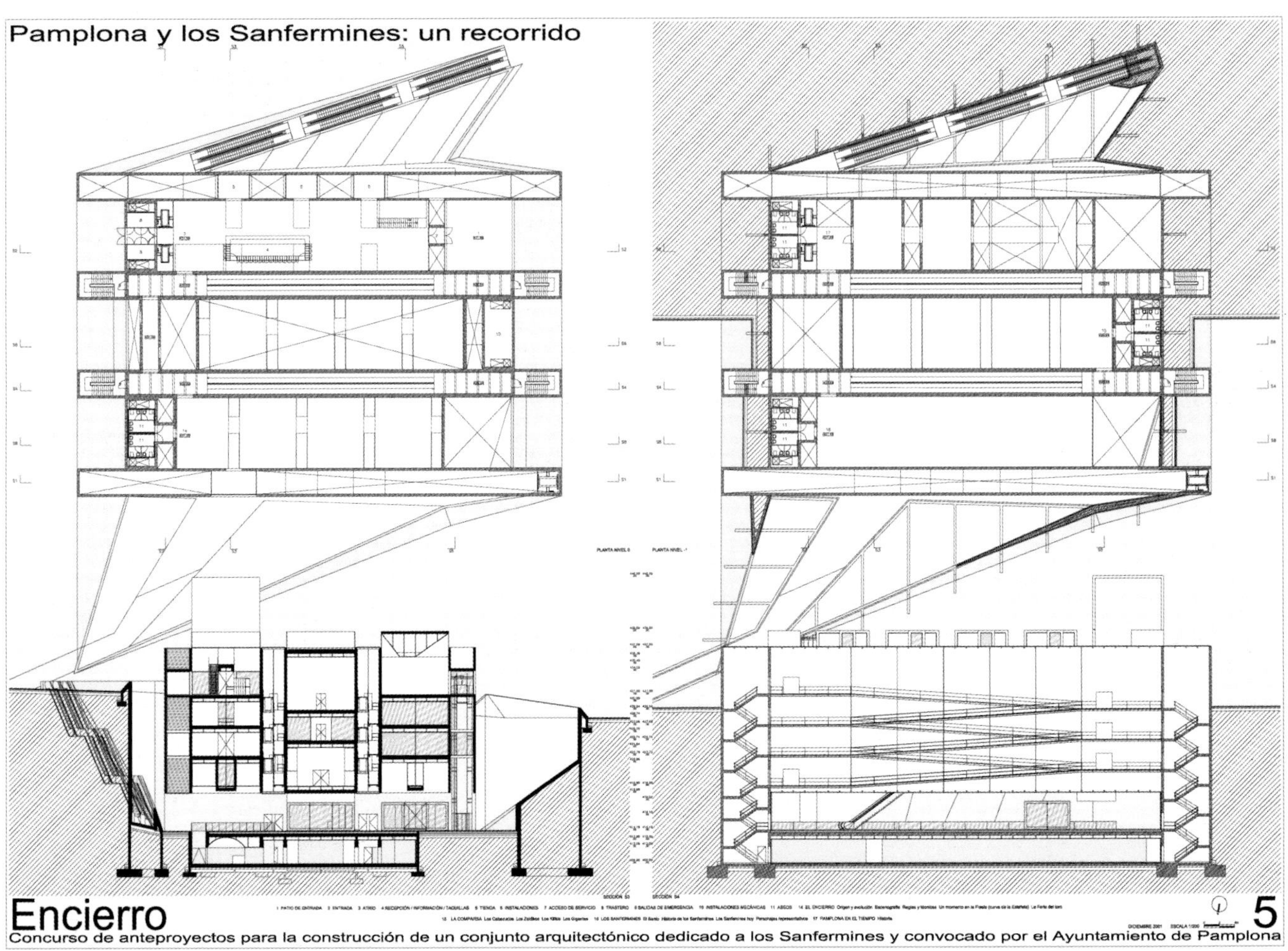

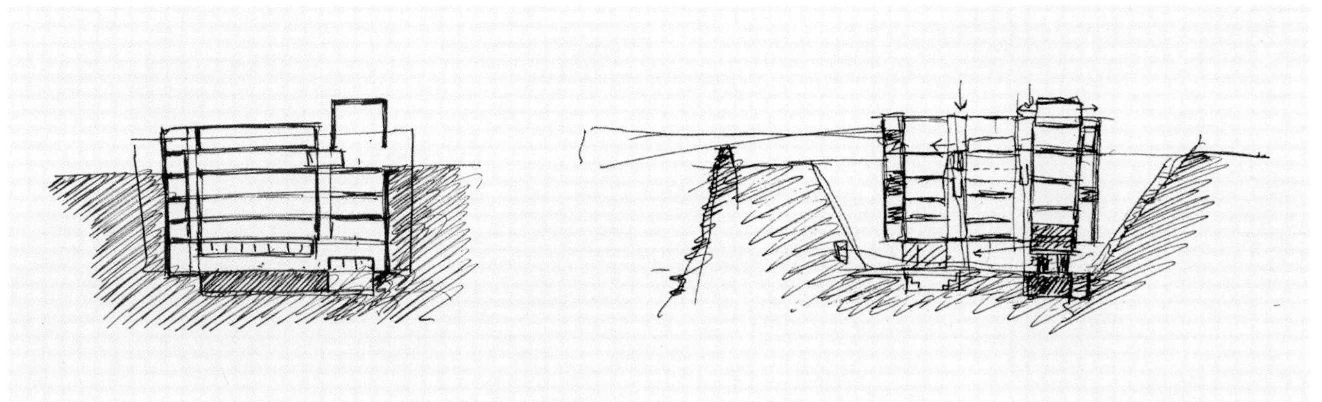

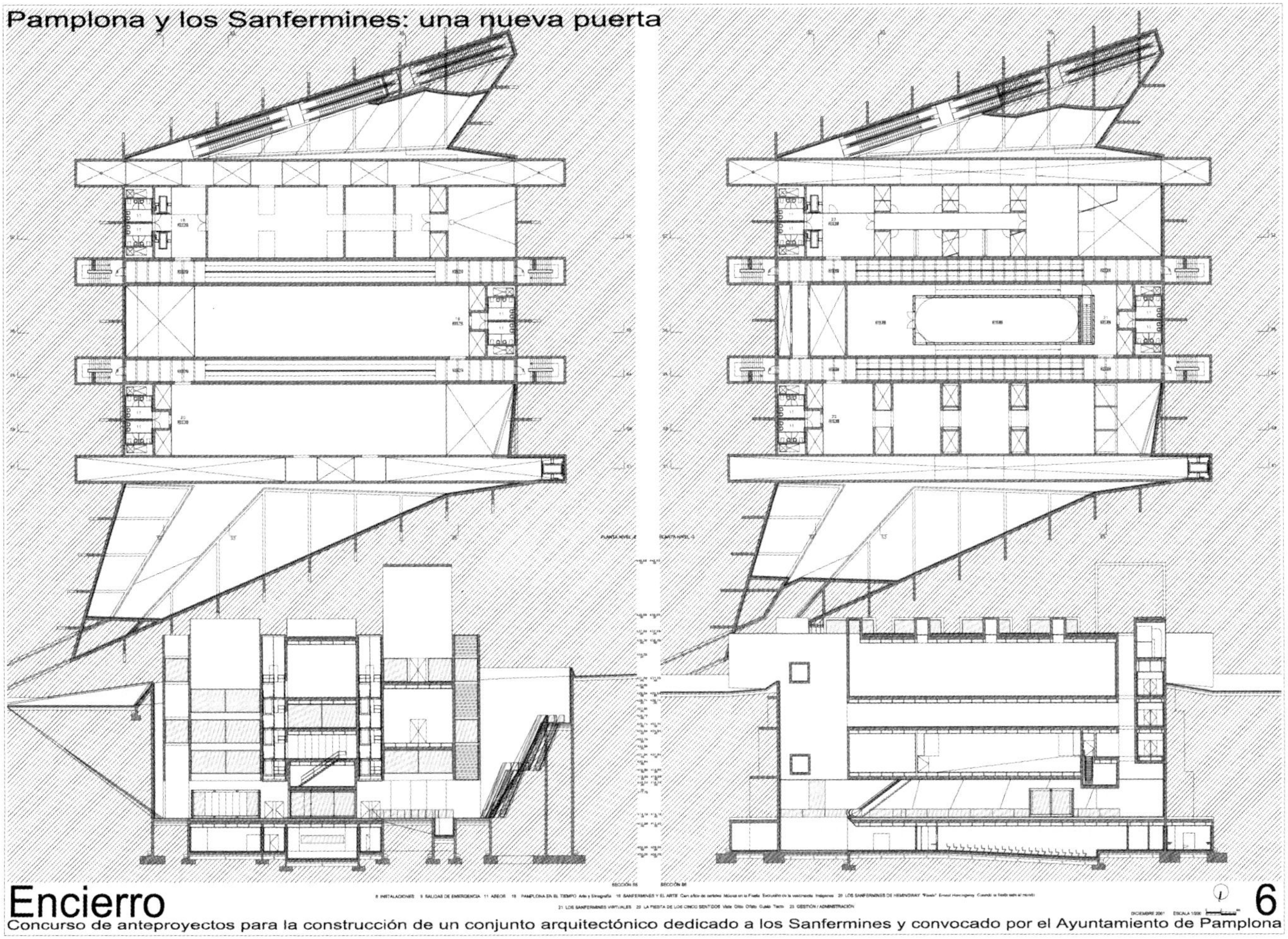

Pamplona y los Sanfermines: una nueva puerta

Encierro

6

Concurso de anteproyectos para la construcción de un conjunto arquitectónico dedicado a los Sanfermines y convocado por el Ayuntamiento de Pamplona

4th (entry from the north side) and 5th level plans, longitudinal and transversal sections.

Facing page:
Study sketches.

Ground and level plans, sections and elevations - the "Encierro" square and the "city observatory" building.

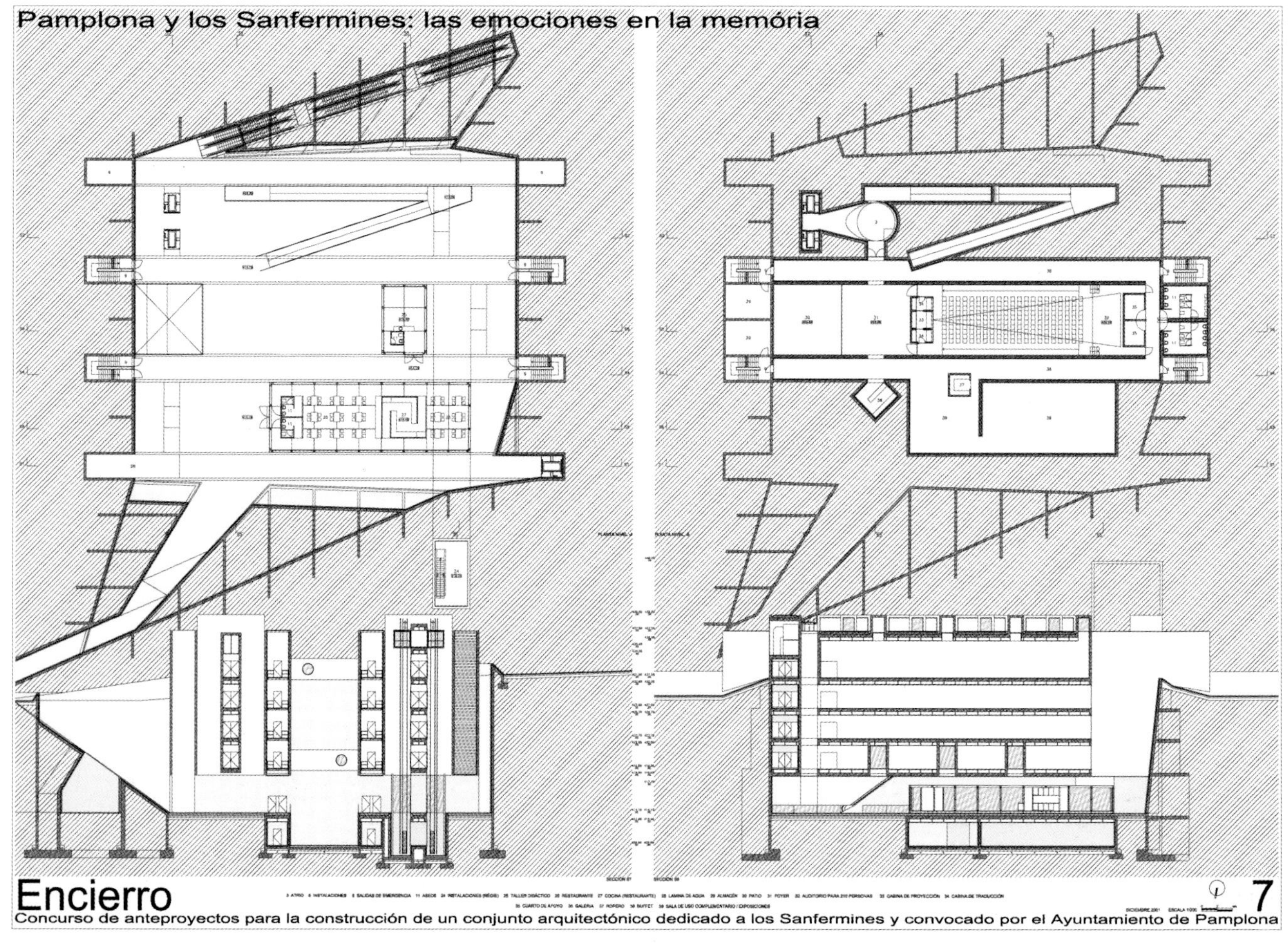

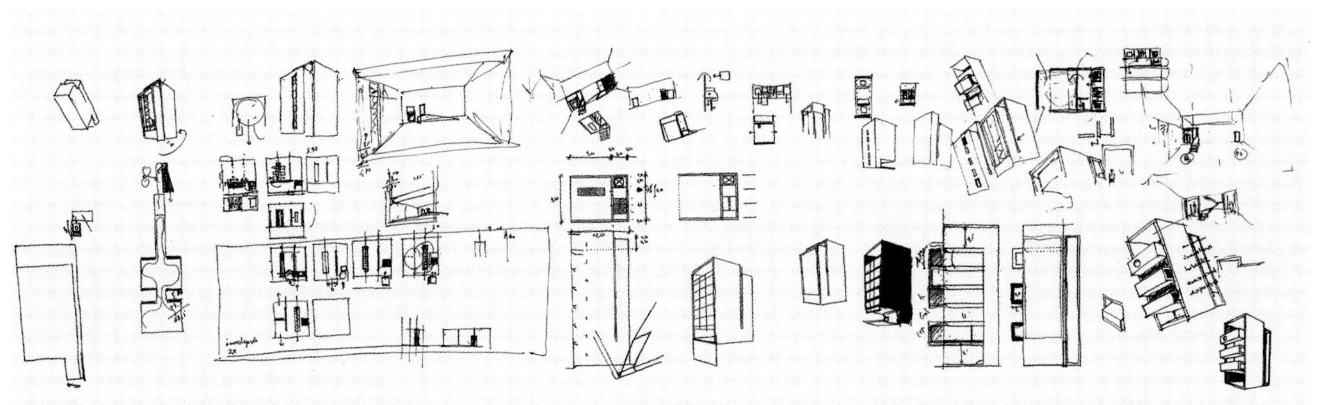

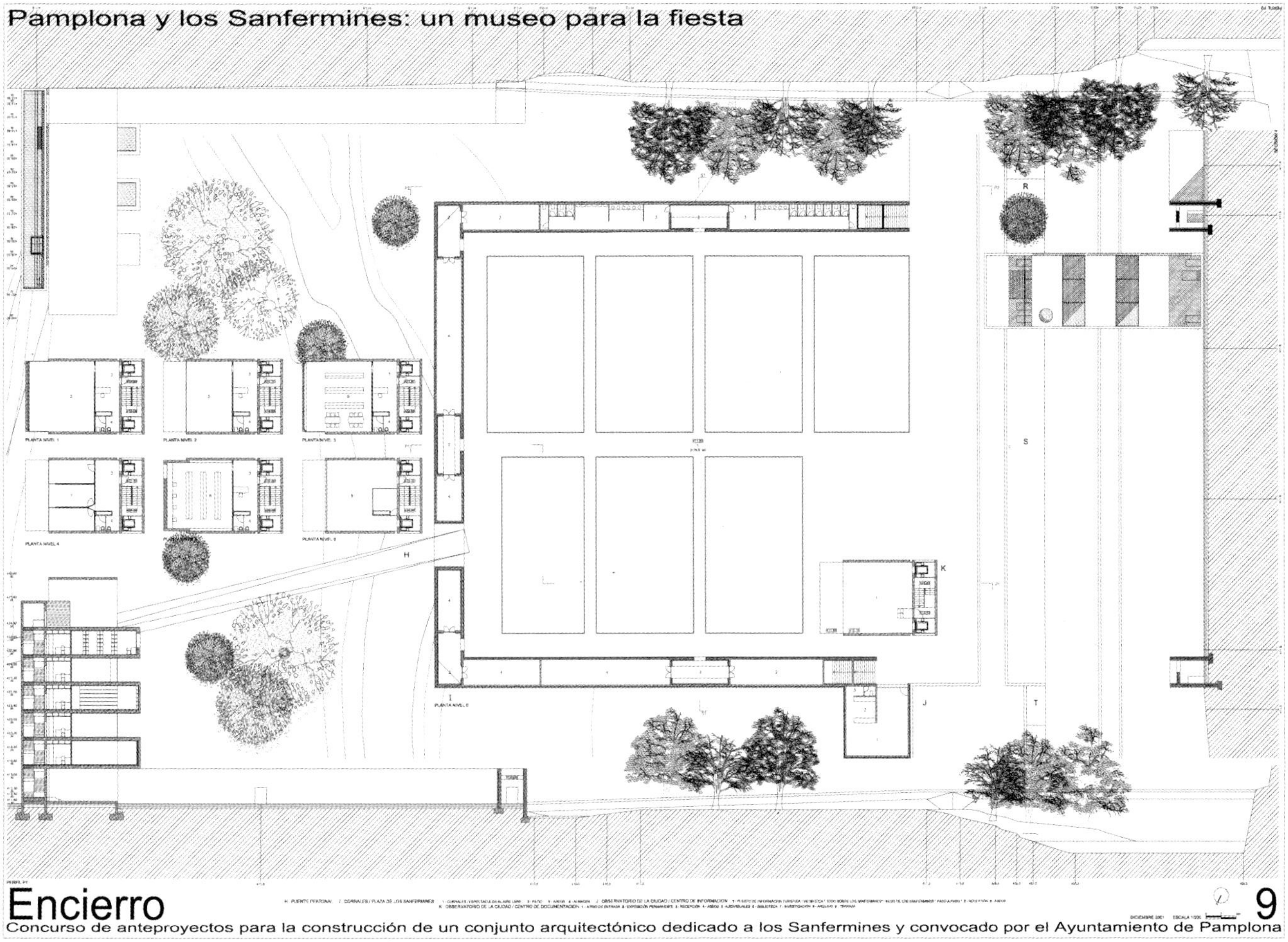

Pamplona y los Sanfermines: un museo para la fiesta

PLANTA NIVEL 1

PLANTA NIVEL 2

PLANTA NIVEL 3

PLANTA NIVEL 4

PLANTA NIVEL 6

PLANTA NIVEL 0

Encierro

9

Concurso de anteproyectos para la construcción de un conjunto arquitectónico dedicado a los Sanfermines y convocado por el Ayuntamiento de Pamplona

Study sketches, concept design.

Study models illustrating the variation in section.

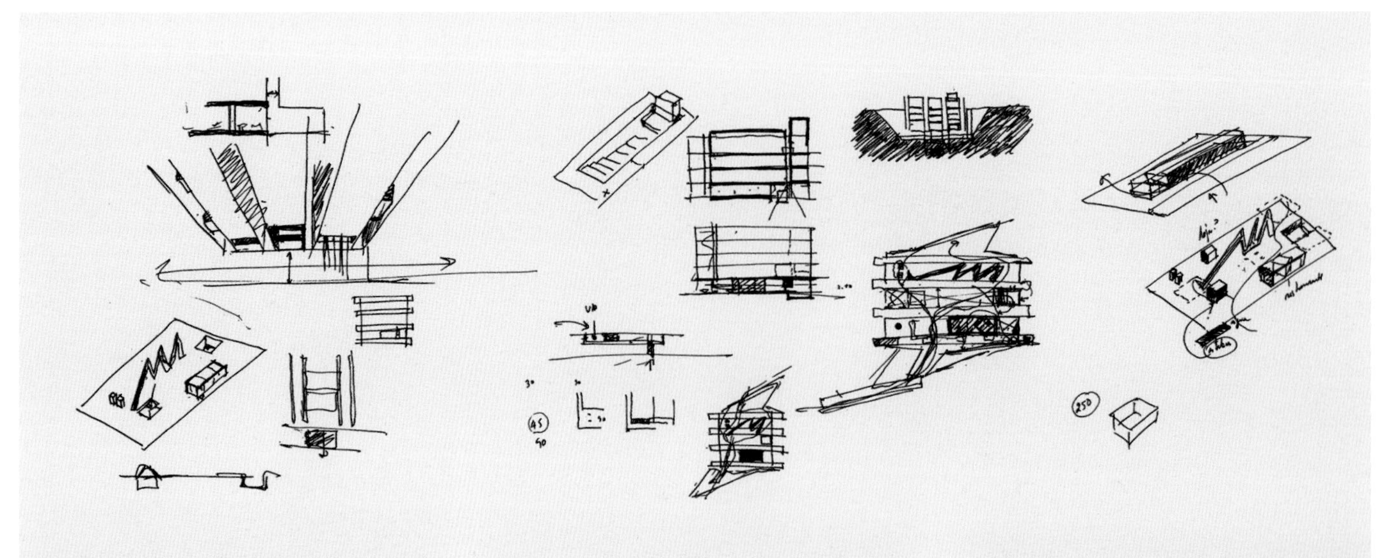

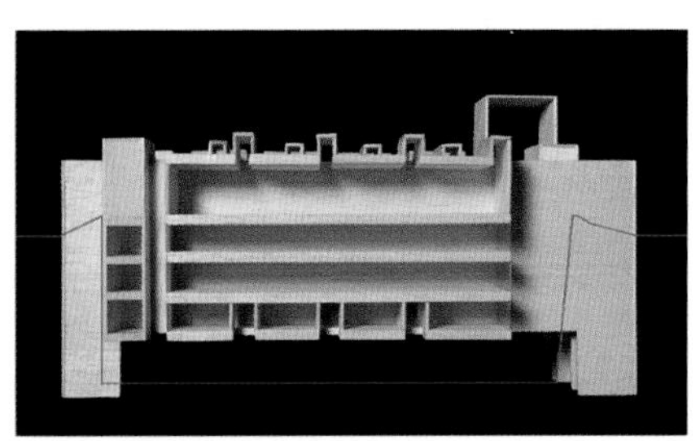

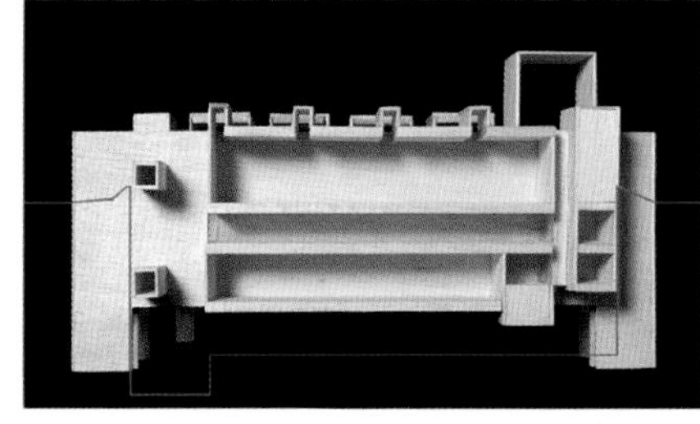

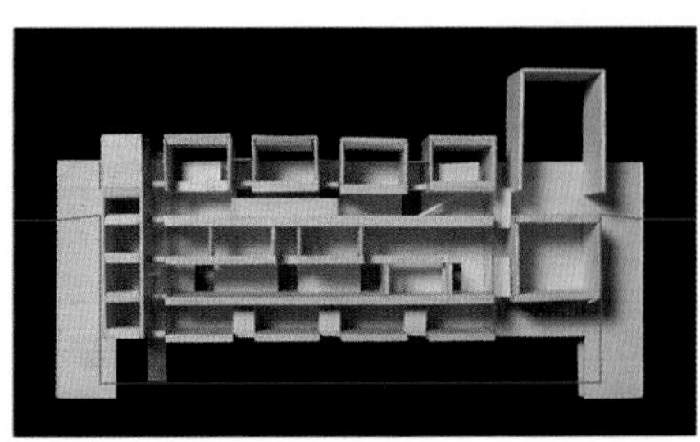

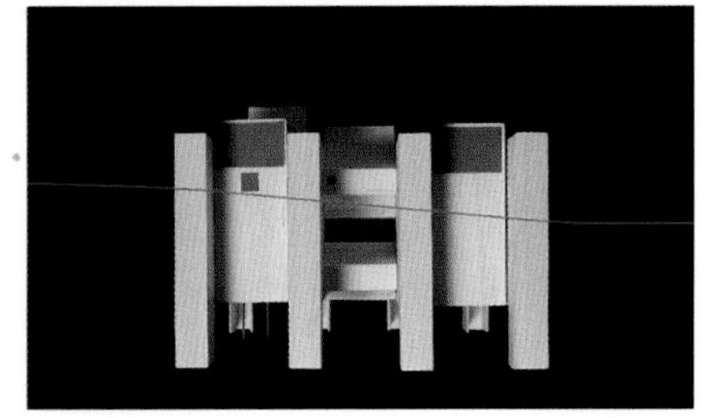

Study model, the building in the site.

Study model, the excavation and building occupying the excavation, Lucio Fontana's painting and collage.

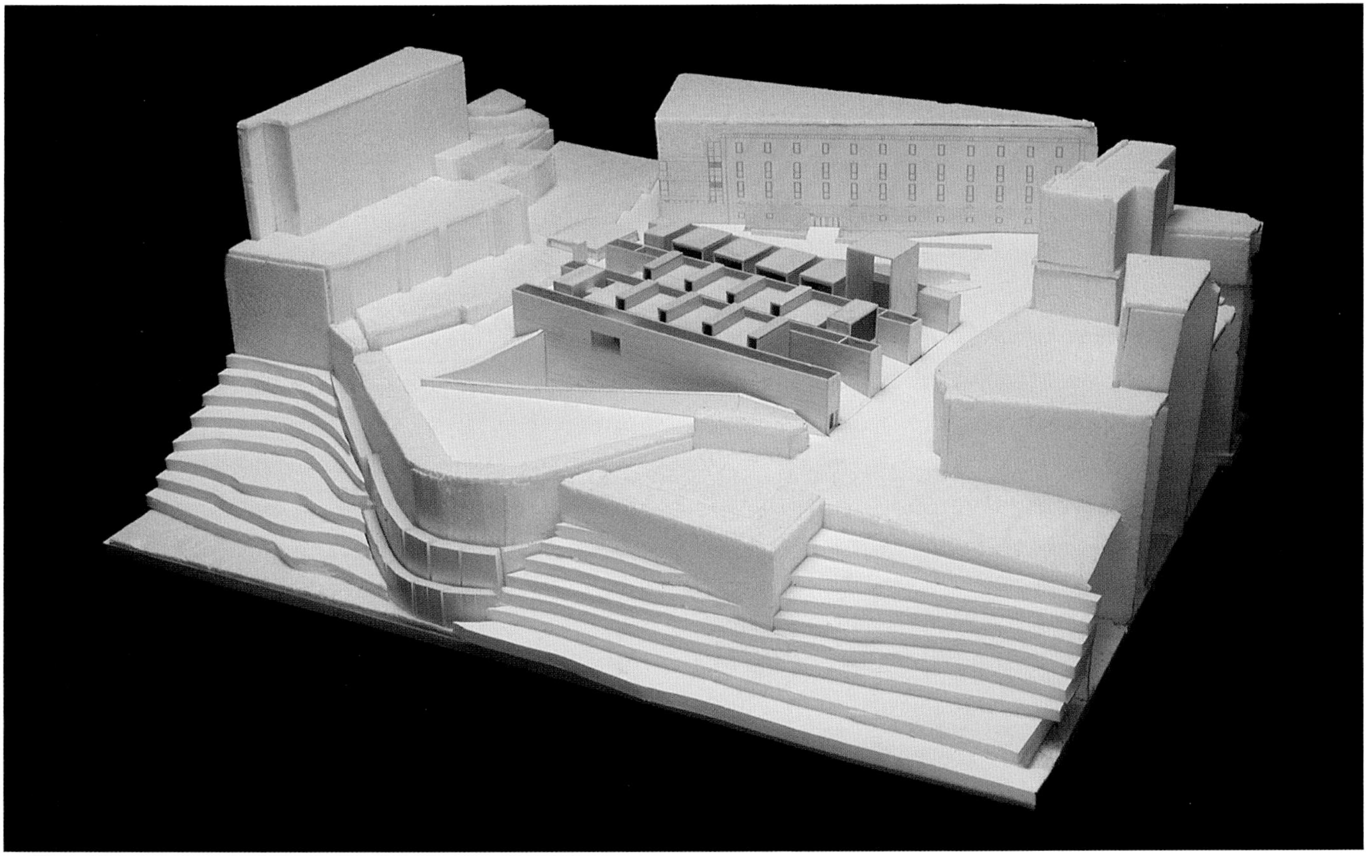

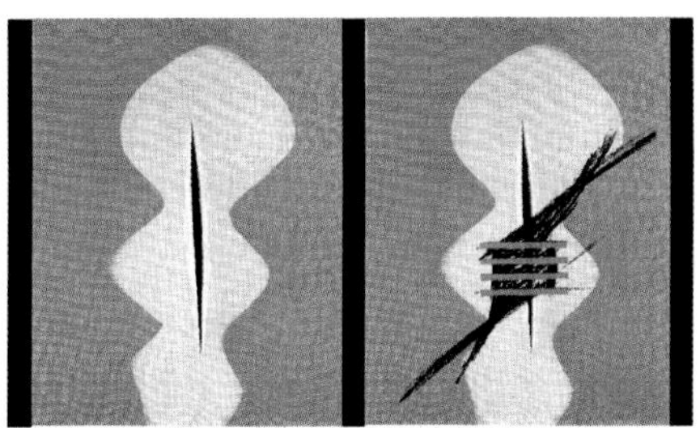

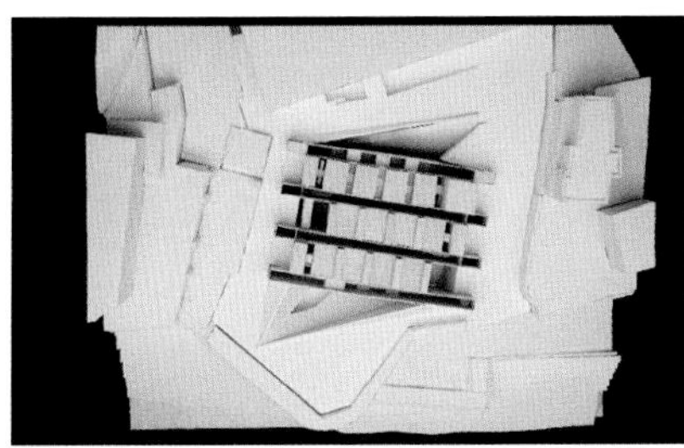

TRANSFORMATION: ACTION AND INTERACTION

Coherence in the design process is a value that goes beyond that of individual solutions to specific problems.
Faced with the inevitable passage of choice, coherence opposes chance, and imposes order to action, thus becoming a means of communicating both significance and practical effects.
As a result a project, even before being a creative action, is the knowledge of an interpretative process, in which ideas are not limited to reflect mere reality, but build it by transforming themselves into actions.
(F.C.)

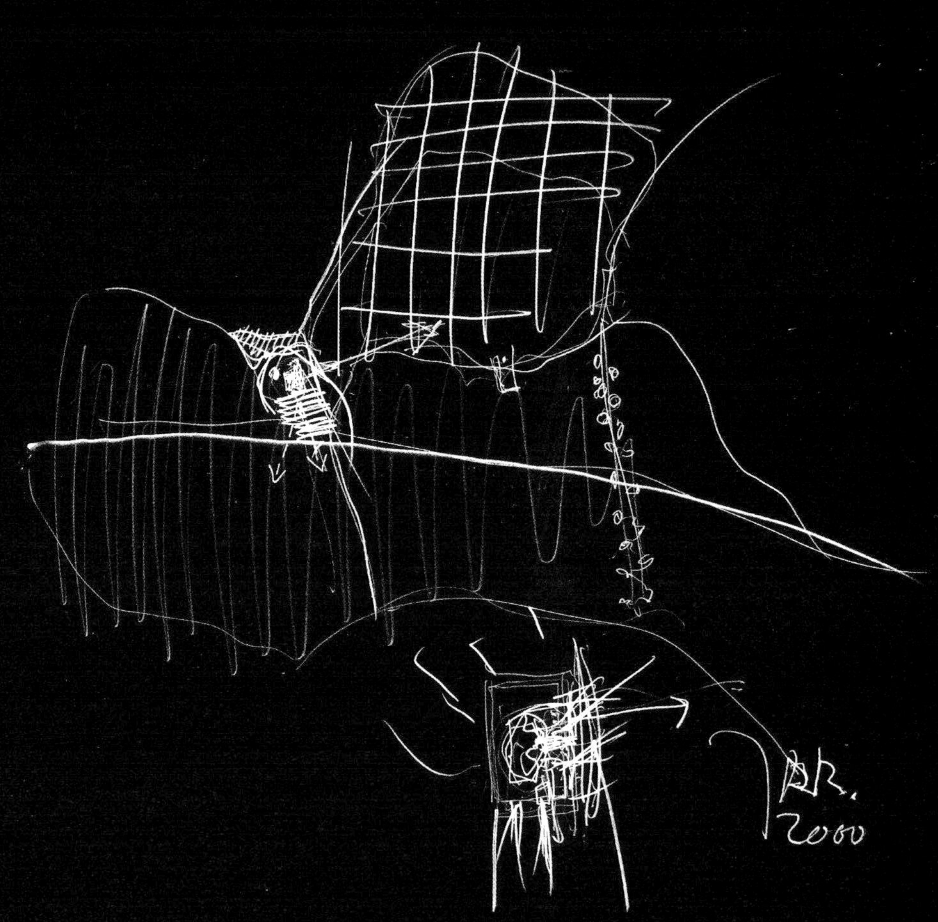
2000

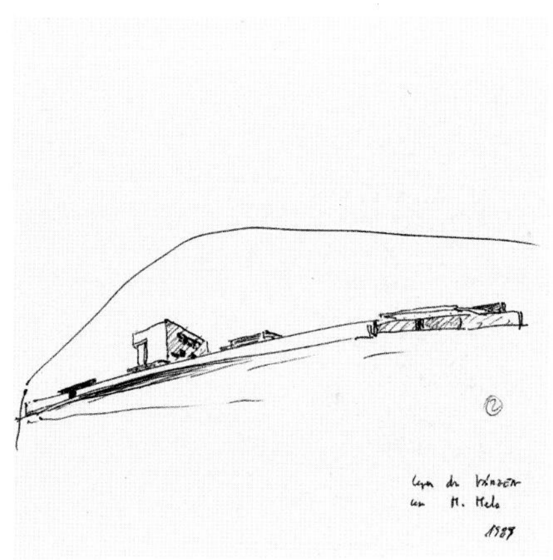

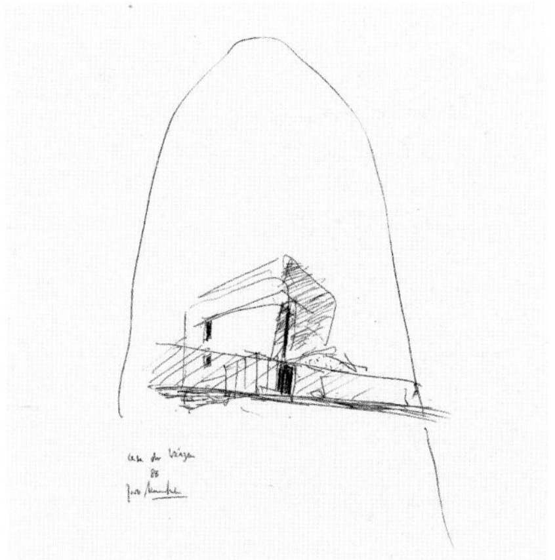

1. House in Lugar da Várzea (I)

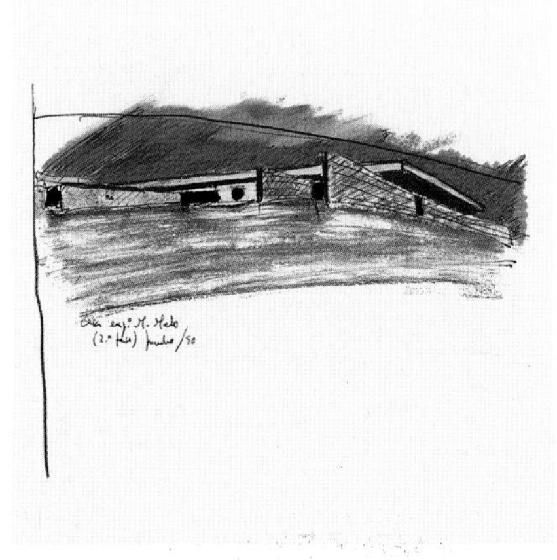

2. House in Lugar da Várzea (II)

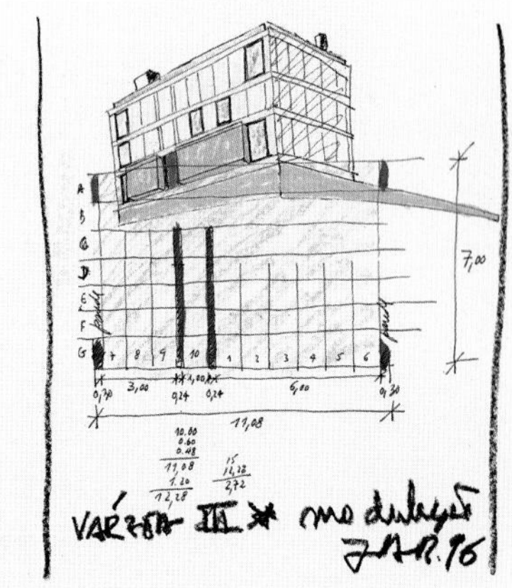

3. House in Lugar da Várzea (III)

1. House in Lugar da Várzea (I)

2. House in Lugar da Várzea (II)

3. House in Lugar da Várzea (III)

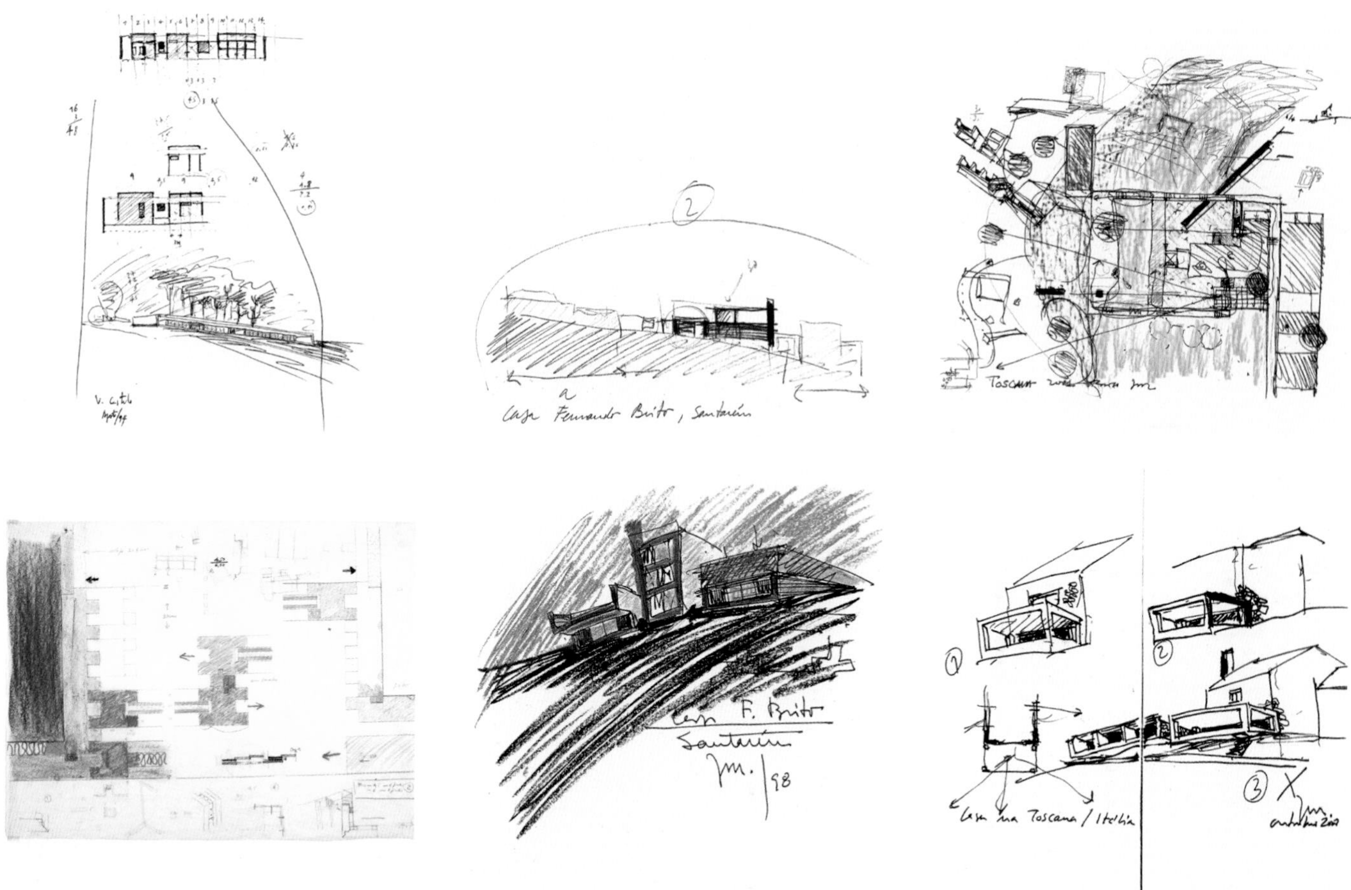

4. House in Lugar do Paçô Carreço

5. House in Santarém

6. House in Montenero, Tuscany

4. House in Lugar do Paçô Carreço

5. House in Santarém

6. House in Montenero, Tuscany

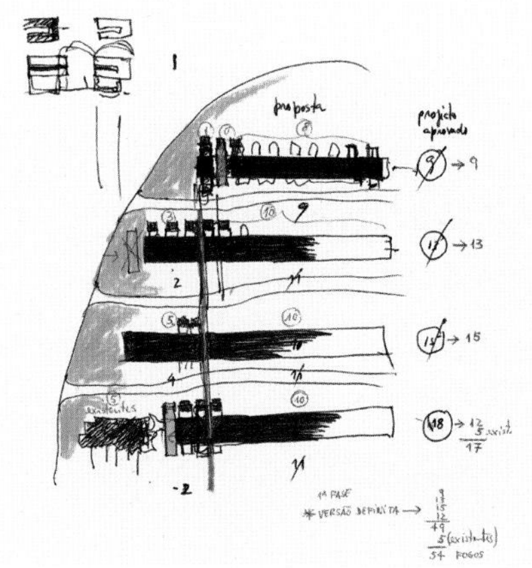

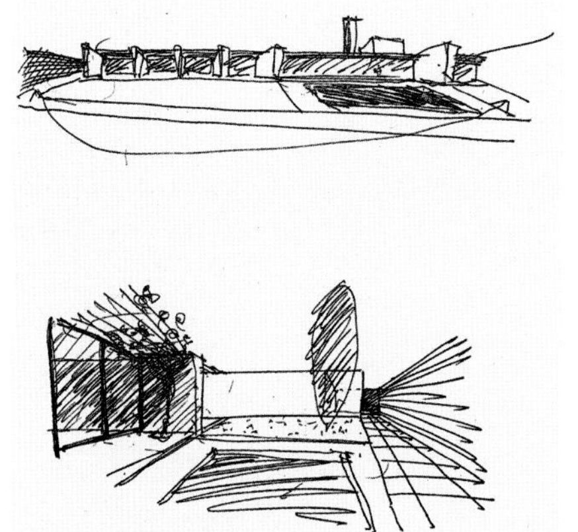

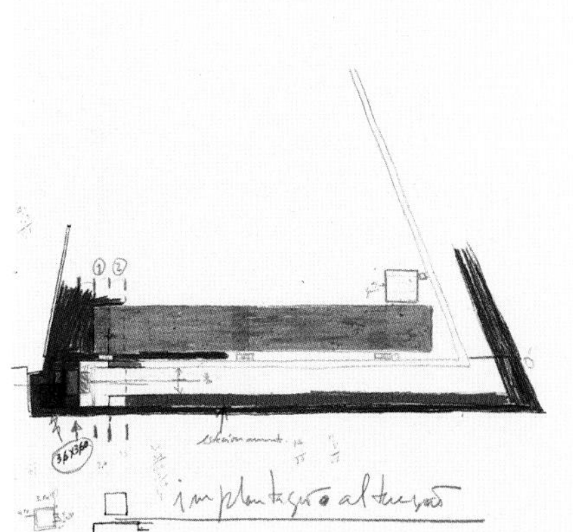

7. Quinta da Barca: Pinhal Houses

8. Quinta da Barca: Marina Houses

9. Social Housing Maia I

7. Quinta da Barca: Pinhal Houses

8. Quinta da Barca: Marina Houses

9. Social Housing Maia I

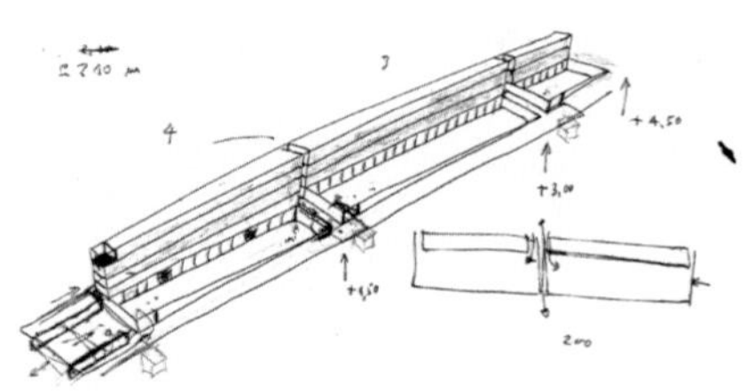

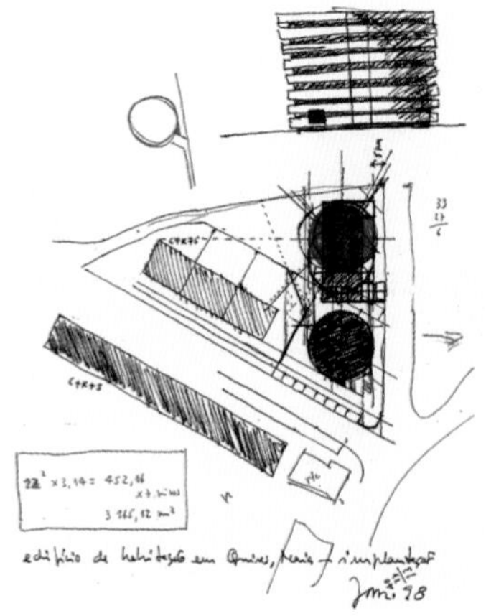

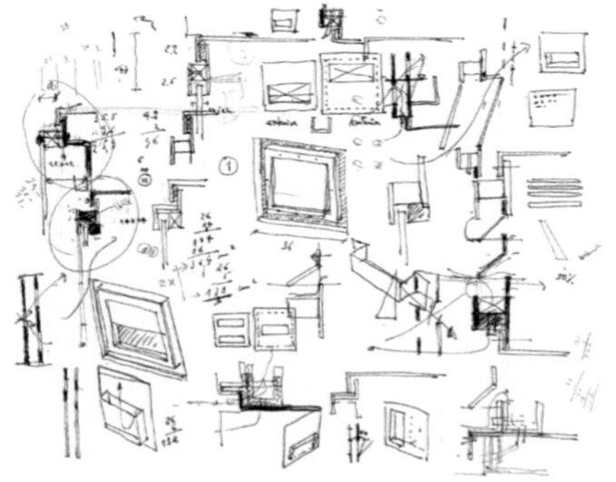

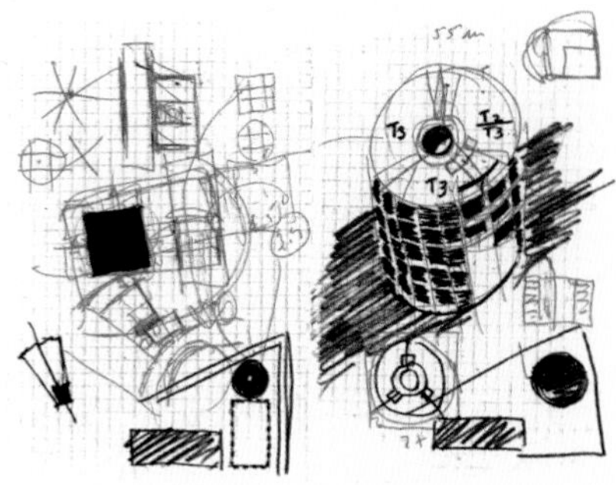

10. Social Housing Vila Nova da Telha I

11. Social Housing Gemunde

12. Portofino Apartment Building

10. Social Housing Vila Nova da Telha I

11. Social Housing Gemunde

12. Portofino Apartment Building

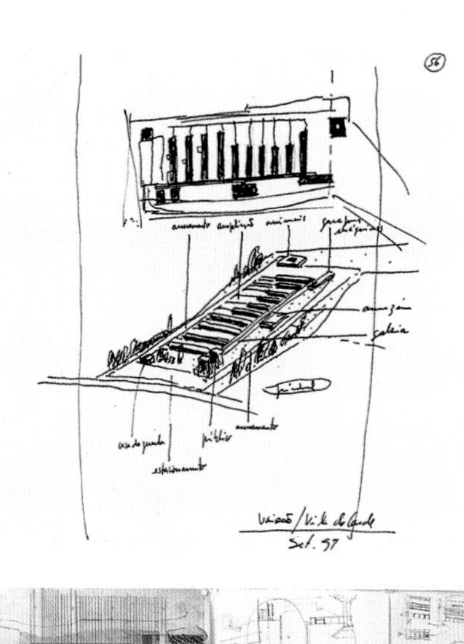

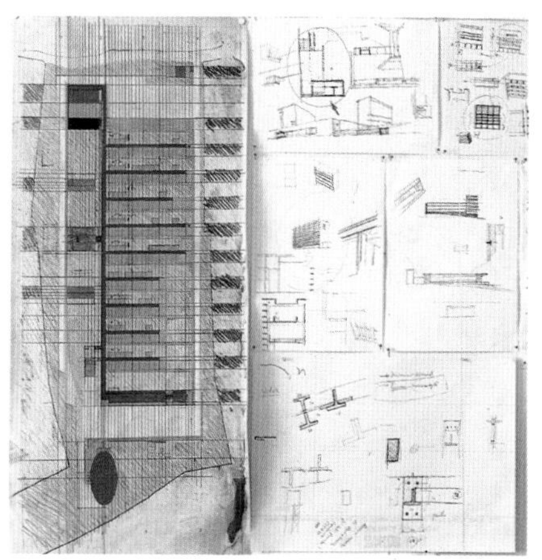

13. LNIV - National Veterinary Investigation Laboratory

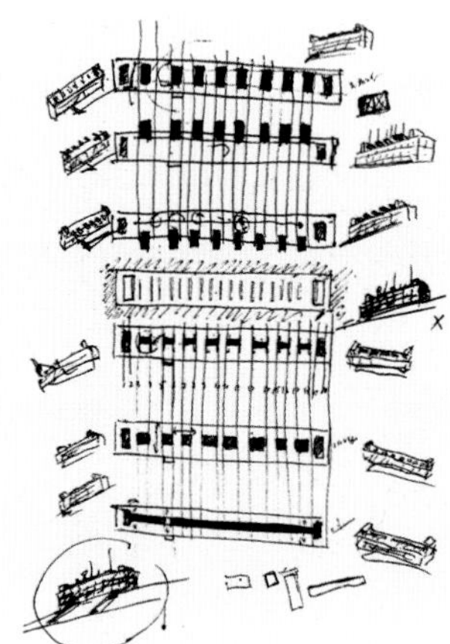

14. ICP - Portugal's Communication Institute

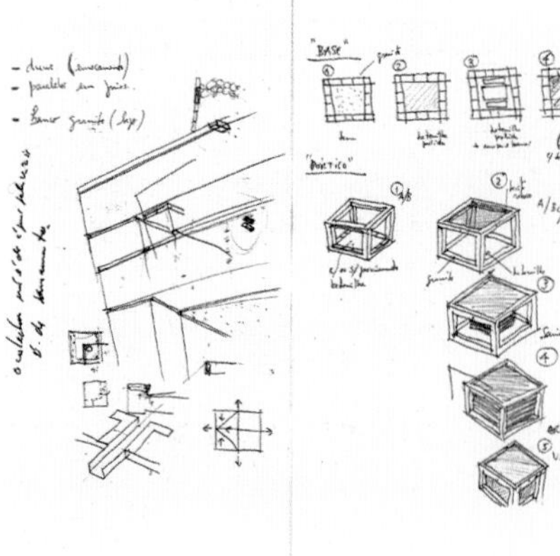

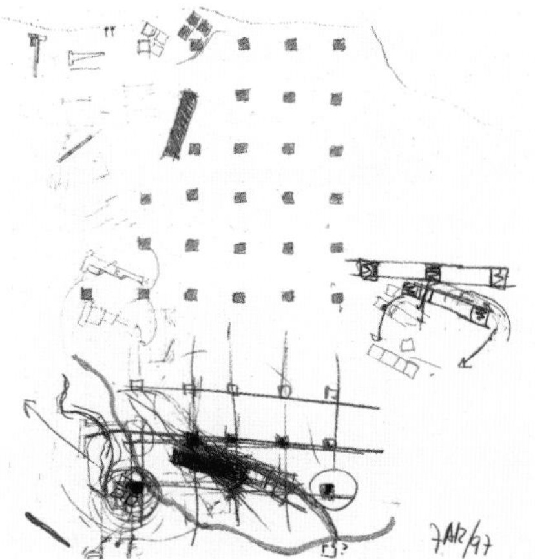

15. Moutidos Leisure Park

13. LNIV - National Veterinary Investigation Laboratory

14. ICP - Portugal's Communication Institute

15. Moutidos Leisure Park

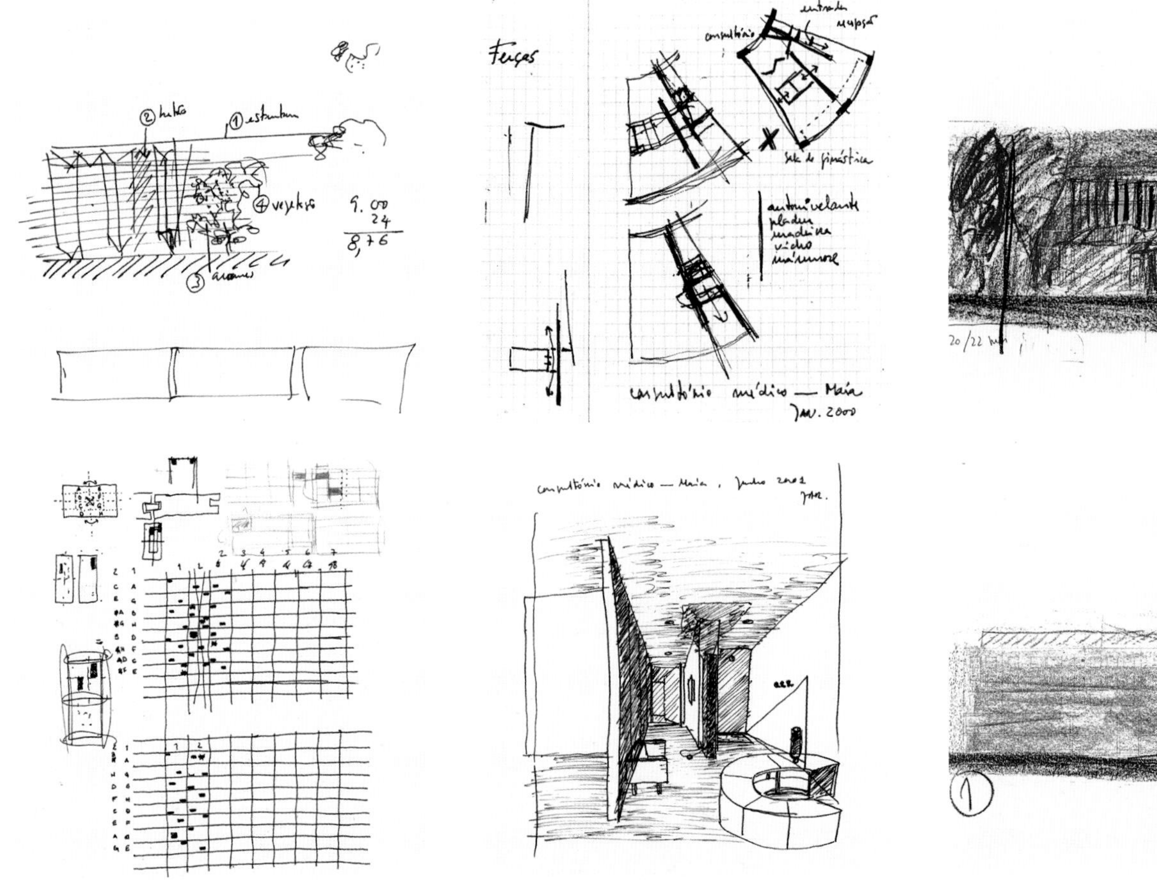

16. Lipor Composting Plant

17. Medical Office

18. Espaço Viso: Office Building

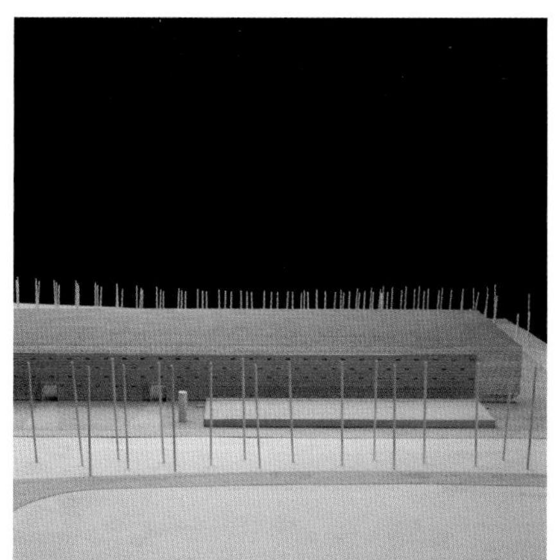

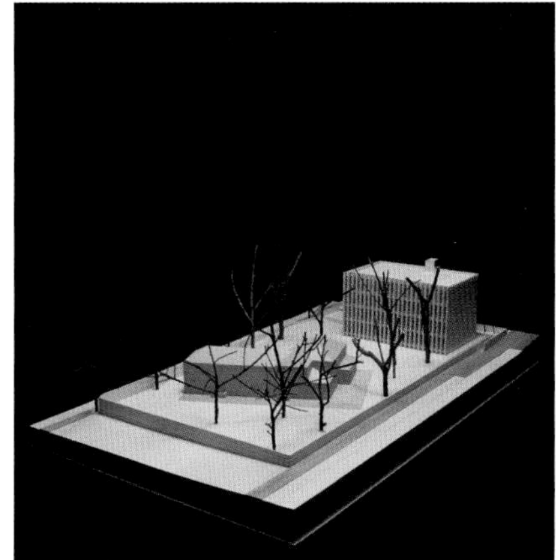

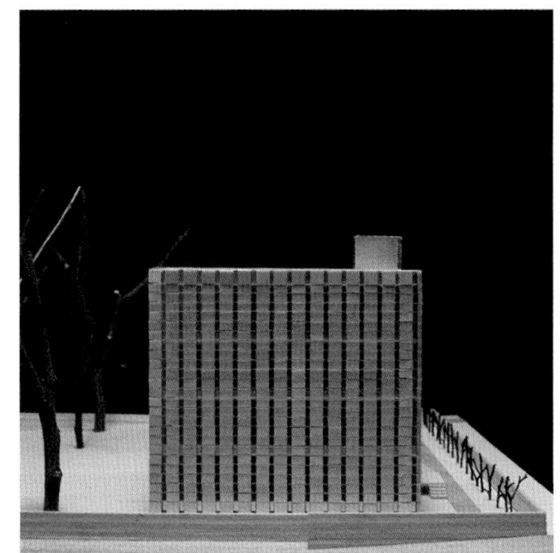

16. Lipor Composting Plant

17. Medical Office

18. Espaço Viso: Office Building

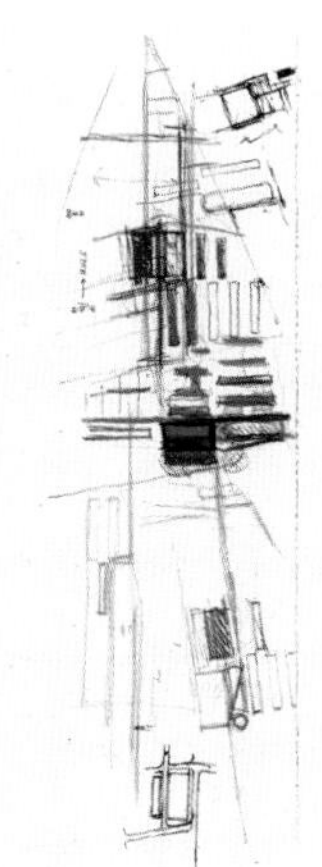

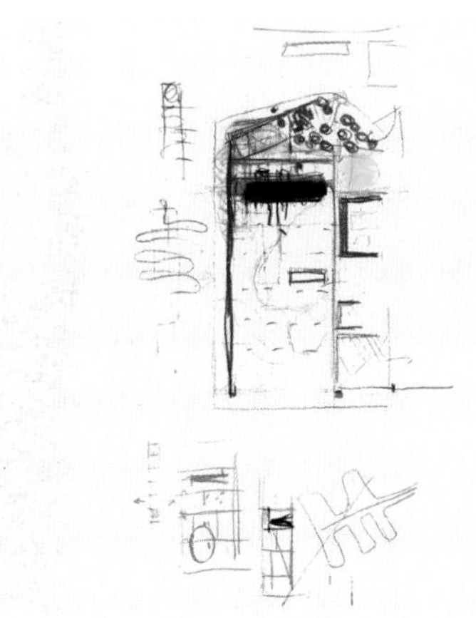

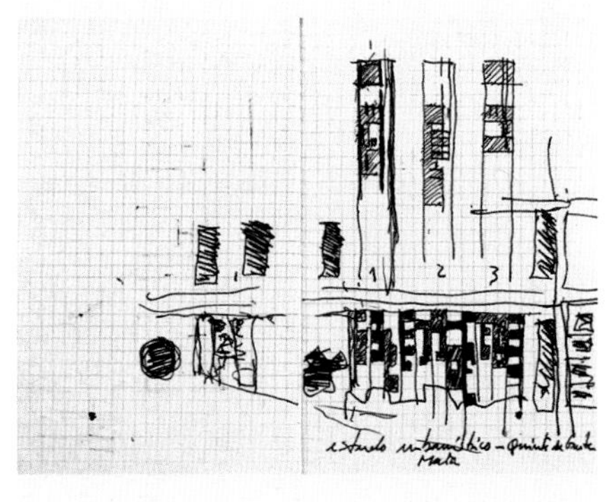

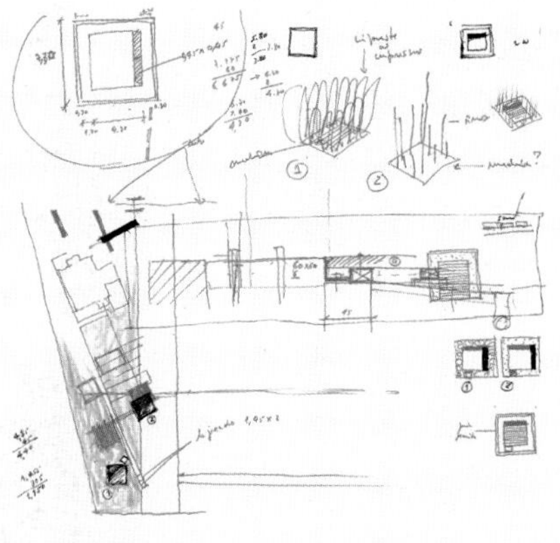

19. Quinta dos Cónegos: Urban Study

20. Vila do Castelo: Detail Plan

21. Vila do Castelo: Urban Park - Garden Areas Renovation

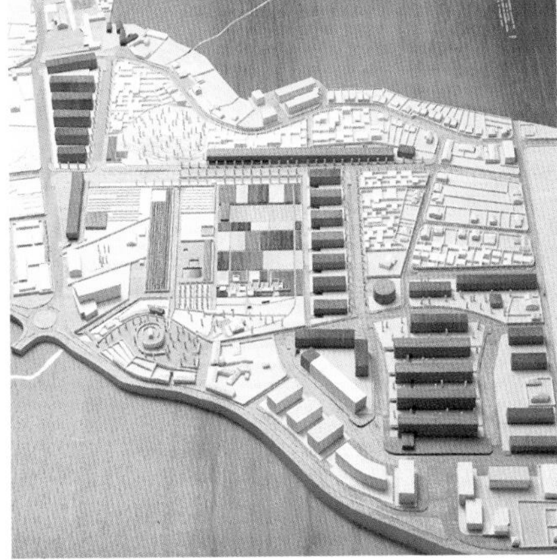

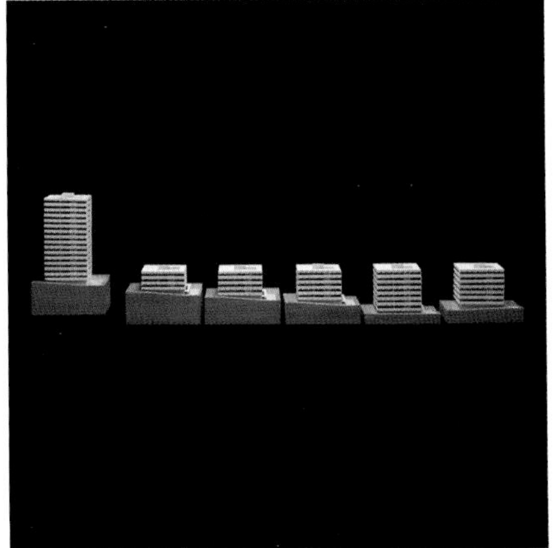

19. Quinta dos Cónegos: Urban Study

20. Vila do Castelo: Detail Plan

21. Vila do Castelo: Urban Park - Garden Areas Renovation

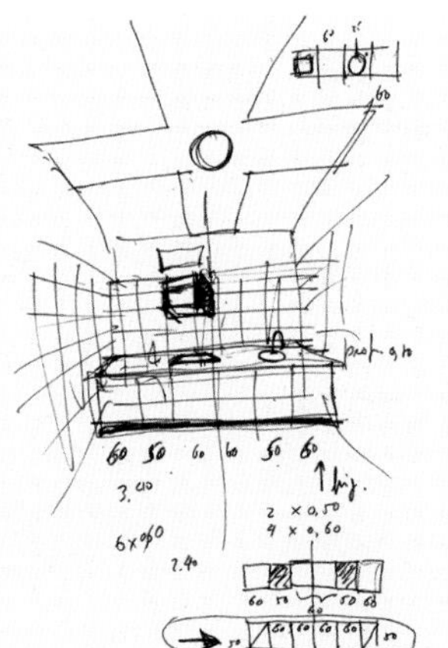

22. Vila do Castelo: Urban Park - Homestead Remodelling

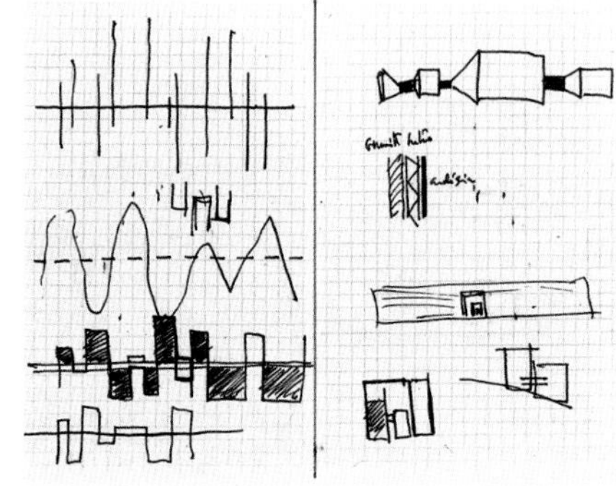

23. Vila do Castelo: Urban Park - Environment Education School

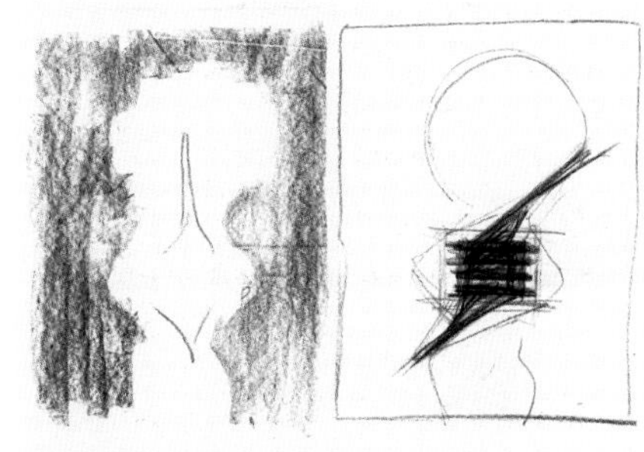

24. Museo de Sanfirmines, Pamplona

22. Vila do Castelo: Urban Park - Homestead Remodelling

23. Vila do Castelo: Urban Park - Environment Education School

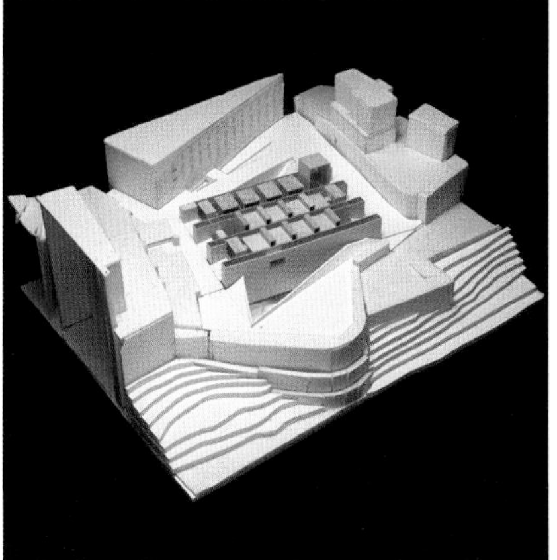

24. Museo de Sanfirmines, Pamplona

CONTRIBUTIONS

António Armesto

Precinct and Taracea[1]
Notes on the work of the architect João Álvaro Rocha

1. House in Mesão-Frio
Penafiel
Design: 1987-88
Construction: 1988-91

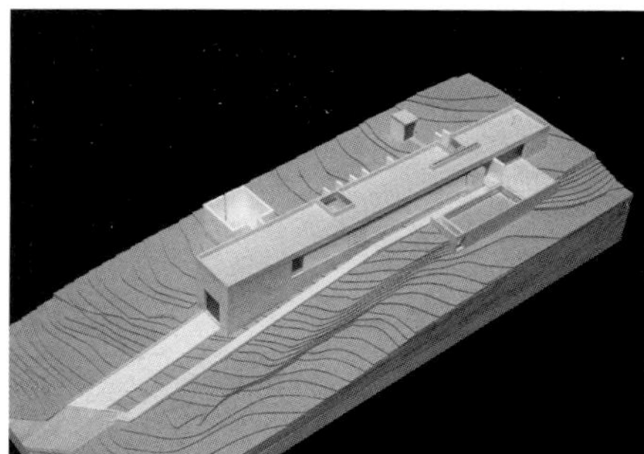

2. House in Santarém (first version)
Design: 1989

Preceding page:
Andrea Simitch,
Untitled (João 2),
Porto, 6 July 1999.

The project as tautology and cultural object
In the work that João Álvaro Rocha has obstinately carried out as an architect over the last two decades, what prevails is architecture.

This statement could be classified as obvious, a concept that closes in on itself and cannot be further discussed, a tautological assertion which is empty, adds nothing to our knowledge of the object under study, and only verifies the formal correction of an analytical judgement. Consequently, our initial statement being an analytical judgement on Rocha's work, it can only be further developed through a description of certain attributes of his works. According to us, this modest enterprise is of critical and cognitive interest. It could be objected that, if the judgement to be formulated is successful in adhering to the reality being described, what has the virtue of being critical and providing knowledge is the work itself, in which case our discourse is superfluous. The reply to this objection could be that this is something that is only confirmed at the end, after and not before. And we feel that it is along this obligatory pathway, overcoming our inhibition to issue an analytical judgement, that the cognitive value of obstinately repeating the obvious lies.

We believe, then, that what architect João Álvaro Rocha does is architecture, and nothing more. This is our argument, which we formulate as a postulate that comes from limiting our view to the projects. But the projects, the buildings, the gardens or the cities are cultural objects. Our analytical judgement can therefore not be made with reference to the explanatory method used in natural science. The right method should not explain but understand these cultural objects. And if there are cultural objects, then they have been conceived and made; they are the results of someone's *poietic* labours, of dynamic processes involving the architect and his collaborators, not in their personal condition, but as social individuals, linked to a reality in which they recognize themselves and which they partially help to build and define. An analytical judgement on cultural objects, then, must necessarily be an interpretation of objective structures (in this case, works of architecture) as manifestations of a set of problematic choices, priorities and values that the authors establish. In other words, the analysis considers the work as the result of the author's civil attitude. But this statement, which in our opinion has a general value, is not made before (although the order in which we write may make it seem that way), but after examining the architectural work created by João Álvaro Rocha and his collaborators. A circular process, then, appears to be inevitable.

If the first evidence obtained from the analysis of João Álvaro Rocha's work is that it never ventures outside what is strictly architecture, the second is that it has a high level of elaboration and clarity. An old academic maxim establishes that the condition for a project to be really complex is for it to be intelligible. And it is intelligible when it is both clear and rich, when it succeeds in ordering a heterogeneous set of facts without unjustly simplifying the problems and imposing an arbitrary order. The search for richness at the cost of clarity very often leads to confusion and disorder. And if richness is sacrificed in a search for clarity, schematism is the result. Rocha shows that he is very familiar with the paradox thanks to which only the conscious use of the tools of his trade guarantees the true complexity of his work.

There is, for example, one element that acts as a syntactic radical in his work and is responsible for its general regularity. We are referring to the gallery, a universal principle consisting, as we all know, of a system formed by two walls, generally parallel, supporting a ceiling. The gallery is a system that provides a regular space for living, from the general form of which different practical alternatives arise concerning the planimetric position and topographic relation. A series of houses such as Mesão-Frio in Penafiel *(fig. 1)*, the first version of the house in Santarém *(fig. 2)*, the first and second version of the House in Santa Maria de Avioso *(figs 3-4)*, explore this principle. They are all based on a narrow, very long gallery, with the space organized in a comb-like arrangement with a lengthway itinerary. In some of the axonometrics of these projects, it is analytically shown how the ceiling can be separated from the walls; where there is no ceiling, the walls form patios between the rooms, and porches appear where the ceiling remains but there are no walls. These are the elementary logical and morphological operations on which the formal architectural project is based. They are the source of the architectural individuality of each of these houses.

In the rest of his work, we will see galleries on different scales, forming a single space or compartments, juxtaposed or superimposed, forming series, etc. And the comb-like arrangement is a recurring element on different scales.

The three houses in Lugar da Várzea *(pp. 10, 20)* make up a small village group and, although each has its own organization, they all reveal a formal structure related to a tripartite order, in which wide and narrow galleries alternate with rooms and patios. The areas between the houses provide not only privacy but a sense of community. The house in Tuscany *(p. 42)*, after its refurbishing and enlargement, also ends up with three volumes, and the same can be said of the house in Santarém *(p. 34)*.

Separations define patios and at times narrow passageways and analytical fissures housing stairs, allowing the light to enter and forming a framework for the landscape. Each project develops a different scale; the first creates the image of a village, the house in Toscana hedonistically takes command of a large amount of territory; some parts of the painter's house are related to neighbouring buildings in their alignment and size, other become private in the patios and finally are converted into a belvedere.

The house at Lugar do Paçô *(p. 26)* seeks a line of topographic inflection, laid back in the wood and converted into a belvedere to contemplate the sea. It is a long house, where floors and ceilings prevail, configuring the house in porch fashion. Elements appear like the pathway that goes from the entrance of the grounds to the house; transversal fissures that become transparent or enlighten; and plastic elements such as the rooms that stick out like back packs on the stratum defined by floor and ceiling.

In many other projects there are fissures welcoming the light in the ceilings of the corridors, accompanying our itinerary. The inside of the corridor thus becomes, for the rooms, an illuminated landscape. At the same time, the concave dihedral formed by wall and ceiling is dissolved, so that the corridor wall becomes separated and becomes an outside wall. The light is therefore of analytical, separating and compositional value.

In the houses, in general, the rooms always appear to follow the same logic. A common spatial module for bedrooms and the kitchen; the living room and dining room occupying one and a half, two or more; the bathrooms accompany the bedrooms and produce what is nearly an urban sequence in the corridor.

The interiors are frequently reminiscent of chapels or cells in a kind of ascetic luxury that is representative of the best architecture. The living rooms combine a panoramic view of the garden or the patio with a zenital or indirect light that reaches the opposite wall, so that when the view is shut-off, it would be possible to imagine the room as a place of worship.

At the Quinta da Barca in Esposende *(pp. 52, 62)*, two types of homes were built. On the one hand, a row of duplex houses with patios, in a comb-like arrangement with regards to the main street. Here again we find a narrow passageway on the ground floor forming a strategic entrance to the internal distribution that helps to adjust the row to the street arrangement. Thanks to the upper floor design, each group takes on the appearance of a linear block, which has the virtue of combining the individual nature of the house with the morphologi-

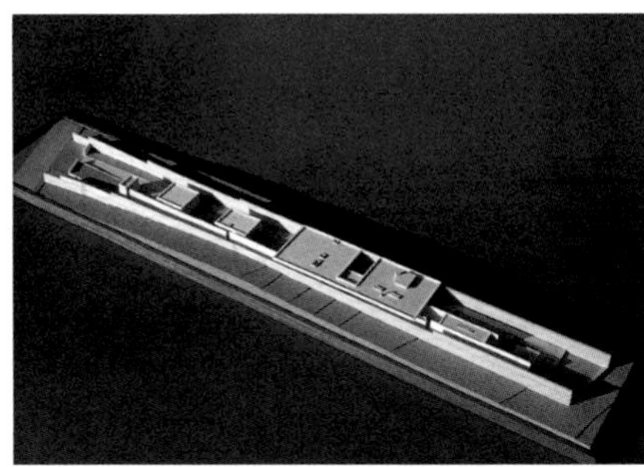

3. House in Santa Maria de Avioso (first version)
Castelo - Maia
Design: 1990-91

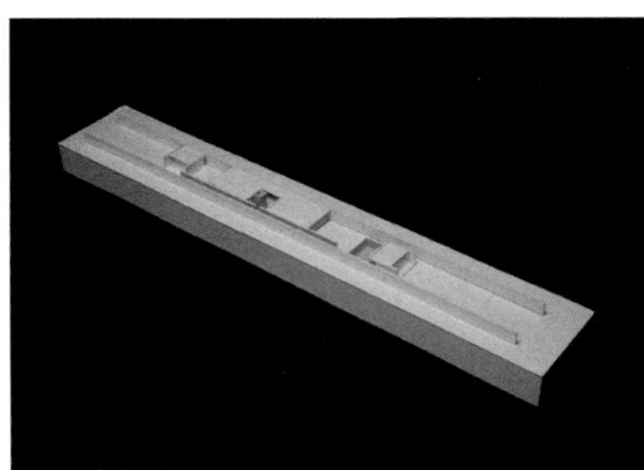

4. House in Santa Maria de Avioso (second version)
Castelo - Maia
Design: 1997

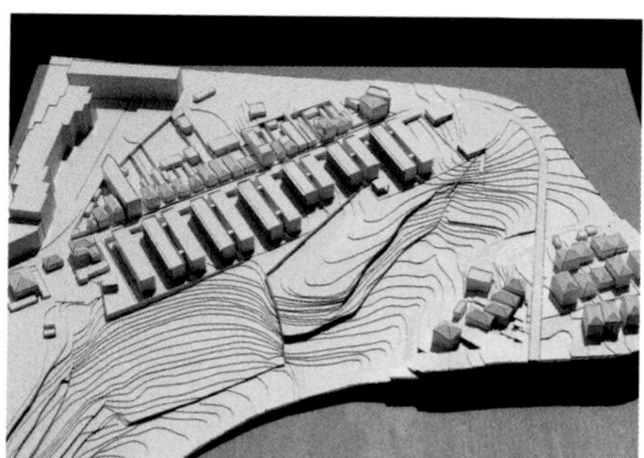

5. Social Housing Senhora da Hora I
(56 dwellings and facilities)
Matosinhos
Design: 1995
Construction: 2001-(underway)

cal unity of the row which, in turn, relates to the scale of the surrounding land. The second group consists of two rows of four spacious patio houses. The precinct is here radically defined to create a precise and ordered universe in which the clarity of the architecture is identified with an intimate joy of living. In this case the passageway, which is at the same time a space between neighbours and an extension of the entrance, reinforces the feeling of privacy and intimacy in the house. But it is precisely because of the architectural individuality of the precinct that each house is acknowledged as a similar part of the group to which it belongs. In this and other projects by Rocha, the validity of the positive tradition of modern architectural culture is clearly perceived, and this alone should be enough to protect them from so many useless controversies.

In his residential blocks, with modest size homes, the architect has perfected a highly adjusted and carefully modulated domestic cell, in two distributing galleries, which can house a variable number of bedrooms. One of their outstanding features is the suppression of the corridor and the appearance of a distribution area with value of its own; the key is the position of the kitchen, which makes it compulsory to pass through the living room, but can also be crossed. There are different combinations of this cell-dwelling, based on a rationalistic linear block with crossover ventilation. In the tender for the social housing project Senhora da Hora I *(fig. 5)* in Matosinhos and, the blocks are in pairs, optimizing the economy of access; in the social housing in Vila Nova da Telha I *(p. 80)*, the four buildings are also grouped into pairs, with a very different sense, around a common area; in the linear block Maia I *(p. 72)*, he has succeeded in releasing a broad surface of land. In a recently completed project in Gemunde *(p. 88)*, the linear block is three times as long as Maia I and forms, with other common elements and services, an ample gardened area. In all his projects, the relation with the topography pays special attention to the ground floor as the base and the urbanization of the unused space. In all these cases, the dialogue between the front and the rear plays a decisive role because, in addition to rationalising the openings, it modulates the scale by creating areas for communal or public use and clearly defines the general image of the whole.

The magnificent Veterinary Investigation Laboratory (LNIV) in Vila do Conde *(p. 106)*, a long drawn-out project with a complex and extensive programme, is built on elements with which we are now familiar. The building is reminiscent of a Carthusian monastery, or a *bastide*, with their same clarity, but it is also reminiscent of a residential *siedlung*, and shows the need to preserve the surrounding meadows and wood. The arrangement defines the scale of the project without the need to build a border; the high building and its neighbour, connected by a pool, contain the social and administrative areas and provide a head for the project that is deployed regularly to the final building, where animal experiments take place, of singular form. The rhythmic separations between the volumes propose a similar development for the surroundings, following an automorphic logic: the arrangement of each laboratory wing is expanded throughout the entire building and further, where it connects to the road. Again, a logical operation is used as an analogy to solve the problem of the different scales.

In the Environment Education School *(p. 174)*, in Vila do Castelo Urban Park, he uses a similar morphological mechanism combining the spine with the chess board, alternating patios and classrooms. The chess board effect is also present in the proposal for the Quinta dos Cónegos *(p. 148)*, whereas the height of the buildings becomes level, like an aqueduct when it crosses a valley, with the exception of the tower, which gives the entire project a sense of direction.

In the Moutidos Leisure Park *(p. 122)*, the project tends to require the limits of the large precinct, concentrating on one side on urban relations and inserting a series of pavilions that, above all, introduce a metrical modulation with a tectonic argument.

A project of modest dimensions such as the Medical Office *(p. 136)* in the Central Plaza de Maia building shows the importance of wall coverings in spatial determination. The smaller the area, the more condensed the details, so the purpose is to dissolve its presence in the general idea and erase all the traces of the effort made to preserve clarity.

We are going to spend some time on one of João Álvaro Rocha's projects, built between 1993 and 1995, and half way, therefore, along his professional career. It is the project for the Communication Institute (ICP, *p. 114*) building on the northern edge of Porto. Like other outer areas of contemporary cities, it is characterized by the heterogeneity of the objects there, by its disarticulation, by unrelated morphologies, by the absence of meaning in the spaces between buildings and the consequent denial of its public nature. But the site is an area physically delimited by a surrounding wall. It is well known that enclosed property, often with extraordinary ashlar masonry walls, is frequent in the Miñho region and other parts of the country.

Rocha was not working, then, with an open site but with walled-in property. This precinct needed a door. A pathway has to lead from the door to the main building. The architect explains that the main building is next to others of the same size, social housing, whereas, like rural dwellings, he creates a low building, a porch for vehicles. Between them, a regular interval three times larger than the main building. But this interval is something more than a space inside the property; it is a pause built by the architect for the site itself. It is an interval between the social housing, represented on this scale by the main building, and the rural housing represented by the concrete porch. When you enter the precinct, you walk up the path next to the porch and are forced to keep at distance from the main building and see it foreshortened. The path is as long as possible; it reaches a modest but dignified architectural ruin at the rear of the property, the preservation of which guarantees a controlled visual background. The view is framed and profound over the ruin, towards the sky. At the end of the path, you climb a low-gradient ramp to the front of the main building. When you cross the hall, there are stairs that climb to the roof, with a view of antennas, and another set of stairs on the other side. The building is involved. It is one more element in a complex architectural situation, greater than its own condition as an object, which, on the other hand, it retains. The architect has not had to work outside the site provided by the promoter; he has not had to design a special plan for the peripheral area, but has made use of what was already on the site; he has restricted himself to working within the precinct. But what the architect has done has transformed the entire surroundings: the rural fragment and the social housing enter into a relationship between themselves and with nature. The project has created an active, significant vacuum.

The outer wall, the trees that have been preserved, the paved paths, the grass, the buildings, are all, like the finished work, pieces that have been harmonically fitted into the precinct. Although these pieces are individually defined, their relative positions, the measurements and distances, how they are separated leads the project to appear to be the result of an assembly following a previously meditated strategy. And this also applied to the distribution of the building: a few different sized areas, well fitted together, with no waste, housing corridors, stairs and different rooms. The outer walls of the building also appear to be marquetry work, exquisitely finished. The large stainless steel window has all the elements required to regulate the ventilation and the light, without being opened. The same window, of a different size, is at the rear, in the corridor. The front of the building is clearly distinguishable from the rear, even though the entire building is covered with carefully fitted aluminium sheeting.

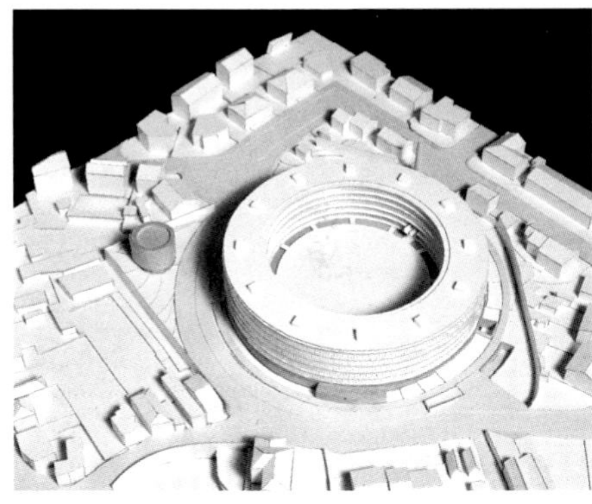

6. Residential Apartment Building (120 dwellings)
Predrouços - Maia
Design: 2000-01
Construction: adjudication phase

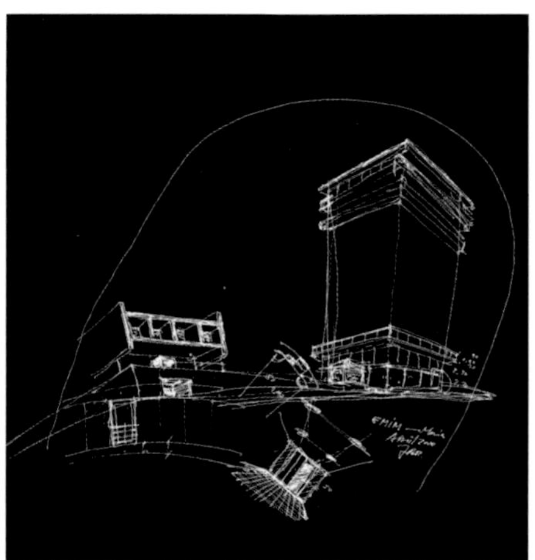

7. EMIM - Office and Commercial Space Building
Moreira - Maia
Competition design: 2000

Many of these descriptions, with some variations, apply to the rest of his work.

In his recent work, circular buildings have appeared, nearly always in association with the relative size and irregularity of some sites. The internal logic is a corollary of the morphology of linear buildings. According to the architect, the cylindrical shape manages to decompress, creating distance from neighbouring buildings, and a punctuation or condensation in relation to different configurations in the surroundings. The building thus emerges individual and powerful, monumental and recognizable, heavily characterizing its location and creating areas for communal or public use. This is the case for the Portofino Apartment Building *(p. 98)* or the two buildings in Pedrouços *(fig. 6)*, although in the latter case the size of the operation presented new issues. This idea of a concentrated building is also found in some office buildings (Espaço Viso, *p. 142*; EMIM office building in Moreira, *fig. 7*) in which it serves an industrial purpose (ADP - Waters of the Douro and Paiva, *fig. 8*, Lipor Composting Plant, *p. 132*). The facades of both buildings are treated in a uniform manner, emphasizing the similarity to drying facilities, silos or other constructions, such as shaded areas or greenhouses.

In the project presented for the Museo de Sanfermines in Pamplona *(p. 180)*, recently adjudicated, Rocha makes use of some of the above, outside Portugal, with a new meaning. Although the programme is not well defined, the idea is to establish a positive relationship between the inner city and the new area across the river, with reference to the famous festival in which bulls and men run through the city centre until they reach the bullring. The precinct and the pathway are once again the architectural elements of this ritual in which life is lived on its most instinctive, disordered and carefree fashion. The project includes a sense of symmetry: it proposes a museum building with a logic similar to the row of houses of the city, which is really a gate and a covered passageway to another urban area on the other side of the river. The new route provides a historic view of the city over its bastions, it stresses on the existence of the river and the park, and gives meaning to the separation between the old inner city and the new. Rocha's work was nearly chosen, but another project was preferred, a large bridge-building that, in our opinion, disguises the banks and thus eliminates the river, darkening the role of the free space outside the old city. I have no doubt that the architects will create a building of quality, but the site will lose the possibility of becoming a perfect vacuum.

A double inventory

Since the scope of the documents associated to João Álvaro Rocha's projects are generous, when we study them with a view to understand them, we are capable of perceiving a more complete reality that overflows their framework. A slow, panoramic overview of his many projects leads us to discover some constants of disorder and also some elements of their potential order. The maps, plans, reports and photographs make up a double inventory which translates the dynamic nature of the present and its problematic condition, and defines the project as a possibility of transformation and clarification.

In the inventory of disorder we find: heterogeneous situations, sometimes the result of natural processes, sometimes of the mixed or mixing way in which urbanization advances over rural and natural areas; the destruction of the signs of certain facts that had vital significance in the past; the loss of meaning associated to the space between elements, making them mere unconnected objects; pure quantitative accumulation; the loss of a sense of direction; the contemporary lack of confidence in the value of outlines and plans; the forgotten concept of urbanity and the public dimension of space; the cultural impotence revealed when architecture is considered as a thing or product. In general, the terms in the inventory of disorder tend towards schematism, noise and no sense of direction.

On the other hand, the inventory of potential order includes: the sun, providing a sense of direction and light; the climate as culture; geographic, orographic and topographic features; geological aspects; the persistence of a historical land division, of paths and roads, of the physical delimitation of property; the presence of woods, meadows, rivers, cultivated fields, villages and certain horizons. Each of these elements of order is articulated with separation, pauses and distances; emptied space on a defined scale. The rural world has its own: the wood, the meadow, the cultivated field, the cottage garden, are all related to the composition of the soil, the climate and certain anthropological characters, so the size of elements and their relative positions are never arbitrary. Certain morphologies and urban layouts also have their own characteristics. We could say that the basis of order is due to the significant nature of these intervals, to their qualitative and structural dimension. And this necessarily implies the well defined condition of limits or borders that have, or aspire to, persistence over time. The quality of these limits, in both senses of the work, creates a rich variety of thresholds between what is intimate and private and what is communal and public. In general, the items included in our inventory of order tend to restore a comprehensive concept: orientation.

It seems clear that João Álvaro Rocha is in favour of this restoration. Restoring implies re-composing the conditions that give us orientation. And re-composing does not imply disregarding life and the site. Quite the opposite, their features are transcribed into his architecture. To do this, João Álvaro Rocha's method appears to be ironic. The project seems to ally itself with all that it finds, with its conventions and fragments, but what it does is change their direction. The architect faces his project with something like and oriental martial art: he takes the disordered impulse of life, the availability of the site and its not always favourable situation, and he redirects them, with no apparent effort, in a concentrated act, with morphological wisdom. In this procedure, we see an intellectual affinity with architect Giorgio Grassi, and in a way with Hilberseimer.

The meaning of technique

Both order and disorder, disorientation and its potential remedy, could be the subject of a taxonomy. And since the thoughts of an architect are always concerned with life, sites and techniques, these disorders and orders could all fall into several of these categories. But life is, in a way, uncontrollable information. Sites are found and can be changed. Technique is a means of altering reality. Technique, then, appears to be the only way of coming to terms with disorder. But the architect's technique is not identified with building but with projects, and in this field there is a level of autonomy that should urgently be acknowledged.

Rocha's work immediately acknowledges this field, its elements and its laws. This field consists of a highly limited number of forms and their possible combinations. The architect responds to complex reality, to order and disorder, to a variety of programmes, to sites and to problems with just a few elements and their combinations. This is the distant, and therefore essentially ironic, approach of the architect's technique. Series of classrooms, patios and porches ordered in spine, chess board and comb-like morphologies, in a radial manner, in patterns reminiscent of keyboards, pentagrams or wheels. The figures resulting from this *ars combinatoria* are subjected to two primary references: one is the perimeter of the precinct and the other is the intersection between the buildings and the natural ground. From here, the routes register the intervals and the vacuums, starting the architectural device that uses nature as a framework, completing the projects according to paradigms taken from the experience that the architect has defined as something specifically his own. In many projects we can find the example of the acropolis or sanctuary: with the definition of the door providing access to the precinct and the main itiner-

8. ADP - Waters of the Douro and Paiva, S.A.
Exploration Buildings
Lever
Competition design: 1999

ary that not only clarifies the spatial relationship between the pieces, but between the latter and the neighbourhood and the distance, the sky and the horizon. Or the example of the shrine, the *stoa*, the *agora*, the monastery and the pre-industrial city against the landscape, with its towers; the aqueduct, the city wall, the village and the silo, etc. These architectural paradigms often solve the problems of scale associated to each project.

A vacuum is just as concrete as solid objects, said Lucretius in his *De rerum natura*. So the architect consciously considers and measures the vacuum. The architect's technique arranges those few elements in relative, topological positions that are isomorphic with life and the site; but not only does he measure the vacuum but he establishes it at its borders, so that technique also includes the definition of the limits, the concrete qualities of which are responsible for the *decorum* of the space defined. And this is, evidently, also applicable to interiors.

To summarize, then, what we call technique in architecture consists of these two aspects. One is based on the formality of the elements and their combinations, *ars combinatoria* that allows us to make topological decisions and can provisionally be conceived with abstraction from matter. The other is derived from the material creation of the limit. But this division is conventional, since both aspects are analogous.

The double wall system similar to English cavity walls appears to have become a European standard, and is regularly used by architects. This system distinguishes between walls with a mechanical function, load bearing walls, and walls intended to delimit spaces, protect and decorate buildings. With this duality, the system of load bearing walls has become like the skeleton-based systems such as a framework or the Domino structure. The problem of the covering thus is of the greatest technical importance. For example, ashlar masonry can be used in its traditional stereotomic modality, or as coating that can be exchanged for steel or aluminium sheeting, without scandal. Never before had the concepts developed by the lucid mind of Gottfried Semper, in his *Der Stil*, been developed so extensively and applied so pertinently. Some people see a stone wall as something "regional" and an aluminium sheet or a large glass window as something "technological". But the discussion, in reductive terms, concerning what is international and what is local, and that involves a large number of critics and historians who are not or do not work as architects, is losing content, if it ever had any.

We have already seen, in different ways, that Rocha places special emphasis on the notion of limits, and therefore on the precinct. The characteristic of the pecinct's limits is not restricted to the outer fencing, since it also involves the entity of the surface area delimited. In view of the aerial photographs of the finished work and the models of the projects, it is evident that each area is framed by precisely delimited lines and borders and also that each area has its own individuality. And this is also true for the entire piece of land, the pathways and ramps, the paved and grassed areas, for the plans, and the rooms, corridors and stairs contained by it, for the walls, inside and out, with the windows and doors, showing the frontiers between the different components by exact juxtaposition; and for the detail plans with the sections of steel, wood, stone or concrete. This similarity creates solidarity between all the elements in the project, in spite of their different size and nature. Both those that appear on the general plan and the details on a 1:10 scale are all necessary for the project. They are also homogeneous, since they are applied the same logic. In other words, they are analogous.

We could say that the pieces are set out in the project as if it was taracea or marquetry work. Precisely, well inserted and well adjusted. The value of each one, including the vacuums, saturates the framework from a conceptual and physical perspective. But what is more remarkable still is that the landscape that enters through the window (fragments of blue and green), or the diffuse light that penetrates the fissures, like a piece of ivory or mother-of-pearl, becomes part of this jigsaw universe. There are concrete experiences in Kahn's or Scarpa's architecture in which this decorative tradition, probably of oriental origin, is clearly perceived. But in João Álvaro Rocha's work, it acquires a unitary and comprehensive significance. We are referring to the analogic operation that converts building details into geography. If we could see all his work together from the air, juxtaposed, one after the other, with the grass framed by path ways, then this meadow would be the equivalent of the board where the artisan fits his marquetry pieces. The ideal dimension of this landscape is not because it is a raw material or natural, but rather because it is an intellectual construction, an artifice, and at the same time a critical call to acknowledge that culture establishes a mental relationship with nature, far from naturalistic affectations. Rocha makes Le Corbusier's dream come true in a different way, by allowing nature to pass beneath and above architecture, but in parts and in a modest fashion, proudly realistic, maybe restoring, without realizing it, the profound strata of an archaeology of the territory's own culture, the profound strata of a tradition.

We have just associated the inventory of disorder with a lack of direction and noise. And we have also said that the architect develops a *poietic* activity to eliminate stridency. We find something similar in the words of the writer Herberto Helder, when he says (condemning our analysis to mutism): "We must wonder if poetry is not an exercise in silence."

[1] *Taracea* is a technique that consists of inlaying pieces of coloured wood or other materials, primarily ivory, into a wooden base to create decorative patterns and subjects. It is similar to marquetry or the Italian technique called *intarsio*.

José Manuel Pozo

Architecture with Thickness

I may not be totally impartial when I refer to João Álvaro Rocha's works, because I hold them in great esteem, and I tend to see them favourably *a priori*. I also appreciate the author's talent and his attitude to architecture, as interesting as his work itself, which is no doubt part of its natural impact.

On the other hand, I hardly feel it necessary to distance myself from his work, in a search for some level of objectivity, since this could lead me to be unfair – which is the general fault of publications concerning current architecture, occasionally centred on good appearance rather than on contents or exemplary attitudes. This alone more than justifies attracting attention to Rocha's work, from which, judging by what he has achieved in the time when he has been working in and out Porto, a great deal is to be expected.

These considerations apart, I begin by making reference to a recent event in which I was closely involved, which provides an acceptable definition for the scenario in which Rocha's work is situated, namely the last project included in this monograph. Since it is merely a project, it lacks the interest of much of his previous work; although it is not his best, it reveals a series of aspects that help us understand the work of this Portuguese master.

The project is that for the Museo de Sanfermines in Pamplona *(p. 180)*. It was one of the three finalists in the public call, but it was rejected in favour or another more "spectacular" project, perhaps very interesting but lacking realism for Pamplona's reality. The fact is that, in view of the result, it would appear that Rocha's proposal, which is possibly very similar to what will eventually be built, was too discreet.

He had concentrated his efforts on complying with the ambiguous and far from concrete "programme", taking special care to consider the location, its history and the site's topographical connotations, with exquisite respect for Pamplona's skyline, which from the Arga is one of the city's few values worth respecting.

A well-known story concerning another master comes to my mind, and is applicable here. When Richard Neutra was visiting Spain in 1954, he met some students from Madrid's school of architecture, which ended in a lively exchange of questions and opinions. One of the students asked him what he thought should be done if an industrial building, a chemical plant for example, had to be built in one of Spain's historic cities, such as Avila. His answer was to commission the project from an architect who was familiar with, and of course loved, the city.

Rocha's will was that of finding a solution for the Museo de Sanfermines which could also solve the city problem relating to a conflictual site; but he did not want his intentions to be apparent. Like all good surgeons, he wanted to go unnoticed: a clean operation and a prompt recovery. That's why he did not win. Because that is the way he is.

It may seem strange to spend so many words on this project, the concrete solution of which is no longer of much interest, since it will not be executed; but I think that it is a valid reference, because it perfectly reflects one of Rocha's personal characteristics, present in all his work: discretion. In a recent exhibition on his work in the Navarra School of Architecture,[1] he himself acknowledged that for him the ideal architectural solution is that of building without altering the landscape, as if constructions exist, but are not on the site.

Respect for the territory and acknowledgement of its leading role, in a Rossian sense, are part of the unquestionable premises for Rocha's work. Anonymity is the source of inspiration, to become a part of the landscape. This is evident even in the materials he uses, which are taken from local sources whenever possible, with no desire for newness, nor loud or colourful imports, nor spectacular formal details and pretentiousness.

In fact, in the few occasions when Rocha has abandoned this rule of conduct, his work has been much less interesting, as may be the case for his renovation of the Vila do Castelo HomesteadFacing*(p. 166),* with the glass volume in the assembly hall, which he was forced to position outside the building because of the amplitude of the programme.

Rocha does not see territory as a framework in which to excel, but rather as a ready-furnished "room" in which he has to look for a place for his architecture. The landscape is already there and has to be respected. In a sense, it is the territory that has to determine the project, which, if possible, should become one more geographical accident. This does not mean that Rocha's work is discreet, almost shy, because, as he himself says, "if one is incapable of understanding or interpreting a place's spirit, one is condemned to fail, to be crushed under the arrogance of soul stealing, or the fear of not being able to touch it".[2]

This combination of respect and decision is the source of the confidence that is characteristic of Rocha's work. Such strong substantiality is quite unusual in the ephemeral and unsure contemporary architecture, with which we all too often have to be satisfied.

There is a passage in one of the oldest books on Earth that comes to my mind when I see the noise and spectacularity of some architectural operations of supposedly extreme beauty or quality, which are presented as exemplary or ideal but practically all of which are lacking in "silence" and tranquillity. They are built no doubt because their excellence (real or imagined) is sung far and wide, but their only apparent quality comes beforehand when due consideration is given to the case in hand.

The text to which I am referring is a poetic passage from the Book of Kings, in which the prophet Elijah is waiting for God: "There came such a violent hurricane that it destroyed mountains and broke rocks in view of the Lord; but the Lord was not in the wind. After the wind, came an earthquake; but the Lord was not in the earthquake. After the earthquake, came fire; but the Lord was not in the fire. After the fire, came a gentle breeze; when Elijah felt it, he covered his face with his mantle, went outside and stood at the entrance to the cave".[3]

The echo of this text can be heard in Rocha's work, and at times in his own words, when he defends the complex simplicity of all that surround us: "Nature also seems simple, but of simply high complexity."

The true meaning of the Miesian "less is more", which has a great deal to do with this admiration for nature, positively shines in Rocha's work, in more than one sense.

In the first place, because of the evident formal simplicity, not simple at all, that gives rise to the noble elegance of all his work.

Secondly, because of the powerful underlying geometry and construction, which make the formal essentiality of the work, which after all is what gives meaning to the "more", making it seem "less", real (with "substance", as he likes to say) and not false, and what supports the formal and functional rigour that is perceived as an unquestionable substrate, and leads to strict order and a "spontaneously geometric" construction.

Rocha considers decorative details as superfluous, because the volumes that result from the structural core should in themselves be a decoration, and produce such intense plastic effects that other details become useless. Although on his trip to America Dudok declared that he would need a lifetime to achieve this "less", this "silence",[4] this was Rocha's starting point, as taught by his masters.

These characteristic notes provide Rocha's architecture with something that is fundamental if what we are looking for is a work of art: rest. His buildings convey tranquillity and seem to have been conceived to occupy the space they fill, just where they are, and to be the subject of serene contemplation, enjoyed at leisure, relishing the materials, the colour and texture of the compositions.

This manifest desire to give architecture density and composure, on a classical background, reminds us no doubt of the ideas defended by Berlage, for whom constructive clarity and the value of walls as fundamental for spatial definition and rest were essential qualities of good architecture; these qualities are also distinctive of Rocha's work. These characteristics also release his architecture from the danger, derived from its formal purity, of being catalogued as minimalist. Rocha would not agree to apply this superficial and somewhat vague concept, used to define countless heterogeneous things, to architecture.

On the contrary, his architecture, in spite of its coherence, does not have a single formal source of inspiration. We can detect many different influences, possibly not the result of intentional formalistic imitations, and also partially incomplete; but his work is still young to fully understand this interference. It is easy to observe these undisguised references, which he makes no effort to avoid: to follow his masters without attempting to hide the fact is part of his nature. It is precisely because of this that I feel it would be interesting to identify some, although by no means all, of these visible references.

Furthermore, if at the beginning I warned of the danger of my judgements lacking in objectivity, I now mention something else that should be taken into consideration in order to better understand these bold, but convinced, considerations on Rocha's architecture.

I have never liked dynastic interpretations of architecture, analysing work in search of details and elements with which to establish a linear and clear chain of influence and schools. It would make sense to identify these formal similarities when considering work from centuries past, but when we consider today's architecture, with the wealth and variety of information now at our disposal, these discoveries are lacking in evidential value.

In other words, I think we should be more concerned with the facts themselves than identifying their origins. In this case, this is an interesting aspect, since the variety of influences is considerable. There are evident and multiple direct references to Mies, particularly in the impressive series of detached homes that we will consider later. Neither does Rocha disguise his admiration for Scandinavian architecture, Asplund in particular, whose cemetery is a constant reference for the Moutidos Leisure Park (Maia, *p. 122*). We can also observe what is perhaps a certain Rossian influence in some of his social housing blocks, in which an ordered and rhythmic succession of small square windows, drawn on the terse skin of a completely plain brick wall, remind us vaguely of some of the compositions of this Italian master, who Rocha claims to admire and respect. We can also establish a certain relation, without being concerned with its concrete origin, between the interior of the series of houses at Várzea, which reaches its peak in house number 2 *(p. 16)* of the series, and the exquisite sensitivity of Japanese architecture, in the play between planes and textures and the subtle succession of areas that is characteristic of traditional Japanese homes.

With these and other influences that we could identify for the rich plasticity of Rocha's work, such as Siza, his building lecturer at the school, or Le Corbusier, the most significant is, without a doubt, derived from Mies, with its simultaneous acceptance of Berlage's concept of constructive clarity, Wright's spatial fluidity and the neoplasticist aesthetics based on the use of planes to de-compose and re-compose space.

In a way, we could consider that Rocha's work has evolved from other masters' ideas and creations, critically seen in the light of the concern for solid buildings (with substance), decisively abandoning the non-geographical value of architecture, which on the other hand is reaffirmed on the territory, and a conscious rationalization of the expressionist dynamics of Wrightian space, understood as it is interpreted by Mies and the Dutch school: Rietveld, Dudok...

This open and fluid space will no longer be centrifugal, as in Mies's Barcelona Pavilion or the Prairie Houses, or Hilversum Town Hall, but linear. Mies's plane movements are more orderly; his compositions with orthogonal walls have been replaced by series of parallel planes, organizing the rooms in a linear fashion. The same applies to small housing projects, with the appearance of fissures and patios that create areas that are simultaneously continual and independent, as on a larger scale, such as the spectacular inclined corridor in the Laboratory building in Vairão *(p. 106)*, an interminable, rhythmic, surprising and vigorous succession of openings and blind walls in a waterfall arrangement that is totally adapted to the ground, to the territory. We even see the same thing in urban projects, such as the blocks of housing in Maia, where the buildings are separated by what are authentic "urban rooms", the same yet different, generating an intimate, closed world, echoing the resources employed by Taut in his Berlin urbanizations.

The spaces that articulate the buildings, from inside or out, are a projection of the same concept on different scales; they create closed, introspective atmospheres with which Rocha brings each project's universe to life, with apparent timidity, or better still reserve or a search for isolation, allowing these buildings to survive in the most disordered and hostile surroundings without suffering from their presence. Whenever he can, he builds thick blind walls, that seem to originate in the earth itself, around them to define each building's own horizon, and they take over the place with all the force of their precise geometry.

On a private scale, the patios, very Miesian and loaded with sensitivity, directly relate these works to Campo Baeza and his masters, Carvajal or Sota, who share Mies's serene vitality and elegance. This relation is also evident in the way in which Rocha uses light, as one more "building material", which he employs to build and modify spaces, and is part of how they are lived in and felt.

We could say much more about the richness and variety of Rocha's works, together with their lack of inhibition and even their possible faults, but the new branches could easily hide the forest, and lead to confusion. I will therefore add just two more things before I enter into a brief summary of some of the details in his work. They are related, but different, issues.

The first is something that powerfully attracts our attention when considering Rocha's work, and it is the enormous variety of his projects, not so much in regards to his programme, which is not that large, but in relation to their size and scope, and the assurance with which he approaches them. We are surprised by the courage and wisdom with which he designs his projects, whatever their size. Between Maia, the park at Moutidos and the way space and the park is ordered at the Vila do Castelo Urban Park *(p. 158)*, there is a remarkable variety of scale to which his pencil seems to adjust as easily as he designs the Laboratory in Vairão of the Composting Plant project for Gondomar *(p. 132)*, or the domestic arrangement in house number 3 at Várzea *(p. 20)*.

It is possible to successfully handle short distances, then medium distances, and then even long distances: this shows an enormous capacity for adjustment, and a great command of the profession, which in fact puts the very existence of architectural divisions into question: architecture of different proportions only exists when the hand designing it has perfect command of scale. And in this art, Rocha is a master.

It is impossible, for example, to establish a valid urban approach and then design an architecture to "fit", just like it is impossible to conceive a project, and then add constructive details to enrich it. And this is the second consideration which I wanted to stress on: Rocha's works are like they are, because they are born that way. For Rocha, decoration is clearly a crime, even if it makes use of "modern" materials and shapes.

This Portuguese architect is convinced that the beauty of nature lies in its internal complexity, which is so "well studied" that mani-

1. House in Mesão-Frio
Penafiel
Design: 1987-88
Construction: 1988-91

fests itself in such simplicity. And that is exactly what he aspires to achieve. But this requires a great deal of work on paper, on models, on the site, studying, watching, meditating...

The conclusion is that good architecture grows in the same way as people do; modern embryology has shown that when children are just tiny embryos in their mothers' wombs, not only has the colour of their hair and eyes already been determined, but even their nails have already been designed: only time, parents and society will help them develop all their qualities. Rocha's work is as it is from the very beginning: the details are not added later to enrich or complicate it; they are born with it, they are an intrinsic part of it. On the few occasions when this is not the case, you can notice that the details are not part of the essence of the project and, as Berlage maintained, since they have neither clarity nor justification, they have no unity and should possibly not have been built.

I end by quoting the words of Rocha himself, uttered during a conference in Pamplona, a good summary of his attitude towards architecture. I'm not sure why, but they seem to be the reason of his coherence.

"Like politicians, architects have to contradict themselves. Today we say one thing and after a time we have to say the opposite. But unlike politicians, these contradictions are a problem for architects."

Not much more needs to be added. I may have said too much already, and clouded the glass through which this work should be contemplated.

Before I end, however, I cannot but include a few specific notes relating to the concrete projects included in this book, although anything that I now add must by force be reiterative and possibly superfluous. And it will certainly not be very useful, because if architecture has to be "lived" to be understood, this Zevian principle is unquestionably true for Rocha's work if we wish to capture any of the emotion that it transmits.

In spite of this, I trust that there is something to be learned from some of the formal and spatial qualities to be appreciated in the projects included in this monograph.

With regards to his detached homes, we have mentioned earlier their fortunate combination of spatial continuity and fluidity with separate spaces, based on a succession of areas, patios and openings that have evidently matured over time in his different projects, from Penafiel *(fig. 1)*, spatially more complex and somewhat confusing with regards to the use of materials, to the exquisite patio houses at Quinta da Barca *(pp. 52, 62)*, in which the architect has achieved remarkable richness of space and form by an exquisite use of materials and the play on movements: spaces arranged in the form of a comb, with gaps breaking the continuity and welcoming the light, which thus becomes a primary factor in the spatial articulation, besides provoking the continual indoor presence of what is outdoors.

Later, this arrangement moves from housing to large buildings, as we can see in the Laboratory project to which we have already referred, or in the project for the Environmental Education School at Maia *(p. 174)*, which has become a fruitful journey entertained by empty spaces and full ones, the material result of his "geometric spontaneity".

On the other hand, isolated exercises unrelated to this concrete spatial research are less interesting from this perspective. Such is the case for the Communication Institute (ICP, *p. 114)* in Porto, the greatest interest of which is without a doubt related to how Rocha takes command of the highly deteriorated landscape on which the building is situated, together with the ease with which he solves an issue that is not characteristic of his usual practice, both with regards to the programme and to the materials employed. Also of less interest for understanding Rocha's architecture is the reform of the Vila do Castelo Homestead, since we are able to appreciate the elegance and skill with which he solves the details and finishes, but the very nature of the commission itself (a reform) forces him to centre his performance on detail, the design of which are not here born with the building process itself, but necessarily have to be added to the existing structure, and forcing him to leave his usual *modus operandi*, as we shall see later. In any case, and although it may seem over-elaborate at some points, the Homestead has elements of exquisite design, such as the large wooden archive box, the copper painting or the kitchen, which again reveals Rocha's extraordinary capacity to undertake all kinds of projects.

Also of great interest is the treatment given to the setting. Although it is also affected by what was there before, the solution provided is, however, less complex than that applied to the Homestead itself.

With regards to Rocha's attitude to the landscape, however, the Moutidos Leisure Park is much richer and more suggestive, with its intentionally essential pavilions, like monuments, its well-studied paving and the spontaneous naturality with which the territory, the wood and the water are handled.

I also think that it is worth referring to the delicate spatial composition of the house at Lugar do Paçô (Carreço, *p. 26*), an authentic modern palace; built on a plinth and crowned by a cornice, this palace dominates the territory with the force of a Paladian villa, the resources and axial arrangements of which it evokes. The linear continuity of the interior area and the exquisite combination of materials and colours, uniform thanks to the geometry and the light, make this house a nearly perfect synthesis of Rocha's architecture.

On the other hand, in another order of things, his economic housing projects, in which he masterly solves two interesting challenges, are also remarkable: first of all, he establishes the conditions for variety in the inevitable programmatic and formal uniformity, with a balanced combination of what is social and what is private, so that users can personalise their homes and perceive their singularity, with a reference to a concrete location, reminiscent of the intentions behind the Dutch town planning that was inspired by Berlage, and by no means anonymous. This supports the second detail to be mentioned: Rocha's groups of buildings and blocks colonise the territory. They are not mere houses lined up in streets and squares, but they are arranged in such a way that the spaces between them are at the service of the homes themselves, of which they form part, providing tranquillity, independence and rest. This is clearly appreciated in the Vila Nova da Telha complex *(p. 80)*, but even more interesting in the Maia I complex *(p. 72)*, where this respectful colonization of the territory is achieved with a single dominating block, similar to the effect at the Communication Institute in Porto, where an authority that imposes rest prevails, the serene calm of modern classicism, is evident.

Finally, after contemplating such extensive, rich and uniformly varied work, so natural and simple that it appears to be easily conceived, all that is left to us here is to follow the advice given by Sota, which Rocha could well have heard: "Before working at the drawing board, you must think. And when you have finished, and are sure, then draw your thoughts."

[1] 20 December 2001.
[2] João Álvaro Rocha, *Memoria del estudio urbanístico del área comprendida entre Nova Ponte y la Avenida Antonio Feijó*, August 2001.
[3] Book of Kings, 19, 9a 11-16.
[4] W.M. Dudok, *To live and to build*, 1954.

José V. Vallejo Lobete

"What can be seen, should not be told"

I often remember these words that Utzon uttered while contemplating the blue of the Mediterranean from his Porto Petro home.

At the end of December 2001, at the Pamplona School of Architecture, Rocha ended the exhibition of his work, with the room packed with students, with similar words. The exhibition showed the same work that is magnificently presented in the pages of this book.

I have no intention of disobeying Jorn Utzon, and tell you about João Rocha's architecture, but to humbly suggest some ideas about this young Portuguese architect's work and personality, the leading figure of a new generation from Porto, following in the wake of masters like Távora, Siza, Souto de Moura.

His work sums up the initial results of a line of thought, a sensitivity, an attitude to architecture which, after the formal contemporary interpretation of the inheritance of the Modern Movement, is based, in my opinion, on clear principles.

1. Deep respect for the tradition of discipline, and I refer to tradition as the practice of Architecture in which values such as the precision of layout, the nature of materials, the execution of details or the vocation for permanence, for the durability of buildings, are considered as fundamental goals.
In this respect, I remind João's recent mention of the luck he had to have an old wall builder on one of his recent projects, one of those builders who used to sing to the stones when working on them, asking them how they should be placed on the wall.

2. Another of the aspects that I feel common in all of Rocha's architectural production is his concern for building a "place", so that nature is analysed and turned into a controlled area and system of reference.

3. Also fundamental in all his work is the attempt to achieve coherence by an architecture that does its utmost to get rid of everything superfluous. Although there exist architectural photographs for all kind of catalogues, in this case we are acknowledging the value of what is authentic, identifying the work with the author's personality. I first met João some years ago, when only the two Maia houses had been published, and was able to read from his serene conversation and sober attire (nothing to do with the uniforms that are so popular in our profession) that his architecture would be absolutely coherent.

But it is during his project classes that his serene enthusiasm for this way of understanding architecture, and culture in general, is most evident. I have had the opportunity to see how students from different cultures and countries, from Cornell University, in the snow of Ithaca, to the Granada school's summer courses in Motril, and a large number of renowned European schools, all end up under the spell of his work, performed with discretion and coherence.

And it is refreshing, in a sceptic and unbelieving cultural (and existential) world, where many hide their mediocrity in the general confusion, to find someone whose personal goal is lucidity.

Val K. Warke

Unpacking

One cannot help being a bit overwhelmed by the complexity of these buildings. It isn't that they *look* complicated. Our initial impression – coolly elegant buildings, crisply neat, a bit self-absorbed, "without a care in the world", and mastered in a glance – this impression collapses with the opening of a door, the first step on a stair tread, or with even just the slightest expansion of our peripheral vision. One is then left to be exposed to the intricate web of interrelationships that can occur between things in space: between body and door, door and window, body and window, window and landscape, landscape and building and body, and so on. All bodies, especially the buildings of João Álavro Rocha.

And it's probably not simply a matter of translation that, in his text, Rocha uses the word "body" to indicate the built condition he seeks to achieve through the design process. This "body" seems to resonate with the "body" the writer Fernando Pessoa describes as both a classical ideal and as a central tenet of "sensationism" in the arts:

"[A]rt is supremely construction and [...] the greatest art is that which is able to visualize and create organized wholes, of which the component parts fit vitally into their places: the great principle that Aristotle enunciated when he said that a poem was an 'animal'."[1]

No, these bodies do not *look* complex, but they certainly *behave* in complex ways. There is even something Janus-like to most of them. Like the two-faced god, they all seem to address two directions simultaneously: inside and outside, public and private, light and dark, rough and smooth, singular and plural, near and distant, earthbound and levitating, toward past and future, city and country.

Urbanistically, these structures are neither reactive – deforming to the pressures of an extant set of conditions – nor exclamatory – preening, oblivious to their surroundings – but are, instead, initiative and assertive: they quietly pose potential strategies for the development of their contexts while imposing unfragmented wholes that tend to catalyze the often ad hoc debris that constitutes their neighbors. In this sense, they are very much like pieces of urban furniture. Identifiable as singular and complete, their siting is clearly tactical. Like Wallace Stevens's "jar" –

I placed a jar in Tennessee,
And round it was, upon a hill.
It made the slovenly wilderness
Surround that hill.

The wilderness rose up to it,
And sprawled around, no longer wild.[2]

– they organize their surroundings, often scaling their environment while measuring their landscapes.

They operate metaphorically and metonymically: the housing slab might also be a city wall; and, made of bricks, it might be itself a brick. In the same way, the site plan and the building detail seem to have equal status, representing information of equal density, and equally concerned with the perceptual effects of their subjects. But, while equally influenced by the visual, if the site plan tends toward the tactical, the detail tends toward the tactile, with materials – like precise bricks and rough stone and polished wood – used both as sensory phenomena as well as abstractions – of precision, of roughness, of oily reflection.

So these "bodies" are also "boxes": simultaneous boundaries of exteriors and interiors. But, in bounding their exteriors, they're often conceived in perspective, inevitably with two vanishing points and frequently from a position somewhere beneath the line where they touch the ground. These views emphasize corners, and they facilitate the continuity of adjacent surfaces (while reinforcing the separateness of opposite sides). Viewed from below, these buildings all seem to aspire to a difficult, earthbound levitation. Like the traditional *espigueiros* populating the countryside, they're humble containers and

Parthenons. In Rocha's hand, perspective is both a mathematical construct and an approximation of perception, both formula and illusion. Far from being merely presentational, this aspect of perspective is clearly integral to these works. The rule of linear perspective is a "fact"that the works consistently *reinforce*, rather than a "fact" the works consistently *manipulate* (as does much of contemporary architecture). These boxes use perspective in that, when built, they practically *define* perspective – picture plane, station point, horizon, and so on – while providing the boundaries of their exteriors.

Within these containers, however, the perspectives we are given to discover inevitably have just one vanishing point, and a horizon that has us standing erect, looking straight ahead. From the freestanding buildings, that horizon is usually emphasized as we look outside from the primary living spaces, with landscapes being meticulously framed paintings. In the courtyard buildings, the interior that is inside is inevitably projected across the interior that is outside. The window, then, is a picture plane that either separates or unites the interior and the exterior.

(As an American, I must confess to a deep admiration for the way in which Rocha makes garages. And the ones at Quinta de Barca represent particularly impressive examples of this type of exterior interiority. In the Pinhal Houses, the simple addition of a set of opposing louvered doors – Janus-like, again – transforms the garages from being tide pools of the public realm into being convertible spaces that can be shaped by their users into spatial extensions of their dining rooms and patios, into shaded and breezy outdoor dining spaces, into easily-supervised play spaces, into porte-cocheres, and so on. In the Marina Houses, the lowered garage door bounds a formal entry space, or, when opened, extends the entry sequence from brightness into shade, provides a contrast of textures with its exterior counterpart, converts into a controlled play space adjacent to the kitchen and dining areas, furnishes a forecourt for the unit's subsidiary maisonette, and, from the interior, expands this meticulously-detailed room into an elegantly-proportioned doubling of itself.)

Interestingly, it's also in the perspectives – drawn horizons and the selected views through the camera lens – that we find *our* bodies, since the images in this text are almost completely devoid of human figures. Clearly intentional, it seems that this absence of the human as object tends to reinforce the presence of the human as subject. This has also occurred in many of the publications of Aldo Rossi, for whom the absence of people from the photographs and drawings was a manifestation of the 'silence' he advocated. Rocha also uses the word 'silence' in describing certain desirable characteristics of architecture. It's not the silence of muteness, but, rather, the silence that occurs in a conversation after one has spoken and another is responding, or is thinking of a response. Architecture's silence permits its participants to "speak": it is the opportunity for response that comes after an articulate assertion. (I need only present here one of the series of *in situ* collages produced by Andrea Simitch during her visits to a number of Rocha's works, in order to demonstrate the complexity of response these works can initiate.)

Perhaps, this opening of a dialogue with the viewer is the reason that, in an analogous way, the text that accompanies these works was not written as a series of descriptions of undertakings as *faits accomplis*, a technique that can place a series of projects in a historical past, and that could possibly frame each project as a closure. This text is instead presented as the unfolding of a series of design insights that serve to involve the reader in their formulation. Reading this text, one is presented with a chronicle of a designer's evolving logic.

Reading this evolving text and engaging these "silent" images – not to mention having been fortunate enough to have visited many of these "bodies" – leads me to believe that the appearance of simplicity in the work of João Álvaro Rocha is actually the image of a complexity that has been well-packed. And that the unpacking – the return to complexity – is, simply, "life".

[1] Fernando Pessoa, "Notes on Sensationism", in *Always Astonished: Selected Prose*, translated by Edwin Honig, City Lights Books, San Francisco 1988, p. 40.

[2] Excerpt from the *Anecdote of the Jar* by Wallace Stevens.

Francisco José Mangado

The Architecture of Precision

The architecture that appears too obvious does not exist because, among other things, it would cease to be architecture or it would simply cease to interest us as such. In my view, something similar occurs with the architecture that organizes its reasons in an exclusive manner, based on opinions outside the discipline itself. In the end, the most interesting architecture is the one to which concepts such as density or intensity can be applied, concepts that endow the work with a content that deserves to be analyzed in a direct and useful manner for those who approach it. This architecture always shows an intelligent and sensitive knowledge of the problems, has an undeniable appeal and becomes more solid with time. If aside from all this, as happens with the work of João Álvaro Rocha, it surprises us gradually and becomes totally visible only after a detailed analysis, all the better. Also this brief writing has been adjusted over and over again until it has reached its final form. This fact (apart from casting a shadow over the capacity of the signatory) indicates that we are before a subject with various readings which are not contradictory but that superpose and strengthen one another. Before a work, let us say this as soon as possible, this attitude removes any doubt about the lack of contents.

The work of Rocha, rich in quantity and contents, is not the result of a predetermined ideological decision that ought to be supported in any given circumstance; and even less of a series of haphazard coincidences. It is rather a display of a rich and subtle way of doing things that searches within the project itself, its circumstances and contents, for just the necessary questions and answers to develop the proposal. In sum, a work that gives relevance to the process. A process which, in the end, is the only aspect that can establish a unity, and not identity, among his works. A process that nurtures itself with architectural realities that for Rocha are still essential. The site, the realization, the constructional approach (very refined in his case), the program – understood both in the ideological sense and in the most pragmatic one – and the architectural references – always shrewdly chosen and manipulated – do not constitute for the architect surpassable concepts or categories that should be sacrificed to meet any one calligraphic purpose. In his projects, the possible stylistic identity (so attractive in these days from perspectives that grant more importance to the way in which the object is presented than to the object itself) does not seem as important as the coherence of concepts, the architectural research and the interest in providing something more with each new proposal. His work still clearly shows that architecture is not a simple discipline, that it is yet not finished and, most of all, that it is too serious to be transformed into yet another object for consumption. Also, that its exclusive objective cannot be to surprise with the last "novelty" but rather to conclude a good work within a process in which time ends up being the most accurate and indisputable judge.

For those of us for whom it is easier to confront the built work itself rather than its critique, to contemplate the projects of Rocha is a healthy exercise. They constitute the work of a "builder" who transforms the theory of architecture into a theory of the project, into true research. His works involve the reader and reveal a certain educational value that, to a great extent, inspires and supports his career as a professor in several academic institutions in different countries.

The architecture to which this monograph is devoted is a precise architecture. Precision as a concept applied to architecture – unlike other closer but more limited concepts such as exactness or perfection (boring and impossible) – suggests that there is still space for contingency and risk, for trial and error. We would be talking about that kind of precision which is present in certain architecture (for instance, in that of masters like Arne Jacobsen) that makes us think (the search for references can always be simplifying) whether we are before a case of synthesis between the Atlantic

1. House in Mesão-Frio
Penafiel
Design: 1987-88
Construction: 1988-91

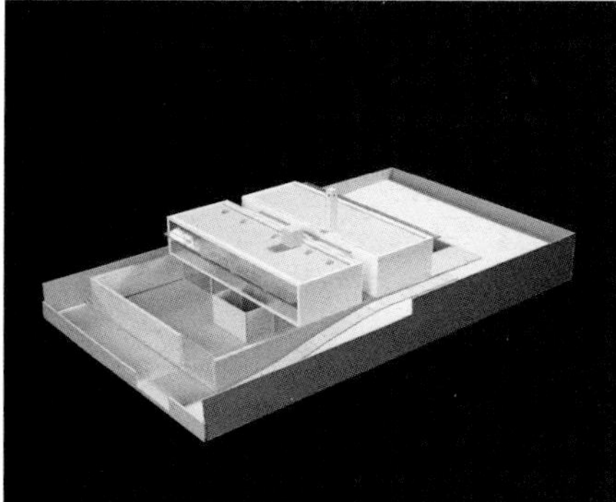

2. House in Praia do Cabedelo
Viana do Castelo
Design: 1996-97
Construction: 2000-(underway)

and the Nordic (both have craftsmanship in common). Synthesis which, overcoming any false syncretism, turns out to be completely coherent and full of good results as those here reflected.

The first symptom of this precise architecture can be perceived in the analysis of the floor plans of the different projects. It is the floor plans that structure and order the essential contents, and their interpretation allows to discover the project's values. Their design relies on the agreement of the main arguments. In this way, one discovers in them the desire that many projects show for "seizing" and occupying the entire site. In the first single-family houses of Mesão Frio *(fig. 1)* or Lugar da Várzea *(pp. 10, 20)*, the floor plan extends as a "magma" and, through the use of stone walls, it takes up the entire perimeter. Previously the plot is transformed into an artificial and architectural space, upon which it is possible to unfold the drawn scheme of the house. Any graphic element, a simple partition wall or a part of the development, acquires value in this unfolding scheme that, consciously planned, occupies everything. In the case of the single-family housing projects in Lugar do Paçô, Esposende *(p. 26)*, or Cabedelo *(fig. 2)*, the general plan is replaced by the definition of certain boundaries, more geometric and contained, less organic, but which come to express the need to resort to a previous architectural and structural frame that may serve as a starting point for the project. The case of the house at Lugar do Paçô is especially paradigmatic because here this frame acquires a literal condition and the lateral limits extend continuously to perform at once as base and roof. The wood boxes that actually contain the house are inserted in this perimeter. In all these cases, it is from the interpretation of the floor plans where one can foresee this abstract and artificial manner of settling on the site.

But the floor plans also serve to explain project decisions that have to do with the problem of the program. Hence, in the case of the Veterinary Investigation Laboratory (LNIV, *p. 106*), any other document or photograph becomes unnecessary (little does it matter how the project is finally materialized) to understand that it is the nature of the program, its functional complexity and the desire to provide a precise answer which have led to the final result. In this project, the solution is not only the consequence of a required attention to efficiency, and the document we are making reference to transmits an ideological attitude which one can easily relate to the concept of precision.

The precision in the architecture of João Álvaro Rocha is equally reflected in its continuous and systematic reference to geometry and order. A sufficiently fragile order, not rigid, that answers to functional needs rather than to ideological premises. This order, alongside other typological and compositional mechanisms such as repetition, gives a logical sense to the entire work, a sensible approach adjusted to the problems set forth. The Pinhal Houses at Quinta da Barca *(p. 52)* or the impressive social apartments of Maia I *(p. 72)* reflect this interest, that has remained constant and has even been intensified in the more recent proposals for the housing project in Vila Nova de Telha *(p. 80)*, in the Pedrouços *(fig. 3)*, or in competition entries such as the one realized for the water board of Douro and Paiva *(fig. 4)*.

Finally, the idea of precise architecture is made evident in the construction of the project. Rocha shows an unquestionable capacity when it comes to taking constructional decisions and, particularly, when these decisions are materialized in the detail. The construction process in all his works is an active, not so much obsessive, concern, and its quality constitutes a basic and natural condition of architecture that cannot be added *a posteriori.* The nature of the architectural object, as physical fact, can never be false. This nature, so close in essence to the procedure of the school of Porto, requires an exhaustive knowledge which, in the case of João Álvaro Rocha and in spite of his youth, is backed by a broad experience in construction. His architecture uses traditional materials like stone or brick, closer to a context where one can find remnants of craftsmanship – as well as other more industrial or specialized ones – though the final solution in many cases is determined by the simultaneous use of both, in a rather attractive and natural symbiosis.

This constructional naturalness does not entail a lack of elaboration, in fact Rocha belongs to that group of architects that are more interested in technique than in technology. In technique because he prefers to explore the possibilities implicit in the direct manipulation of the different materials and to establish a dialogue between them, than simply incorporating the subproduct of the last catalogue or the last technical publication. The constructional details are not casual facts, in fact, it is from the details that the keys and interests that define the project are explained. And whereas in the first projects one can notice a certain excess and profusion of details, in posterior ones, they appear only there where it seems practically impossible to do without certain elaboration, this is, on the limits. The exterior and interior window frames, the stairs and their handrails, attract the continuous and careful attention of the author and, in every case, the solutions aim at providing an answer, with the least amount of elaboration, to as many problems as possible. Thereby the solution for the interior window frames also serves for the wood cladding and for the wardrobes; and the solution for the exterior window frames incorporates the protection system built with the same material, or the elementary corner bead extends horizontally constituting the encounter between the floor paving and the walls. All the details take part in that appropriate relationship between means and ends, that conceptual balance which so well illustrates the concept of precise architecture here described.

I would not like to conclude this comment about the work of Rocha without making reference to two concepts that, in my view, are related to it. The first has guided the length of this text, and it has to do with the idea of precision. The architecture we are contemplating pursues simplicity. A simplicity which should not be understood as a pursuit of minimals (in no way are we facing a simplistic architecture or one that can be easily qualified as minimal), but as an architecture that equals decantation, research, a back and forth process, with the purpose of giving an adequate answer to accurate questions. Rocha does not belong to the world of invention or improvisation but rather to the world of intelligence and sensitive knowledge. Simplicity so understood – as linked to the process and to the acknowledgment of the fact that questions and answers are neither easy nor immediate – supports research and rejects speculation contemplated as a mere game without contents.

But in order to support this way of doing architecture it is necessary to have the most valuable material and unfortunately, at this moment, most scarce in architecture: time, that material the project needs in order to survive. Time to work. João Álvaro Rocha, I am certain, is an architect sensitive to this need and this absence because he is aware that without time architectural decisions are unlikely to be as accurate and precise as he intends. When one observes the abundance of decisions that accumulate in the elaboration of the floor plans of his projects, or the exquisiteness displayed in his details or in the use of materials, the density and quality of his work in sum, one sees that only from a perspective that is conscious and enjoys taking each and every decision, that does not renounce to giving all the necessary time, is it possible to obtain results such as the ones that so accurately illustrate this monograph.

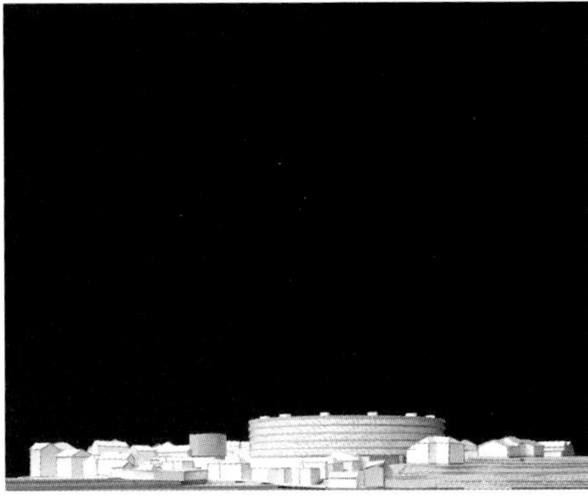

3. Residential Apartment Building (120 dwellings)
Predrouços - Maia
Design: 2000-01
Construction: adjudication phase

4. ADP - Waters of the Douro and Paiva, S.A.
Exploration Buildings
Lever
Competition design: 1999

Luis Ferreira Alves, photographer

"Ostinato Rigore"

These beautiful words by Leonardo, to which Eugénio de Andrade lent the resurrection flames, came furtively up to my mind on the path that was leading me to João Álvaro Rocha. And, like anchors, they have remained in this writing inspired by friendship and admiration.

I do not refuse, but take caution in this doing, that is not mine, so far away and so incapable am I of specialized, aesthetic or technical criticism, so opaque to fashion hermeneutics.

My images are the only form of criticism I know.

Architectures of poor grammar are retained in images of indolent façades, weary searches and academic framings: no personal involvement in them.

In João's works, everything is quite the opposite; they accept successive re-beginnings and just as many unpublished journeys; they not only resist, but compel the movement that goes from the whole to the unit, and ends up in the minuscule portion of matter in which the design is revised... still.

This is the result of an ethic of fight, the fight for the building, at the building site, the strict defence of the initial drawing and its fragile and indecisive journey among the depreciating contingencies that the act of building brings about.

That is a fierce attitude that has been growing generation after generation, since Carlos Ramos has lit up the School. An attitude in which João excels with *ostinato rigore*.

Outsiders say, and they are many, that the "School of Porto" is an evidence; insiders, vehemently refuse that label considered empty of content. And those, like myself, half outside, half inside, believe that one should search and question. Like Jorge Dias searched, in vain, the cultural foundations of our identity or Eduardo Lourenço that lost himself in the labirith of our longing.

One may not get there, but the journey is worthwhile in itself.

And this moral, which already is an aesthetic, could also be, who knows, a foundation.

Porto, February 2002

Appendix

Works and Projects

1.
Factory Unit Support Building
Viana do Castelo
Design: 1980
Construction: 1981

2.
Residential Complex
Vermoim - Maia
Design: 1982

3.
Religious Home
Sameiro - Braga
Design: 1982-84
Construction: 1984-85

4.
Residential Complex
Vermoim - Maia
Design: 1983-84

5.
"Boa Vontade" Building
Viana do Castelo
Design: 1983-93
Construction: 1993-95

6.
Police Department
Lamego
Design: 1983

7.
Sales Stand
Frankfurt International Fair, Germany
Design: 1983
Construction: 1984

8.
Dr Sá Lopes House
Vizela
Design: 1983

9.
City Park: Swimming Pool - Tennis
Lamego
Design: 1983-86

10.
Restaurant on the Beach: interior design
Matosinhos
Design: 1984

11.
TLP - S.ª da Hora's Telephone Communication Building (extension)
Matosinhos
Design: 1984
Construction: 1985-86

12.
TLP - Maia's Telephone Communication Building (extension)
Maia
Design: 1984
Construction: 1985-86

13.
Carreiros Pavilion
Porto
Competition design: 1984

14.
Furniture Design
Braga
Design and Construction: 1985

15.
House in Silva Escura
Silva Escura - Maia
Design: 1985
Construction: 1986-88

16.
City Park: Fountain
Lamego
Design: 1986

17.
City Park: Tea House - Restaurant
Lamego
Design: 1986-88

18.
Cafe and Garden
Viana do Castelo
Design: 1986-87

19.
Funerary Chapel
Taipas - Guimarães
Design: 1987
Construction: 1989

20.
Residential Building
Argaçosa - Viana do Castelo
Design: 1987
Construction: 1988-2001

21.
House in Mesão-Frio
Penafiel
Design: 1987-88
Construction: 1988-91

22.
Allotment
Vermoim - Maia
Design: 1988

23.
Residential Apartment Building
Vila do Conde
Competition design: 1988

24.
Partial Urban Plan
Abelheira - Meadela
Viana do Castelo
Design: 1988-89

25.
Two Houses in Lugar da Várzea
Vermoim - Maia
Design: 1988-89
Construction: 1990-93

26.
Furniture Design
Porto
Design and Construction: 1989

27.
Residential Complex and Facilities
Gondifelos - Famalicão
Design: 1989
Construction: 1994-97

28.
House in Santarém (first version)
Santarém
Design: 1989

29.
Interior Remodelling of a Bookstore
Porto
Design: 1989
Construction: 1989

30.
Beach Support Buildings
Esposende
Competition design: 1989

31.
Felga House
Gondomar
Design: 1990

32.
Remodelling of a Dwelling
Castelo - Maia
Design: 1990
Construction: 1991

33.
House in Santa Maria de Avioso (first version)
Castelo - Maia
Design: 1990-91

34.
Office Furniture Design
Porto
Desing and Construction: 1990

35.
Layout of the Exhibition "Contemporary Portuguese Architecture, years '60-'80"
Fundação de Serralves, Porto
Desing and Construction: 1990

36.
João Paulo II Social Centre - Support Building
Apúlia - Esposende
Design: 1991

37.
Furniture Design
Porto
Design and Construction: 1991

38.
LNIV - National Veterinary Investigation Laboratory
Vairão - Vila do Conde
Design: 1991-93
Construction: 1994-98

39.
Student Housing
Coimbra
Competition design: 1991

40.
Carvalhido House
Trebosa - Barcelos
Design: 1992

41.
ICP - Portugal's Communication Institute Northern Headquaters, Porto
Design: 1993-94
Construction: 1994-95

42.
TLP - Building in Rua do Falcão
Porto
Competition design: 1993

43.
Interior Remodelling of a Dwelling
Miramar - Vila Nova de Gaia
Design: 1994

44.
Residential Allotment
S. Mamede do Coronado
Santo Tirso
Design: 1994

45.
Agricultural Warehouse and Keepers Home
Quinta da Carrapata
Fundão
Design: 1994-95

46.
Furniture Design
Porto
Design and Construction: 1994

47.
Cultural Building in the Palácio de Cristal Grounds
Porto
Competition design: 1994

48.
House in Lugar do Paçô
Carreço - Viana do Castelo
Design: 1994-95
Construction: 1995-97

49.
Furniture Design
Porto
Design: 1994

50.
Competition for Residential Complexes in Matosinhos and Senhora da Hora 1 (dwellings)
Matosinhos
Competition design: 1995

51.
ICP - Portugal's Communication Institute: Plan of the Installations in Barcarena
Barcarena - Oeiras
Competition design: 1995

52.
Social Housing Matosinhos I (132 dwellings and facilities)
Matosinhos
Design: 1995
Construction: 2001-(underway)

53.
Social Housing Senhora da Hora I (56 dwellings and facilities)
Matosinhos
Design: 1995
Construction: 2001-(underway)

54.
Quinta da Barca - Pinhal Houses
Esposende
Design: 1995-96
Construction: 1997-(underway)

55.
Social Housing Vermoim I (30 dwellings)
Maia
Design: 1996

56.
Impersa - Warehouse and Office Building
Vila do Conde
Design: 1996-97
Construction: built without respecting the design

57.
House in Santa Maria de Avioso (second version)
Maia
Design: 1997

58.
Social Housing Vila Nova da Telha I (12 dwellings)
Maia
Design: 1996
Construction: 1997-2000

59.
House in Praia do Cabedelo
Viana do Castelo
Design: 1996-97
Construction: 2000-(underway)

60.
Social Housing Maia I (15 dwellings)
Maia
Design: 1996
Construction: 1997-99

61.
Gas Station
Bagunte - Vila do Conde
Design: 1996-97
Construction: 1997-(construction interrupted)

62.
Social Housing Maia II (44 dwellings)
Maia
Design: 1996-97
Construction: in adjudication phase

63.
Quinta da Barca - Marina Houses
Esposende
Design: 1996-97
Construction: 1999-2001

64.
Social Housing Vermoim II (48 dwellings)
Maia
Design: 1996-97
Construction: 2000-(underway)

65.
University Student Housing
University Campus in Alto da Ajuda
Lisboa
Competition design: 1996

66.
House in Lugar da Várzea (III)
Vermoim - Maia
Design: 1997-98
Construction: 1999-(underway)

67.
Moutidos Leisure Park
Maia
Competition design, final design: 1997
Construction: 1998-2001

68.
Two Houses
Rua João de Barros
Porto
Design: 1997
Construction: 1999-(underway)

69.
Quires Urban Park (first version)
Vila Nova da Telha
Maia
Design: 1997

70.
Social Housing Vila Nova da Telha II (32 dwellings)
Maia
Design: 1997
Construction: 1998-(underway)

71.
Social Housing Moreira I (21 dwellings)
Maia
Design: 1997
Construction: 1998-(underway)

72.
Social Housing Moreira II (48 dwellings)
Maia
Design: 1997
Construction: 1998-(underway)

73.
Interior Decoration and Furnishings for the Pinhal Houses
Quinta da Barca
Esposende
Design: 1997
Partially Built

74.
CAE - Business Support Centre
Câmara Municipal da Maia
Design: 1997-98
Constraction: in adjudication phase

75.
Social Housing Gemunde (66 dwellings)
Maia
Design: 1997
Construction: 1998-(underway)

76.
Urban Study of Rua Corga - Urban allotment
Aguas Santas - Maia
Design: 1998

77.
Vila do Castelo: Urban Park - Homestead Remodellig
Maia
Design: 1998
Construction: 1998-2001

78.
Vila do Castelo: Detail Plan
Maia
Design: 1998-2001

79.
House in Santarém (second version)
Santarém
Design: 1998-99
Construction: 2000-(underway)

80.
Commercial Store
Porto
Design: 1998

81.
Quinta dos Cónegos Urban Study
Maia
Design: 1998

82.
Residential Apartment Building
Águas Santas
Design: 1998
Construction: 1999-2001

83.
Quinta dos Cónegos: Urban Study II
Câmara Municipal da Maia, Maia
Design: 1999

84.
Garage Complex and Garden in Quires
Vila Nova da Telha, Maia
Design: 1999

85.
Limited Competition for the Contract Job Design Construction of the Bank interceptor of the Douro River between de D. Luís I Bridge and the Gaia Litoral Treatment Plant
Vila Nova de Gaia
Competition design: 1999

86.
Quinta dos Cónegos Urban Study III
Câmara Municipal da Maia
Maia
Urban design: 1999

87.
Social Housing Vila Nova da Telha III (24 dwellings)
Maia
Design: 1999-2000
Construction: 2001-(underway)

88.
Sports Pavilion (first version)
Vila Nova da Telha
Maia
Design: 1999-2000

89.
Portofino Apartment Building (21 dwellings)
Quires, Vila Nova da Telha
Maia
Design: 1999-2000

90.
Vila do Castelo: Urban Park - Garden Areas Renovation
Maia
Design: 1999
Construction: 1999-2001

91.
Detail Plan of the Eastern area of the designated Lidador town plan, in Moreira e Vila Nova da Telha
Maia
Design: 1999-(underway)

92.
Imoesfera - General Study of a Residential Complex and Sports Centre of High Revenue
Maia
Urban study: 1999

93.
Residential Apartment and Commerce Building
Pedrouços - Maia
Design: 1999-2000

94.
ADP - Waters of the Douro and Paiva, S.A. Exploration Buildings
Lever
Competition design: 1999

95.
Vila do Castelo: Urban Park - Environment Education School
Maia
Design: 1999
Construction: 2001-(underway)

96.
Medical office
Interior Remodelling
Maia
Design: 2000
Construction: 2000-01

97.
Lipor Composting Plant International Public Competition
Gondomar
Design: 2000

98.
Sogenave - Warehouse Building
S. Pedro Fins - Maia
Design: 2000

99.
Single Family Home
Quinta dos Sete Sonhos Estate
São João da Pesqueira
Design: 2000

100.
EMIM - Office and Commercial Space Building
Moreira - Maia
Competition design: 2000

101.
Residential Apartment Building (120 dwellings)
Predrouços - Maia
Design: 2000-01
Construction: in adjudication phase

102.
Council Shop
Maia - Predrouços
Design: 2000-01
Construction:
in adjudication phase

103.
Urban Study (360 dwellings and facilities)
Guardeiras - Maia
Urban study: 2000

104.
Urban Study of the Surrounding Areas to the Municipal Market
Ponde Lima
Urban study: 2000-01

105.
Turist information office and Exhibition Gallery
Ponde Lima
Design: 2000
Construction design: (underway)

106.
Urban Allotment
18 Single family Homes
Santa Maria de Avioso
Maia
Design: 2000

107.
IAFE - Business Support and Formation Institute Headquaters building
Maia
Design: 2000-01
Construction design: (underway)

108.
House in Montenero
Castel del Piano
Montenero, Tuscany
Italy
Design: 2000-02

109.
VIP House
Quinta dos Cónegos Estate
Design: 2001-(underway)

110.
Quires's Urban park (second version)
Vila Nova da Telha - Maia
Design: 2001

111.
Espaço Viso - Office Building
Senhora da Hora
Matosinhos
Design: 2001-(underway)

112.
Turistic Complex - Golf and Residential Complex (240 dwellings)
Alfena - Valongo
Design: 2001-(underway)

113.
House remodelling
Porto
Design: 2001-(underway)

114.
Residential Complex (150 dwellings)
Curia
Design: (underway)

115.
Residential Apartment Building
Nogueira - Maia
Design: 2001-(underway)

116.
Sports Pavilion (second version)
Vila Nova da Telha - Maia
Design: 2001-(underway)

117.
General Plan study of the Quinta do Pinheiro Estate
Paços de Ferreira
Urban plan study underway: 2001-02

118.
Museo de Sanfermines
Pamplona
Spain
Competition design: 2001

119.
Johan Stevens House
Carreço - Viana do Castelo
Design: 2002
Construction design: (underway)

120.
Funeral Chapel
Viana do Castelo
Design: 2002

121.
Office and Commerce Building
Maia
Design: 2002

122.
Residencial Complex
18 Single Family Homes
Vilar do Pinheiro
Vila do Conde
Design: 2002

123.
Park Metro Staion, Viaduct and Urban Insertion
Maia
Design underway: 2002

124.
Zona Industrial I Metro Station, Urban Insertion and Viaducts
Maia
Design underway: 2002

125.
I.S.M.A.I. Metro Station and Urban Insertion
Maia
Desing underway: 2002

126.
Mandim Metro Station and Urban insertion
Maia
Design underway: 2002

127.
Ribela Metro Station
Maia
Design underway: 2002

128.
Residencial Complex
12 Single Family Homes
Padrão de Moreira - Maia
Design underway: 2002

129.
Residencial Complex
30 Single Family Homes
Quinta de Pisões
Santo Tirso
Design underway: 2002

Porto, July 2002

List of Associates and Collaborators

Associates
José Manuel Gigante (1988-95)
Francisco Portugal e Gomes (1987-2001)

Collaborators
Alberto Barbosa Vieira
Alberto Montoya
Ana Luisa Teixeira
Ana Sofia Ribeiro
Ana Sousa da Costa
António Luís Neves
Camilo Rebelo
Carla Garrido de Oliveira
Cristina Emília Ramos e Silva
Francesco Craca
Francisco Portugal e Gomes
Helena Limas
João Ventura Lopes
Jorge Pereira Esteves
José Eurico Salgado dos Santos
Juan Cabello Arribas
Luís Tavares Pereira
Manuel Fernando Santos
Maria João Lima
Nicolau Lima
Paula Barros
Pedro Ruano de Castro
Pedro Tiago Pimentel
Ricardo Cruz
Roberta Albiero
Rosana Caro
Sónia Campos Neves
Stefano Ferracini
Susana Souto
Susana Vilela
Tiago Carvalho
Tiago Macedo Correia
Victor Oliveira

External Collaborators

Engineers
Adalberto França
Alfredo Costa Pereira
Ana Paula Neves
António Manuel
António Paz do Vale
António Rodrigues Gomes
Chia-Yau-Cheng
Conceição Abreu
Constantino Matos Campos
Encarnação Ferreira
Fátima Pimenta
Francisco Brito
Isa Angelo
João Carlos Bacelar
José António Lameiras
José César de Sá
Júlio Veloso Cardoso
Laurindo Guimarães
Luciano Cucchi
Luigi Pezzoli
Manuel Luís Brito
Manuel Pedro Melo
Maria Manuela Castro
Marilia Sousa
Nuno Calheiros Vaz
Odete Almeida
Paula Ranhada Castro
Paulo Oliveira
Paulo Queirós Faria
Paulo Sousa
Rui Fernandes Póvoas
Rui Lobão
Susana Tomás
Tomás Cruz Pereira
Vasco Peixoto Freitas

Architects
Arrigo Tognon
Maria de Conceição Melo

Budget Surveyors
António Manuel Barbosa
Jorge Pereira
José Ramalho

Bibliography

Articles on single projects

1987
Utópica, no. 2, Venezia.

1988
Concurso de Arquitectura PLEA, Porto;
Jornal dos Arquitectos, no. 68, Associação dos Arquitectos Portugueses, Lisboa.

1989
Quadernos D'Arquitectura i Urbanisme, no. 179, Colégio de Arquitectos da Catalunha, Barcelona.

1990
Architécti, no. 7, Editora Trifório, Lisboa, 1990;
Architectures à Porto, Pierre Madraga Ed., Paris;
Obradoiro, no. 17, Colégio de Arquitectos da Galiza, La Coruña.

1991
Casabella, no. 579, Electa, Milano, May 1991;
Architectural Houses - Country Houses, Edições ATRIUM AS, Barcelona;
Portugal 1990s – Arquitecturas, Colégio Oficial de Arquitectos de Andaluzia, Sevilla;
La scuola di Porto, Stella Polare Guide di Architettura, Clup-CittàStudi, Milano;
Portugallo - Architettura, gli ultimi vent'anni, Electa, Milano;
Architécti, nos 11-12, Editora Trifório, Lisboa.

1992
Páginas Brancas, II, AEFAUP, Porto;
Obradoiro, no. 20, Colegio de Arquitectos da Galiza, La Coruña.

1993
Architécti, no. 22, Editora Trifório, Lisboa;
Architécti, nos 23-24, Editora Trifório, Lisboa.

1994
Architécti, no. 27, Editora Trifório, Lisboa.

1995
Anuário de Decoração - Arquitectura, Interiores e Design, Estar Editora, Lisboa, 1994-95;
Costruire, no. 146, Ed. Abitare Segesta, Milano;
Tectónica, no. 11, ATC, Ediciones SL, Madrid.

1996
Anuário de Decoração - Arquitectura, Interiores e Design, Estar Editora, Lisboa, 1995-96;
Architecture Today, no. 90, Architecture Today PLC, London;
Casas Atlânticas, Editorial Blau, Lisboa;
DiseñoInterior - Interiors, Architecture and Design, no. 54, Globus Comunicacion, Madrid;
ON Diseño, Barcelona;
Architécti, no. 32, Editora Trifório, Lisboa.

1997
Seminário Energia Ambiente e Arquitectura, *Estudo de caso*, Computação Gráfica SA;
Costruire, no. 166, Editrice Abitare Segesta, Milano, March 1997;
Werk, Bauen + Wohnen, July-August 1997;
Edifícios solares passivos em Portugal, INETI, Lisboa;
Architécti, no. 35, Editora Trifório, Lisboa;
Architécti, no. 38, Editora Trifório, Lisboa.

1998
Area - Rivista Internazionale di Architettura e Arte del Progetto, Progetto Editrice Srl, Milano, September-October 1998;
Arquitectura Viva, Arquitectura Viva SL, Madrid;
AV Monografías, no. 72, Arquitectura Viva SL, Madrid;
Casas +, Estar Editora, Lisboa;
Architécti, no. 41, Editora Trifório, Lisboa;
Architécti, no. 42, Editora Trifório, Lisboa;
Architécti, no. 43, Editora Trifório, Lisboa.

1999
Casas de Portugal, Press Fórum, Lisboa;
Jornal Expresso, Lisboa, 13 February 1999;
Casas Internacional, Kliczowski Publisher, Buenos Aires;
Minimalist Interiors, Watson Guptill, Barcelona;
Proyetos 1998-99, Universidad de Navarra, Pamplona;
Architécti, no. 47, Editora Trifório, Lisboa;
Architécti, no. 48, Editora Trifório, Lisboa.

2000
Arq./a - Revista de Arquitectura e Arte, year I, no. 2, Ordem dos Arquitectos SRS;
Conceber - Maia + Habitação, annexed to *Arquitectura e Vida*, Loja da Imagem, Lisboa, April 2000;
Arquitectura e Vida, year I, no. 2, Loja da Imagem, Lisboa;
Proyetos 1999-2000, Universidad de Navarra, Pamplona;
DPA 16 - Abstracción, Edicions UPC, Barcelona;
Casas del Mundo, Könemann, Barcelona;
On Diseño, no. 214, Barcelona;
Arq./a - Revista de Arquitectura e Arte, year I, no. 4, Ordem dos Arquitectos SRS.

2001
Dicionário de Personalidades do Porto do séc. XX, Porto Editora, Porto;
Revista Espaços, Data Espaços Editores SA, December 2001;
Jornal Expresso, Lisboa, 14 July 2001;
Arquitectura e Vida, year II, no. 18 , Loja da Imagem, Lisboa;
Arquitectura Portuguesa Contemporânea, Edições Asa, first edition, Porto;
Arquitectura & Construção, Casa Cláudia, Lisboa, September 2001;
Modern Construction Handbook, Spring, Wien-New York;
AV Monografías, no. 86, Arquitectura Viva SL, Madrid;
Jornal Independente, Lisboa, 4 October 2001.

2002
J.A - Jornal dos Arquitectos, no. 205, Ordem dos Arquitectos, Lisboa;
Anuário de Arquitectura, 5, Estar Editora, Lisboa;
AA - Arquitecturas de Autor, T6 Ediciones -- Escola Técnica Superior de Arquitectura da Universidade de Navarra, Pamplona.

Articles on João Álvaro Rocha

1983
J. Paciência, "A propósito de uma exposição", in *Jornal dos Arquitectos*, nos 16, 17, 18, Associação dos Arquitectos Portugueses, Lisboa.

1986
M. Chaves, "Um Prémio, Dois prémios, Três prémios", in *Jornal de Notícias*, no. 5, August 1986, Porto;
J. Paciência, "O gosto pela Arquitectura", in *Jornal dos Arquitectos*, no. 45, Associação dos Arquitectos Portugueses, Lisboa;
M.G. Dias, "O fórum da 1ª Exposição Nacional de Arquitectura AAP: Um acontecimento", in *Arquitectura Portuguesa*, no. 6, Lisboa;
J.M. Pedreirinho," 1ª Exposição Nacional de Arquitectura - as leituras possíveis", in *Jornal de Letras*, no. 189, Lisboa;
Jornal dos Arquitectos, nos 63, 64, 65, Associação dos Arquitectos Portugueses, Lisboa;
J.A. França, "Gulbenkian III", in *Colóquio Artes*, no. 70, Lisboa;
A. Rodrigues, "Gulbenkian: a exposição dos 30 anos", in *Jornal de Letras*, no. 212, Lisboa;
A. Queirós, "Arquitectos do Porto premiados por trabalho urbanístico em Lamego", in *Jornal de Notícias*, 21 October 1986.

1987
M. Bérida, "L'école de Porto: colloque, exposition à Clermont-Ferrand", in *AMC*, no. 16, Paris;
J.M. Pedreirinho, "Ganhou a descentralização", in *Jornal de Letras*, no. 283, Lisboa;
M. Mendes, "Porto: École et Projects 1940-1986", in *Architectures à Porto*, Pierre Mardaga Editeur, Paris.

1988
T. Ferreira, "Uma leitura de tendências", in *Jornal dos Arquitectos*, no. 68, Associação dos Arquitectos Portugueses, Lisboa;
F. Naves, "Nova Arquitectura Portuguesa - uma geração em movimento", in *Jornal "Semanário"*, Lisboa, 16 April 1988;
E.P. Barroso, "Inventar uma identidade e algumas recordações", in *JN*, Porto, 15 December 1988.

1989
A. Silva, "Energia passiva aplicada à habitação social vai entrar em acção", in *JN*, Porto, 26 November 1989;
"Sliding", editorial, in *Quaderns*, no. 179, Colégio de Arquitectos da Catalunha, Barcelona;
J. Paciência, *Exposição nacional de Arquitectura - anos 80, Jornal dos Arquitectos*, nos 77, 78, Associação dos Arquitectos Portugueses, Lisboa;
A.A. Costa, "Em torno das primeiras obras", in *Revista dos Arquitectos*, no. 2, Associação dos Arquitectos Portugueses, Lisboa;
D.C. Melo, "O Simulacro do Risco", in *Revista dos Arquitectos*, no. 2, Associação dos Arquitectos Portugueses, Lisboa, 1989;
J.V. Caldas, "Um guia dos anos 80", in *Jornal Expresso*, Lisboa, 15 April 1989.

1990
J. Gigante, "Entre o sentimento e a razão", in *Discursos de Arquitectura*, FAUP, Porto.
J.C. Portugal, "Agora é deixar que a obra se complete", in *Discursos de Arquitectura*, FAUP, Porto.
K. Frampton, "In Search of a Laconic Line: a Note on the School of Oporto", in *Discursos de Arquitectura*, FAUP, Porto;
M. Toussaint, "I Trienal de Arquitectura – Sintra", in *Jornal dos Arquitectos*, nos 83, 84, Associação dos Arquitectos Portugueses, Lisboa;
J.V. Caldas, "Sintra: casas modernas", in *Jornal Expresso*, Lisboa, 10 February 1990;
M. Toussaint, "16 obras no maio de quê?", in *Architécti*, no. 7, Trifório, Lisboa, December 1990;
P.V. Gomes, "Demasiada Arquitectura", in *Architécti*, no. 7, Trifório, Lisboa, December 1990.

1991
P.V. Gomes, "Trinta anos de Arquitectura: paradoxo", in *Jornal Expresso*, Lisboa, 8 June 1991;
M. Toussaint, "XVIII Trienal de Milão - breve apresentação da representação portuguesa", in *Jornal dos Arquitectos*, no. 106, Associação dos Arquitectos Portugueses, Lisboa, 1991;
J.B. Rodeia, "O fim da inocência", in *Jornal dos arquitectos*, no. 106, Ordem dos Arquitectos, Lisboa;
M. Toussaint, "Projectos recentes de David Chipperfield", annex to *Jornal dos Arquitectos*, nos 97, 98, cycle of articles on "Arquitectura na Cidade", Ordem dos Arquitectos, Lisboa;
M. Mendes, "Arquitectura Portuguesa Recente - conjuntura, contingência, coincidências de um território", in *Jornal dos Arquitectos*, no. 100, Ordem dos Arquitectos, Lisboa;
W. Wang, "Entre Formulas Y Formulaciones", in *Portugal 90's - Arquitecturas*, Colégio Oficial de Arquitectos de Andaluzia, Sevilla;
M. Mendes, "Recente Architettura Portoghese (una geografia diffusa, alcune coincidenze)", in *Casabella*, no. 579, Electa, Milano, May 1991.
M. Toussaint, "Corte Anatómico", in *Architécti*, nos 11, 12, Trifório, Lisboa.

1992
M. Toussaint, *Architettura e Natura*, exhibition catalogue of the "XVIII Triennale di Milano", Electa, Milano;
M. Toussaint, "Outra ENA", in *Jornal de Arquitectos*, no. 110, Ordem dos Arquitectos, Lisboa.

1993
M. Chaves, "Um Projecto", in *Jornal dos Arquitectos*, no. 128, Ordem dos Arquitectos, Lisboa;
M. Mendes, *A pretexto da exposição do projecto do Laboratório Nacional de Investigação Veterinária*, leaflet on an exhibition, Lisboa-Porto.

1994
M. Toussaint, "A lógica da restrição", in *Architécti*, no. 27, Editora Trifório, Lisboa.

1995
M. Pizzuto, "Cuore di Pietra", in *Costruire*, no. 146, Editrice Abitare Segesta, Milano;
C.Q. Eirás, "Casa en Carreço", in *Tectónica*, no. 11, ATC, Ediciones SL, Madrid;
M. Toussaint, "Breve guia de 43 obras de arquitectura", in *Anuário de Arquitectura, Interiores e Design*, Estar Editora, Lisboa.

1997
M. Pizzuto, "Frequenze in scatola Istituto di Telecomunicazione", in *Costruire*, no. 166, Editrice Abitare Segesta, Milano, March 1997.

1998
A. Ravalli, F. Benincasa, "Casa a Carreço - House in Carreço", in *Área-Rivista Internazionale di Architettura e Arti del Progetto*, Progetto Editrice Srl, Milano;
A. Angelilo, "Identidad Y Cambio - Breve informe sobre la arquitectura portuguesa", in *Arquitectura Viva*, no. 59, Arquitectura Viva, Madrid;
P.V. Gomes, "Breve informe sobre la arquitectura portuguesa", in *Arquitectura Viva*, no. 59, Arquitectura Viva, Madrid;
M. Toussaint, "Casas Portuguesas - Portugese Houses", in *Casas +*, Estar Editora, Lisboa.

1999
M. Alves, "Senso e sensibilidade - Quinta da Barca", in *Casas de Portugal*, Press Fórum, Lisboa;
P.M. Barata, "Casas de Estudantes", in *Jornal Expresso*, Lisboa.

2000
B. Ferrão, "Privilegiar o todo sobre a parte", in *Arquitectura e Vida*, year I, no. 2, Loja da Imagem, Lisboa.

2001
M.G. Dias, "Simples e Civilizado", in *Jornal Expresso*, Lisboa, July 2001;
V. Consiglieri, "Arquitectura sem fronteiras", in *Arquitectura e Vida*, year II, no. 18, Loja da Imagem, Lisboa;
J.B. Rodeia, "Pulsares da Terra", in *Jornal Independente*, Lisboa, October 2001.

2002
M.G. Dias, "O habitar colectivo - 2", in *J.A.*, no. 205, Ordem dos Arquitectos, Lisboa, March-April 2002;
"Parque Urbano de Moutidos - 36.000 m^2 de área verde e lazer", in *Jornal da Maia*, 14 March 2002;
P. Vallejo, "La arquitectura como expresion de la idea", in *AA - Arquitecturas de Autor*, T6 Ediciones, Escola Técnica Superior de Arquitectura da Universidade de Navarra, Pamplona.

Texts by João Álvaro Rocha

1997
Projecto (notas para um percurso), text for the aptitude test at Porto University, Porto.

2001
No limits, Memoria Motril 2000, Escola Técnica Superior de Arquitectura, Granada;
"Edifício da Faculdade de Arquitectura da Universidade de Navarra", in *Jornal dos Arquitectos*, Ordem dos Arquitectos, Lisboa.

2002
"Uma nova existência", in *Arquitectura e Vida*, year II, no. 25, Loja da Imagem, Lisboa;
"Arquitectura sem excesso, Separata Mercados - Construção e Obras Públicas", in *Jornal de Notícias*, Porto, 28 March 2002.

Exhibitions

1986
"III Exposição de Artes Plásticas", Fundação Calouste Gulbenkian, Lisboa;
"I Exposição Nacional de Arquitectos", Associação de Arquitectos Portugueses, Lisboa.

1988
"IV Bienal das Produções Culturais Juvenis da Europa do Mediterrâneo", Bologna.

1989
"Exposição Nacional de Arquitectura", Associação dos Arquitectos Portugueses, Lisboa.

1990
"I Trienal de Arquitectura - A arquitectura em manifesto", Câmara Municipal de Sintra, Sintra.

1992
"La vita tra cose e natura: il progetto e la sfida ambientale - XVIII Triennale di Milano", Milano;
"III Exposição Nacional de Arquitectura", Associação de Arquitectos Portugueses, Lisboa.

1997
"Portugal Arquitectura do Século XX", Deutsches Architektur Museum, DAM Prestel, Frankfurt.

1998
"I Bienal Ibero-Americana de Arquitectura e Ingeneria Civil", Madrid.

Awards

1988
Prémios Nacionais de Arquitectura, Associação de Arquitectos Portugueses, Lisboa.

1989
Prémios Nacionais de Arquitectura - Primeiras Obras, Associação dos Arquitectos Portugueses, Lisboa.

1993
Prémios Nacionais de Arquitectura, Associação de Arquitectos Portugueses, Lisboa.

1998
Prémios FAD Arquitectura i Interiorisme 1998, On diseño, Barcelona.

1999
Sixth Mies Van Der Rohe Award for European Architecture, Fundació Mies Van der Rohe, Barcelona.

2000
Prémios FAD Arquitectura Interiorisme 2000, On diseño, Barcelona.

Photographic credits

All photographs are by Luís Ferreira Alves except:

Pages 9 (bottom right), 44, 49, 105 (bottom right), 136, 147 (bottom centre), 176, 178, 188, 189, 195 (bottom and top right), 207 (bottom and top centre, bottom and top right) by Arménio Teixeira.
Pages 17 (bottom), 147 (bottom right), 179, 205 (bottom right) by João Álvaro Rocha.
Page 19, 111, 201 (bottom left) by Francisco Portugal e Gomes.
Page 81, 83 by António Luís Neves.
Page 42 by Francesco Craca.
Page 193 (bottom left) by Sérgio Antão.
Page 105 (top left) by Engil S.A.
Page 115 by Manuel Ventura.